INDIAN AMERICANS

ETHNIC GROUPS IN AMERICAN LIFE SERIES
Milton M. Gordon, *editor*

INDIAN

MURRAY L. WAX
University of Kansas, Lawrence

AMERICANS

Unity

and

Diversity

PRENTICE-HALL, INC., ENGLEWOOD CLIFFS, NEW JERSEY

INDIAN AMERICANS

Unity
and
Diversity   WAX

© 1971 by Prentice-Hall, Inc., Englewood Cliffs, New Jersey

P: 13–456970–9   C: 13–456988–1

Library of Congress Catalog Card No.: 71–146886

Current printing (last digit):

10   9   8   7   6   5   4   3   2   1

Printed in the United States of America

PRENTICE-HALL INTERNATIONAL, INC., London
PRENTICE-HALL OF AUSTRALIA PTY. LTD., Sydney
PRENTICE-HALL OF CANADA LTD., Toronto
PRENTICE-HALL OF INDIA PRIVATE LTD., New Delhi
PRENTICE-HALL OF JAPAN, INC., Tokyo

Dedicated

To the memory of my father, Abraham Wax,
Alav HaShalom—
his ethnic identity was engraven on his soul;

To my mother, Helen Wax Cook,
may her years be many and her rewards great;

To my wife, Rosalie Hankey Wax,
who contributed in so many ways to whatever
merit there will be found in this book.

Foreword

The problem of how people of diverse racial, religious, and nationality backgrounds can live together peaceably and creatively within the same national society is one of the most crucial issues facing mankind, second in importance only to the overriding problem of international war itself. Indeed, these two problem areas, while not identical, are, from the viewpoint of recurring social processes of group interaction, interrelated at many points. The United States of America, as the classic example of a highly industrialized nation made up of people of diverse ethnic origins, constitutes, both in its history and its current situation, a huge living laboratory for the serious study of various underlying patterns of ethnic interaction—patterns which produced in this country both corroding failure (particularly with respect to the treatment of racial minorities) and certain modified successes which, however, have by no means been free of a residue of unfulfilled personal hopes, psychological scars, and unjustified hardships for those who were not born with the majority sociological characteristics of being white, Protestant, and of Anglo-Saxon cultural origins.

The explosion in the 1960's of the Negro's or black American's anger and growing revolt against centuries of white prejudice and discrimination have shocked the nation out of an attitude of mass complacency with regard to ethnic group relations. Now, not only social scientists, academic liberals, and well-meaning humanitarians, many of whom had waged valiant battles against racism before, but also millions of other Americans in all walks of life are becoming aware that to devalue another human being simply on the grounds of his race, religion, or national origins, and to act accordingly, is to strike at the very core of his personality and to create a living legacy of personal hatred and social disorganization. All the great religious and ethical traditions have spoken out prophetically against ethnic prejudice (however weak their followers have been in implementation). Now it has become increasingly clear that sheer self-interest and the desire to preserve a viable nation sternly countenance the conclusion that prejudice and discrimination are dubious luxuries which Americans can no longer afford.

We have spoken of the social scientific knowledge to be derived (and, hopefully, to be creatively used) from intensive study of American ethnic groups. There is another reason to commend such focused scientific attention. The history and the decisive contributions of the various racial, religious, and national origins groups to the warp and woof of American life is not a story that, to say the least, has been overly told in American publication or pedagogy. The important pioneer studies on the Negro of E. Franklin Frazier, John Hope Franklin, and Gunnar Myrdal, and on the white immigrant of Marcus Hansen, Oscar Handlin, and John Higham, all stem from either the present generation or the one immediately preceding it. In the main, American minority ethnic groups have been, by patronizing omission, long deprived of their past in America and of a rightful pride in the nature of their role in the making and shaping of the American nation. It is time for a systematic overview, group by group, of this long neglected portion of the American experience, one that on the one hand avoids filiopietistic banalities and, on the other, does justice to the real and complex nature of the American multiethnic experience.

A final and equally compelling reason for instituting a series of studies of America's ethnic groups at this time is that more adequate theoretical tools for carrying out the respective analyses are currently at hand. In my book, *Assimilation in American Life*, published in 1964, I presented a multidimensional approach to the conceptualization of that omnibus term "assimilation" and endeavored to factor it into its various component processes, at the same time offering certain hypotheses concerning the ways in which these processes were related to each other. Such an approach appears to facilitate dealing with the considerable complexity inherent in the functioning of a pluralistic society. Furthermore, studies of social stratification or social class which have burgeoned to become such an important part of American sociology in the past few decades have made it abundantly clear that the dynamics of ethnic group life, both internally and externally, constantly involve the interplay of class and ethnic considerations. And, lastly, the passage of time, producing a third generation of native-born children of native-born parents even among those ethnic groups who appeared in large numbers in the last great peak of emigration to America in the early part of the twentieth century, has emphasized the need for considering generational change and the sociological and social psychological processes peculiar to each successive generation of ethnic Americans.

For all these reasons, I am proud to function in the capacity of general editor of a series of books which will attempt to provide the American public with a descriptive and analytic overview of its ethnic heritage in the third quarter of the twentieth century from the viewpoint of relevant social science. Each book on a particular ethnic group (and we include the white Protestants as such a sociologically definable entity) is written by an expert in the field of intergroup relations and the social life of the group about which he writes, and in many cases the author derives ethnically himself from that group. It is my hope that the publication of this series will aid substantially in the process of enabling Americans to understand more fully what it means to live in a multi-ethnic society and, concomitantly, what we must do in the future to eliminate the corrosive and devastating phenomena of prejudice and discrimination and to ensure that a pluralistic society can at the same time fulfill its promised destiny of being truly "one nation indivisible."

MILTON M. GORDON

Preface

This book offers an orientation to the contemporary situations and problems of American Indian peoples. It also attempts to provide the reader with a guide to the kinds of information which are available about Indians. Anyone who hopes to influence or alter U.S. government policies toward Indian peoples ought to be aware of such basic issues as how "Indian" is to be defined and the consequences of one or another definition; he also ought to know the numbers of Indian persons so defined, their conditions of health and welfare, and how much governmental monies have been allocated in their names. In the text and appendices of this book the reader will either find the information or learn where to obtain it.

In this volume, I supply enough historical background so that the reader can debunk some of the mythologies about Indians (e.g., the myth of the traditional Indian culture), and enough so that he can perceive the historical roots of present difficulties. However, my primary focus is not historical, and I have not tried to summarize the extensive anthropological and ethnohistorical literature. I have tried to furnish sufficient references and have mentioned the major bibliographical aids, so that the interested reader can find his way to the better monographs or even to primary source materials.

Many persons—whether they are themselves Indian or not—are distressed by the contemporary conditions of the greater part of the Indian population of North America. Large numbers of Indians are living in poverty and are subjected to discriminatory treatment in hiring, criminal justice, and social accommodations. In the United States, the relationships between the Indian tribes and the federal agencies which have the responsibilities for assisting them in various ways—the Bureau of Indian Affairs, the Indian Public Health Service, and others—have often been dissatisfying to both parties, and there continues to be a persistent strain of authoritarianism and even racism in some federal and state offices. In Canada, many Indians and Eskimos are disturbed by the proposal to terminate their special legal status.

As the reader will observe, too many of the programs that were to have been of benefit to Indians have instead been harmful to them. And, all too often, the same programs reappear generation after generation, because those who design them have no familiarity with Indian peoples or with their historical relationships to Whites. During the four centuries from Cortéz to the present, many reformers have conceived of Indian culture as the source of Indian difficulties, rather than looking to the patterns of interaction between Indians and invaders.

I have not indulged in the popular sport of indicting Whites and Euro-American civilization for the treatment of Indian peoples. During the course of history, almost every people has been guilty of outrageous acts of cruelty and has itself been the victim of such acts. That many Indian peoples were subjected to horrifying treatment scarcely needs to be said again, although it may help if we trouble to recall how many of the European settlers were themselves refugees from harsh, brutal, even genocidal regimes. Thus, the very Scots who were to settle the Hudson's Bay territories and thereby displace the Métis and the Plains Indians were refugees from the genocidal policies of the British monarchy under James I, and theirs is by no means an isolated case. We do not wish to deny the sufferings of the Indian peoples, but to realize that neither suffering nor guilt provide a sufficient basis for analysis and planning. All too often, the guilt felt by sympathetic Whites has led them to institute programs that fail to benefit Indians and leave the planners disillusioned.

If Indians are to better their lot, and if concerned non-Indians are to be of assistance to them, both parties must become reasonably familiar with the historical and present realities. This book is designed to present information that will be of assistance toward furthering that end.

MURRAY L. WAX

Contents

Part Two

CONTEMPORARY UNITED STATES TRIBAL COMMUNITIES

CHAPTER FOUR

Contemporary Plains Reservation Communities

CHAPTER FIVE

A Tribal Nonreservation People: The Oklahoma Cherokee

Part Three

INDIANS AND
THE GREATER SOCIETY

Acknowledgments

The materials on the Cherokee of Northeastern Oklahoma derive from the Indian Education Research Project sponsored by the University of Kansas under contract with the U.S. Office of Education. The principal investigator was Murray L. Wax and the field research on the Tribal Cherokees and the schools was conducted by Mildred Dickeman, Robert V. Dumont, Jr., Lucille Proctor, Elsie Willingham, Kathryn RedCorn, Rosalie H. Wax, and Clyde and Della Warrior; the advice and counsel of Albert Wahrhaftig and Irwin Deutscher were helpful. Dumont did the pioneer work in analyzing the interviews of the household survey reported in this book. Robert L. Bee prepared an early draft of the chapter, "Pan-Indian Responses to Invasion and Disruption." In manuscript form, the book has been read by Robert V. Dumont, Jr., Nathan Glazer, Milton M. Gordon, C. Hoy Steele, and Rosalie H. Wax; as a result of their helpful criticisms, I have made a series of revisions of the original text. The manuscript was typed by Mary Wolken and Barbara Johnson. To all of the foregoing persons I acknowledge my gratitude and appreciation, while insisting that the responsibility of this text is mine alone.

For permission to reprint the indicated tables, I am grateful to the following publishers and authors: University of Texas Press (publisher of the *Handbook of Middle American Indians*, edited by Robert Wauchope), Tables 2–1 to 2–4; University of North Carolina Press (publisher of *Social Forces*), Table 2–5; Richard N. Adams, Table 2–1; Anselmo Marino Flores, Tables 2–2 and 2–4; Arden R. King, Table 2–3; Pierre L. van den Berghe, Table 2–5; and Albert L. Wahrhafting, Tables 5–8 and 5–9.

HISTORICAL DEVELOPMENTS
AND COMPARATIVE
RELATIONSHIPS

Part One

INTRODUCTION

Throughout the Americas—North, South, and Central—are millions of peoples who are referred to as Indians. In the past (and still today) most of these peoples did not refer to themselves by this word, but instead labeled themselves as members of small bands or villages of kith and kin. In like manner, the peoples who inhabited Europe during the Middle Ages would not have referred to themselves as "European" or "French" or "German," but instead would have spoken in terms of their membership in a family household and their residence in a local region. The categories of being *White* (European), or *Black* (African), or *Indian* (native American) were to come about as a consequence of the exploration, trade, conquest, and settlement which brought the Europeans into intimate and prolonged contact with other peoples of the world. This expansion is typified by Christopher Columbus, and it was he, seeking a direct route to "the Indies" (i.e., Southeast Asia), who labeled the American natives as *los Indios*. The Spanish conquistadores who accepted his geographic conjectures and followed his routes also continued his nomenclature, and so the native Americans acquired their name of *Indian*.

Background: Historical and Ecological

To the social scientist, the native peoples of the Americas have appeared markedly diverse. For example, in linguistic terms, the native languages can be classed into about a dozen stocks (each as distinct from the other as the Semitic from the Indo-European), and within each stock into languages as distinct as English from Russian, so the Americas were linguistically as diverse as the Euroasian land mass. (Most of the classifications of Indians into tribes, nations, or peoples have been linguistic, e.g., Siouan, Iroquoian, Athapaskan, rather than political, e.g., the Six Nations.) Likewise, the Indians have been heterogeneous in their level of native technology and complexity of social organization, ranging from the large and civilized societies of Central America and the Andes (Maya, Aztec, Inca) to the small and relatively primitive societies of the Paiute, Seri, or Fuegian. That the Spanish and other European invaders could perceive this diversity as a unity, and so maintain the single term *Indian* is significant of a constancy of relationship. Regardless of the heterogeneity both of the invaders from Europe and of the natives of the Americas, the pattern of their relationship was to prove so constant that it could be characterized as a confrontation of *Indian* and *White* (a conceptual issue to which we will be returning later). To seek a parallel elsewhere, we can note how the slave trade transformed the Ibo, Hausa, Yoruba, and other peoples of the African west coast into simply *Negroes* (the Spanish term for "black").

As we shall observe in the course of this book, there have been significant differences in the ways that Whites and Indians related to each other. In some cases, the invaders sought to exterminate the natives—sometimes simply to rid the land of troublesome tenants, and sometimes for the sport of hunting a human quarry. At other times, the invaders sought to assimilate the natives by Christianizing them or forcibly detribalizing them (through religious missions, compulsory schooling in isolation from their kin, and economic sanctions). Frequently the natives were driven and corraled into regions of the country which the invaders had found unsuitable for their own settlement and exploitation. Meanwhile, there was interbreeding that was sometimes sanctioned as concubinage or even marriage. There were even handfuls of Whites who settled among Indians and found the native ways so congenial that they assimilated, and hundreds of thousands of Indians have assimilated into the national society of their locality.

Given the original diversity of the natives of the Americas and the varieties of treatment to which they have been subjected, there is a problem in deciding who or what group should be categorized as "Indian." For example, in terms of descent, there have been a number of eminent figures in U.S. life with a significant degree of Indian blood in their veins, e.g., Will Rogers, the humorist, Jim Thorpe, the athlete, Maria Tallchief, prima ballerina assoluta, and Jack Dempsey, the prize fighter, not to mention corporation executives, political leaders, and the like. In Central and South America, it is equally true that many prominent men have had some or considerable Indian ancestry. Yet, in all areas of the Americas, one basic referent of "Indian" has come to mean the enclaves or bands who are culturally unique and socially isolated. In Perú, Venezuela, and many other Latin American countries, *los Indios* are the politically impotent, economically impoverished, culturally traditional, and socially enclaved groups who do not participate in the Hispanicized life of the national society. The participants in that society view the *Indio* as an inferior beast in contrast to the *Mestizo* (who bears Indian blood in his veins but has become Hispanicized). Even within the United States, the tendency in many regions is to denote by "Indian" not those who are of Indian descent yet successful by the standards of the national society, but only those who are impoverished and ethnically distinct. Thus, many Dakotans use "Indian" to denote Sioux they perceive as poor and "backward," while northeastern Oklahomans use "Indian" in the same perception of Tribal Cherokee. This should alert us to the fact that, as a word in ordinary language, "Indian" (or *Indio*) sometimes refers to a distinct ethnic group but more often refers to a series of social processes of an invidious character. Hence, to study Indians is to study a historical sequence of relationships which began when the Europeans invaded the Americas in the fifteenth century.

THE SPANISH CONQUEST

When Cortéz and his armada landed in 1519 at what is now Vera Cruz, and a few years later the brothers Pizarro descended upon what is now Perú, the Spaniards encountered the dominant and most civilized societies of the Americas. Technologically, these societies rested on a foundation of settled agriculture, including a large variety of domesticated plants and elaborate techniques of cultivation, such as terracing, irrigation canals, and "floating gardens" (*chinampas*). The stone ceremonial structures of these people still impress us with their size and artistry, but equally significant are the fantastic systems of stone terracing, extending elaborately over miles of the steepest mountainsides. Comprehension of their social organization is more difficult, since except for the archaeological record, we are forced to rely on the narratives of the Spanish invaders, their associates, and those of their mixedblood offspring who became literate and recorded the tales of their maternal kin. Scholars are not even certain of the populations of these societies: estimates for Middle America range from 3 to 15 million persons. In any case, it is clear that these societies were organized quite differently from their European counterparts, although they had independently achieved a high degree of division of labor and cultural sophistication. Their social tenacity may be judged from the fact that after five centuries of military, political, and social pressures, there remain today villages of Indians in the Peruvian Andes which display direct linkages to their cultural past, despite the total disappearance of the civilized (Inca) state of which they were aboriginally a unit.

During the sixteenth century, the Spanish had emerged as the leading military power of Europe. Engaged for generations in conflicts with the Moors, Dutch, and Turks, not to mention raiders of all ethnic varieties, the Spanish had become resourceful experts in a formidable military technology which included steel weapons and body armor, the horse equipped as a cavalry mount with saddle and stirrups, the crossbow, gunpowder and cannon, and seaworthy warships. Against this armament the Indians had vast numbers, but otherwise only wooden clubs, spears and arrows tipped with stone, and shields of hide; equally important, the Indians were divided in their allegiances and their counsels, and the Spanish were quick to capitalize upon these divisions. The Aztecs were the predominant minority in a political state containing national groupings who felt oppressed and were ready to combine with a powerful liberating force. Moreover, the Aztec leaders were perplexed as to whether the Spanish might be divine conquerors, and so were uncertain whether to submit or fight. Similar problems vexed the Inca Empire further to the south in the Andean highlands. In consequence, the Spanish were able to assume control over the major Indian political states, although these states had established large and fierce armies. Once the states had collapsed, some Indian tribes emerged as guerrilla fighters and were able to inflict grievous injuries upon the invading Europeans as they attempted to settle and exploit the country. However, by this time it was too late to influence the basic patterns of conquest and political domination.

The conquistadores believed "the Indies" to be a treasurehouse, and the Indians, unfortunately for themelves, had in fact been attracted by and worked with gold. The aggregates of pure gold which Cortéz wrested from Moctezuma were fantastic, and led to rumors of even more fabulous hordes elsewhere in this unknown territory. With fanatical energy, the Spanish embarked on expeditions throughout the Americas, making incredible journeys and leaving behind them a trail of blood. Some found loot, others found trouble, and, in time, some found mineral lodes. As early as the sixteenth century, the Spanish were mining silver in the Sierra Madre Mountains of what is now Mexico and were enslaving Indians to labor in the mines and to grow crops to feed the mineworkers.

Some conquerors have merely looted and departed (as the Vikings usually did until they settled Normandy); others have displaced the previous rulers and set themselves in power (as in the repeated invasions and conquests of India); but the Spanish had come to stay and to impose on the natives—whom they regarded as heathen and barbarian—their own civilized and Christian style of life. While the conquistadores sought wealth, the Spanish missionaries, protected and aided by the Crown, sought converts. Dominicans, Augustinians, and (somewhat later) Jesuits journeyed widely among the Indians in order to bring them the Christian message, a task defined as assimilating them to the culture of Spain and incorporating them within its national system. Thus, the missionaries functioned not only as priests, but even more as agricultural extension agents, teachers, and local lords. Ultimately at their disposal was the Spanish might, so they could order recalcitrant Indians to be flogged and nomadic populations forced into settlement. On the positive side, the missionaries brought wondrous additions to the native agricultural repertoire: domesticated animals—horses, sheep, cattle, and swine; orchard crops—peaches, pears, apples, and oranges; and cereals—wheat, oats, and barley. To those Indian groups who were already settled agriculturalists and whose environment approximated that of Spain, the benefits must have seemed spectacular.

Native agriculture already represented a superb tradition of the domestication and hybridization of flora native to the Americas (no animal seemed worthy or fit for domestication except the dog and llama of the Andes). The Indians were already cultivating such roots as "Irish" potatoes, sweet potatoes, manioc, and arrowroot; such fruits and vegetables as tomatoes, melons, pumpkins, beans (snap, lima, and kidney), squash (Hubbard, zucchini, butternut), peppers (tabasco, cayenne), and pineapple; and the master grain, maize (corn). In addition, they were utilizing such other plant products as cotton, (American) chestnuts, chocolate, cocoa, peanuts, tobacco, quinine, and rubber. To the dedicated Indian agriculturalists, the Spanish missionaries must have seemed divine beings, bearers of moral and technical blessings, and it should not surprise us that the presence of the missionaries was actively sought by many tribes. Conversely, some of the missionaries regarded the Indians as ideal populations among which to institute utopian commonwealths, and Dominican Bishop Vasco di Quiroga tried to establish the Utopia of Sir Thomas More among the Tarascans (leaving traces still visible in Michoacán). Time was to provide disenchantment, because many of the missionaries—regarding themselves as the bearers of civilization and piety—learned little of the languages, etiquettes, or customs of the peoples they considered lustful savages, with the consequence that the enforced intimacy of mission conditions brought to both sides only continual shock and offense. Added to this was the authoritarian role of the missionary and his reliance upon corporal punishment. In a number of cases the Indian tribes revolted against the mission, and the station could only be reestablished by the exercise of considerable force.

The missionaries tried unsuccessfully to protect their Indian converts from contact with other facets of the Spanish program. For example, those Spanish who wished to establish themselves as gentry, operating mines or plantations (*encomiendas* with *repartimiento*), required cheap and docile laborers whom they presumed to recruit—sometimes forcibly—from among the Indian natives. Soldiers and the other bachelor males wanted Indian women as prostitutes and concubines. The style of living of the Spanish soldiers and settlers was lusty and zestful, featuring abundant consumption of wine and spirits, and the missionaries tried to keep their flocks from involvement with this pattern. Yet the secular program of settlement placed only modest barriers in the way of Indian assimilation. While the towns of New Spain were dominated by the gentry—*gente de razón*, a high estate which prided itself upon its superior Spanish descent—the remainder of the town population was a polygot mixture of poor Spanish, Negro, and Indian, together with their hybrid offspring (mulatto, mestizo), and entry into this social world was easy, as it merely required the abandoning of previous social ties, rather than the mastery of new cultural traits.

Meanwhile, in the area closest to our interest in this book, the northern region of Spanish settlement, other Indian groups affected by the changes underway perceived in them an exciting opportunity. Horses were well adapted to the plains of New Spain, and it was not long before some Indian tribes developed the skills of horsemanship and evolved into a kind of horsenomads. The nature of the people from whom the Apache emerged can now only be guessed—in the near past they may have been small bands of pedestrian hunters and gatherers in the desert; in the distant past they were situated much farther north—but late in the seventeenth century they began to appear as equestrian raiders preying upon the towns and mission stations of New Spain. It was soon evident that their activities were beyond the capacity of the Spanish to control. The civil government was incompetent and inefficient, with the result that vast areas had to be abandoned during the eighteenth century, owing to the pressure of the raiders. (Meanwhile, the adaptation expanded northward, as the Comanche acquired the horse and began to raid the Apache, as well as targets in their own neighborhood.) Not until the end of the Civil War were the Apache restrained, when an arduous campaign of the U.S. Army finally tracked them down so that they could be disarmed and confined to reservations.

Mexico was to remain under Spanish governance until 1821, and we may note that at the time she achieved her independence, some of her northern tribes (e.g., the Opata) were on the road to total assimilation and disappearance. Other tribes (e.g., the Yaqui and the Pueblo) had, through a combination of geographic isolation and stubborn insistence upon preserving their solidarity, been able to hold at bay the various attempts to integrate them into the new national society, and were, if anything, more militantly and self-consciously organized than when the Spanish first arrived. Still other tribes (the Apache and Comanche) had adopted cultural instrumentalities introduced by the Spanish (the horse as a cavalry mount, metal weapons, guns) and were enjoying a cultural efflorescence at the expense of those who had hoped to settle the country in Spanish fashion.

THE NATURE OF INTERACTION

In the remainder of this chapter, we will be sketching some of the early contacts between various Indian groups and the incoming Whites. Since the primary focus of this book is upon the Indians of North America—especially the U.S.—we must neglect developments from Mexico southward. Nonetheless, we should bear in mind that, compared to the history of Indians in this hemisphere, and even compared to the history of Indian–White contacts, the national political boundaries are relatively recent, and the contacts did not follow their delineation. We have already noted that the Apache came to flourish in a zone that would now be spoken of as Arizona, New Mexico, Chihuahua, and Sonora, i.e., the southwest of the U.S. and the northwest of Mexico. We should also remember that the Apache and other tribes of North America were "backwoods barbarians" in comparison with the civilized societies of Indians further to the south, thus occupying a cultural position akin to that of the Germanic tribes in relationship to the Rome of Julius Caesar. Yet, just as in ancient Europe, significant cultural traits had diffused widely. For example, tribes as far north as the St. Lawrence River were cultivating maize and beans, plants that had originally been domesticated in a more southern climate.

For students of ethnic group relationships, the study of Indians can be especially valuable because history has presented us with a series of controlled comparisons. Different kinds of Europeans (Spanish, French, Dutch, English) came into relationship with different kinds of Indians (even the Russians established relationships with Alaskan Eskimos); later, the various American nations (the U.S., Canada, Mexico, Brazil, Colombia, Perú, and so on) not only established varying legal regulations governing the position of the Indian enclaves, but crystallized different social patterns for Indian–non-Indian relationships, and even evolved diverse definitions of who was to be regarded as an "Indian." Since, in this book, we focus upon the small Indian minority of the U.S., we shall necessarily be overlooking the intricacies of relationships affecting the huge Indian populations further south in this hemisphere.

In the sections which comprise the remainder of this chapter, I have tried to emphasize the ways in which the Indian tribes responded to the Whites' presence. One myth that has long distorted the perception of Indian affairs, and has been pervasive even among anthropologists, has it that the Indian societies were static until the coming of the Whites, whereupon they deteriorated under the pressures of conquest and contact. Scholars have been oriented toward seeking out the aboriginal Indian, the culture "before the coming of the Whites." Strictly followed, such a condition would have excluded the most significant and exciting chapters of Apache and Comanche history, as well as that of other peoples, such as the Iroquois and Sioux. (It would also have excluded such ecological adaptations as the spread of maize cultivation throughout the northern hemisphere and such political developments as the Aztec Conquest of Middle America.)

I have tried to stress the modalities of trade or of other interaction between Indians and Whites, of how each appeared to the other, and of the degree of insight which the Whites gained into Indian life. Much depended on whether the Europeans came as single men (explorers, traders, envoys) who proceeded to marry or establish stable liaisons with Indian women, or whether they came as married couples. In the former case, there was much further opportunity for the man to acquire a sympathetic understanding of Indian social life. Here, as a precondition, we should not overlook the White perception of the wealth and hierarchy of the native society. The Spanish conquistadores were happy to marry into the families of those they described as Inca royalty, just as the English John Rolfe was happy to wed Pocahontas, the daughter of a personage regarded as a monarch. Later, on the western frontier, "squaw man" was a term of derogation, as was "Halfbreed," the child of the union.

THE YAQUI

In 1553, Diego de Guzmán ranged northward on a slaving expedition along the coast of the Gulf of California. At the Yaqui River he fought a brief battle, and a soldier in his party wrote that nowhere in the New World had he seen such bravery as that exhibited by these Indians. Later Spanish captains, who returned with larger forces, had similar experiences. In the early seventeenth century Hurdaide led a force of 2,000 Indian allies on foot, plus 40 Spanish on horseback, and was soundly defeated by the Yaqui. He mustered all his resources and raised the largest army ever seen in northwestern Mexico, 4,000 Indian foot and 50 Spanish cavalry. A bloody battle ensued that lasted a whole day and night, and the Spanish were again routed; yet, after their victory, the Yaqui asked for peace and invited the presence of Jesuit missionaries. This was to remain the pattern of Yaqui life: stubborn insistence on independence—and willingness to fight for that goal with terrifying tenacity and courage—but great interest in the culture of the invaders.

The Jesuits found the Yaqui a highly receptive people. Their population of about 30,000 had been dispersed in some 80 *rancherias*; it was now baptized and concentrated in eight new towns. Agricultural cultivation was improved and intensified, and soon the fertile river bottoms were producing sufficiently for a considerable surplus to be exported. However, in time, the area of Spanish settlement *(hacendados)* crept close to the Yaqui border, and civil authorities began pressing to divide the Yaqui lands (which were held in common), to require payment of tribute and taxation, and to open the area for settlement. In 1740 the Yaqui "revolted" and killed or chased away all Spaniards other than "their" Jesuits. When, in 1767, the Jesuits were expelled from New Spain, leaderships devolved upon the Yaquis themselves and, although they had continually to defend themselves against Spanish and Mexican attempts at conquest and absorption, they remained fundamentally autonomous communities for over another century.

The Yaqui preserved the agricultural innovations that had been instituted by the Jesuits and the habits of diligence of good peasants. During the eighteenth and nineteenth centuries, thousands of Yaqui were migrating throughout the region and establishing a high reputation as industrious and capable workmen in the mines, on the haciendas, and in the fishing industry. Meanwhile, the Yaqui were elaborating the Christian dogma to fit their own situation. Every Yaqui was identified with one of the eight towns, and each town was given a sacred origin related to the Bible. Thus, the Yaqui believed that Jesus had been born in one of the eight towns, Belem (Bethlehem), and had traveled in the Yaqui country, curing and helping folk in the face of the hostility of evil beings. The Yaqui also elaborated a cult of the Virgin, whom they merged with a chthonic goddess—a divine being identified with the fertility of the region—and with the cross itself. Each town had a military society whose ritual and symbolism was organized about that of the Virgin of Guadalupe.

In 1828, after Mexico had become independent, the Occidente government enacted three laws designed to integrate the Indians into the new state. These laws expressed an idealistic philosophy. The notion was that it had been Spanish insistence on distinctions of race and birth which had perpetuated the separate castes, and that declaring that all persons born in Mexico were citizens guaranteed equal participation in political life would eliminate the division between Indians and other Mexicans. The laws proposed equitable distribution of land into individual parcels, with title being given to each landholder. While the legislators thought of themselves as moved by a spirit of equity and consideration for individual rights, the response of the Indians indicated a far different orientation to the situation. As independence from Spain was being gained, the Yaquis and their neighbors had visualized an autonomous Indian nation, and their leader, Juan Banderas, had reported a vision of the Virgin of Guadalupe leading its troops. Accordingly, they drove the non-Yaqui from their territory, and the Mexican government was not able to establish a pretense of sovereignty there until 1833. During the next half-century, the Sonoran authorities made ineffectual attempts to enforce the laws for integration, but the Indian towns resisted the distribution of lands, as this would have destroyed the economic and spiritual) basis of their communal integration. The latter half of the nineteenth century embodied continual conflicts between the Yaqui and the government. There were cries to exterminate the Yaqui, but there was also the realization that they were important contributors to the economic welfare of the region. In 1868, General Morales achieved a brief peace by a policy of ruthless destruction and massacre, and the system of land distribution was begun. But in a few years the Yaqui were again fighting, now under the inspired leadership of Cajeme. Not until 1887 was he defeated and executed, at which point organized resistance by the Yaqui ceased, although guerrilla activities from mountain fastnesses were to continue for over another generation.

It should be realized that, throughout these actions, the Yaqui were united by a vision of the eight sacred towns as an independent and autonomous region wholly under their own control. The land was thought to be under the control (or ownership) of the town, and was managed under the guidance of the ritual specialists. At the same time, it should not be inferred that the Yaqui were parochial, or that their national policies merely reflected the views of the "conservatives." Quite the contrary, the Yaquis had come to range rather widely, and many were fluent in Spanish. Cajeme, for example, had fought with General Ignacio Pesqueira against the French, and prior to the revolt had been appointed by him as alcalde mayor of the Yaqui and Mayo towns.

The Mexican government now instituted a policy of dispersing the Yaqui as widely as possible while colonizing their lands with outsiders. Thus pushed by the government, as well as propelled by their own disposition, the Yaquis soon spread throughout Mexico and the southwestern states of the U.S. However, peace and order did not descend on their native land, and even as late as 1926 (four centuries after Guzmán's expedition) the Mexican government was still undertaking military campaigns in the region. Whenever they could, Yaquis were attempting to return to their native soil and resurrect the system of eight towns. In 1939, President Cárdenas established the north bank of the Yaqui River and the Bacetete Mountains as exclusively for the Yaquis (the fertile coastal plain to the south of the river was by then completely in the hands of outsiders), and the Yaquis were able to reestablish settlements where three of the original towns had been. Meanwhile, Yaqui communities in the U.S. were becoming permanently established, and in the 1960's the one on the outskirts of Tucson numbered several thousand people and had organized itself for purposes of ceremonial and of community development.

THE IROQUOIS AND
THE FUR TRADE

Whereas the Spanish had sought precious metals, adventurers from England, France, and the Netherlands sought furs. The trade began early and, throughout the sixteenth century, French companies were competing among themselves for control of the St. Lawrence route. In return for beaver and other pelts, the Europeans offered guns, ammunition, knives, hatchets, kettles, cloth, rum, and trinkets. As Indians applied themselves to trapping, they quickly exhausted local resources and began to travel and trade farther afield. Armed with weapons conveyed by the Whites, they could more easily intrude upon territories which had been the habitat of other tribes, and this served to increase the rate of intertribal conflict as well as to stimulate the need for new weapons. Meanwhile, as the White settlers began to occupy the seaboard, their farming, logging, and hunting also contributed to a decline of the animal populations.

By the seventeenth century, the fur trade was in vigorous swing; in order to take better advantage of the Hudson River, the Dutch, who were based on New Amsterdam, established Fort Orange (at what is now Albany). Thereby, they were brought into a more direct relationship with the *HoDeNoSauNee*, the League of the Five Nations. Known by the French as *Les Iroquois*, the League consisted of the Seneca, Onondaga, Cayuga, Oneida, and Mohawk. Its peoples had been living in settled villages near streambeds where the women could plant their gardens of maize, beans, and squash. In addition to serving as warriors, the men contributed fish and game (especially wildfowl) to the diet. The machinery of their League was primarily an arrangement for maintaining peace and harmony among the member tribes, and, except for issues of conflict among tribes, affairs were largely in the hands of the separate tribes and villages.

By the middle of the seventeenth century, the Iroquois had become intensive participants in the fur trade and had exhausted the beaver of their own territory. When they looked about them in order to continue this attractive enterprise, they perceived the Huron confederacy, which was thriving on a system wherein agricultural products from southern tribes were exchanged for pelts secured by the northern tribes, and these in turn were traded to the French. The two confederacies came into conflict, and in the process the Iroquois were the first to consolidate their union from a largely ceremonial association, concerned with domestic harmony, into an aggressive military (and commercial) alliance. Indian fighting had previously involved small bands of warriors seeking fame and ritual benefits, but the Iroquois now proceeded to field massive expeditions which annihilated their neighbors and scorched their lands. The targets were offered the alternative of submission, including adoption into a member tribe of the League; while most of the Huron were dispersed, a significant bloc was received into the League.

The Iroquois assault was deadly. Some neighbors, e.g., the Erie and the Susquehannock, were wiped out; others migrated westward, precipitating vast shifts of Indian population. The French trade was sorely crippled, while the English, as successors to the Dutch, received the benefits of the League. Meantime, other tribes sought the assistance of the League in protecting themselves from the English colonists. Early in the eighteenth century, the Tuscarora, fleeing from North Carolina, joined the League as the Sixth Nation. A number of other tribes (Tutelo, Saponi, Delaware, Shawnee, Nanticoke) came under the hegemony of the League, and it appeared for a brief time as if it would encompass all the tribes bordering the seaboard settlements. But the Creek, who represented the powerful confederacies of the Southeast, were too confident of their own strength, while the Canadian tribes were too closely allied with the French.

As superintendent of Indian affairs for the northern tribes, the English appointed a young man named William Johnson. Settling among the Iroquois, he learned Mohawk, and took a Mohawk girl to wife. He sent Joseph Brant (Thayendanegea), her brother, to a mission school, and then appointed him as his assistant. Together, Johnson and Brant rose to positions of leadership in the League, and the former was knighted for leading a group of Iroquois at Lake George during the French and Indian war. The Iroquois were becoming both powerful and acculturated: 11 Indian nations were living with the Seneca, numerous Whites were intermarrying, and a distinctive blend of cultures was emerging. Joseph Brant became well established in both societies. He was commissioned a colonel in the British army and appointed a sachem of the League. In 1775 he journeyed to England and sat for a portrait by the famous artist, Romney.

But there were factions among the Colonists who were not pleased by the success of the Iroquois. Land speculation companies and White farmers looked hungrily at the lands occupied by the League and intruded whenever they could, hoping for a sign of weakness. The Crown valued its alliances with the powerful Indian nations, wished to enlist them on its side against the French, and hoped to avoid the necessity of sending troops to fight the Indians. Hence, from its side was issued the Royal Order of 1763, sealing off the western lands and leaving them to the Indians. The Order was not received well among the Colonists, and was one of the grievances that was to lead to the Revolutionary War. During the conflict, the League, following its successful system of neutrality in the wars of the Whites, tried at first to hold itself aloof. Brant, however, was loyal to the Tory cause and carried the Mohawk, Seneca, Cayuga, and Onondaga along with him, while the Oneida and Tuscarora joined the revolutionary colonists. The League was split; the Great Peace of the Six Nations had been ended.

In response to the incursions of the Mohawk, Washington sent General John Sullivan on a campaign against the Iroquois. A scorched earth policy was followed which destroyed the basis of one of the most advanced Indian societies of North America. Scores of brick and stone homes were demolished; orchards were girdled and axed; acres of corn, beans, and melons were ruined. Sullivan's officers drank toasts which demanded, "Civilization or death to all American savages," but it is clear that only the latter was intended. When peace was declared, the treaty made no provision for the Indian allies of the British, but instead granted to the new American nation title to the entire Northwest, in disregard of its occupants. Speaking for the Iroquois, Joseph Brant refused to conclude peace until the rights of the Six Nations were recognized. But the settlers and land speculators saw in the end of the war the signal that the frontier had been cleared for their advance westward. Thus, the new nation inherited the same perplexities that had troubled the British. Invasions of Indian lands and maltreatment of their native residents provoked conflict with the Indians, whereas the national government preferred the friendship of Indian allies. Unhappily, the actions of settlers and speculators could not be controlled; they threatened to organize the border as new states and secede, and there were not sufficient troops (or funds to pay them) to restrain the migrants and limit the trespass. Brant and the Mohawk fled to their English friends in Canada, and were joined there by other refugees from the Six Nations.

ECOLOGICAL ADAPTATIONS
AND DISPLACEMENTS

To the European invaders, the North American continent appeared as "a wilderness." In the face of widespread occupancy by Indian tribes, this testifies to a fundamental difference in patterns of land usage by the European and North American peoples. Except for such skillful and devoted agriculturalists as the Pueblo and the earlier Hohokam of the Southwest, the North American tribes tended either to be hunters-and-gatherers (e.g., the Paiute and the Eskimo) or, more frequently, to rely on a modest horticultural base supplemented by intensive hunting, fishing, and gathering. Cultivation for these latter tribes was confined to small areas, such as the river bottoms, while large areas of forest and grassland seemed untouched (in fact, the forests were subjected to an annual burning of undergrowth which rendered them more parklike and thus more hospitable to herbivores). Since areas were not fenced, or borders demarcated and guarded, and since tribal land was held in common (rather than being "private property"), vast areas of land must have appeared to the invaders as having no owners and being unutilized.

In all intensive agriculture, the fundamental problem is restoration to the soil of the fertility absorbed by the process of cultivation and harvest. When fields are located so as periodically to be flooded by rivers —or by irrigation canals from rivers—then the layer of silt that is deposited may serve to renew the soil; this system provided the basis for the agriculture of Egypt and Mesopotamia, as well as much of the Americas. In North America, the location of gardens along stream and river beds ensured a high level of moisture and a sustained level of fertility. A different solution to the problem of maintaining soil fertility had been evolving in Europe. With metal axes to clear forest land, metal tipped plows to break the sod, animals for draught, dairy, and manuring, and a rotation of land usage to allow the land to regain its fertility by laying fallow and serving as pasture, the European system could sustain an intensive agriculture wherever a temperate zone had sufficient rainfall in the spring. Blended with crops that had been domesticated in the Americas, the resultant agriculture could support a high density of population—always providing that agriculturalists of the proper temperament were available. This pattern of agriculture required a certain type of man, one who (like the Pennsylvania Dutch) "loved the soil" and took pride in patient and skillful drudgery. While many of the missionaries (from Jesuits to Quakers) were to set forth this type of man to the Indians as an ideal, most of the early invaders were in fact adventurers disinclined to devote themselves to diligent farming. Besides, it should not be forgotten that such agriculture requires a stable political system, so that the farmer can be sure, not only of the immediate harvest, but of being able to bequeath to his heirs the plot he has husbanded.

To enterprisers of an agricultural bent, the uncultivated forest and grass lands of North America represented another kind of asset. Especially in the Southeast, where rainfall was abundant and the growing season long, the land could be made the basis of a plantation, i.e., an agricultural factory using large quantities of cheap (or forced) labor in order to produce crops (such as cotton or tobacco) for export and sale. Initial attempts were to operate these plantations either with indentured servants from England or with the forced labor of Indians, but neither proved satisfactory; it was only with the beginnings of the African slave trade that the system became really profitable. However, sustained mono-crop cultivation has always proven especially debilitating to the soil, and the process is aggravated when the laborers have no interest in husbanding the land. The hitherto uncultivated soils of the Southeast represented a natural treasure from which extraordinary yields could be obtained in the initial years. But in a surprisingly short period of time, the original fertility was exhausted and the yields became minimal. This deterioration served to generate enormous economic pressures for westward expansion into areas previously uncultivated: each stretch of virgin soil represented a huge potential profit to a plantation owner, and all that was needed for occupancy was the displacement of some small band of Indians who scarcely seemed to be using the ground.

Indian vulnerability to such pressures was increased by their decimation from disease. The microorganisms which plague human beings evolve and flourish in response to the densities and interaction of human populations. In the European world the density had been relatively high and travel intensive, and a number of organisms had come into existence for which Indians had little native resistance. Tuberculosis, measles, smallpox, mumps, scarlet fever, diphtheria, whooping cough, and other infectious diseases were spread to the Indians by contact with the Whites, and the resultant plagues killed or debilitated great numbers. (Reciprocation by Indians seems to have been confined to the Central Americans communicating to the Spaniards a more virulent form of venereal disease.) Some Whites utilized the Indian vulnerability to European diseases as a basis for "bacteriological warfare" in order to rid the area of their Indian neighbors; thus, Georgians "donated" a large quantity of clothes from smallpox victims to the Cherokee, with results quite as they had foreseen. Be that as it may, in some cases the invaders did encounter not a "wilderness" but a desolate and abandoned land where Indians had been smitten by a pandemic.

THE DAKOTA HORSENOMADS

Bringing horses with them, Spanish colonists moved northward to the Rio Grande Valley in 1598. The colonists did not remain, but the horses did. They were accustomed to a desert climate, being of Moorish breed, and they went wild, roving the southern Plains in herds. We have already noted the emergence of the Apache as mounted raiders of the settlements of New Spain. Over the decades, horses and the skills of horsemanship traveled further northward. Inhabitants of the northern Plains had been settled villagers (such as the Mandan), practicing a mixed economy of horticulture and (pedestrian) hunting. By the eighteenth century, these villagers had to cope with a new neighbor and enemy, the Indian horsenomad. The nomads lived almost as parasites to the bison, residing in skin tipis and equipping themselves with other light and durable articles of animal origin. Their young men were competitive and aggressive, traveling long distances swiftly and quietly across the Plains, searching for horses and scalps, loot and fame.

A number of tribes from different areas and cultural backgrounds vaulted onto the horse and cantered into the Plains: Blackfoot, Arapaho, and Cheyenne from the northern prairies; Comanche from the western foothills; Crow from within the northern Plains. The eastern peoples may have been responding to push as well as pull, since tribal dislocations had accompanied development of the fur trade and expansion of the Iroquois. Regardless of their source, the various tribes found a new and rich life in seeking the bison as mounted hunters. Of the Dakota, the earliest into the Plains were the Tetons, while their relatives remained east in the Mississippi basin, participating in the trade with the French. By the end of the eighteenth century most of the Dakota had made the transformation, although the eastern branch preserved its relationship with the French, serving as Indian middlemen in an exchange of guns, ammunition, and trade goods for buffalo robes, dried meat, horses, and pelts.

The Teton became the scourge of the northern Plains, acquiring a reputation for irascibility, impetuosity, and stealthy ferocity. The settled agriculturalist tribes, which had built a rich ceremonial existence and complex societal organization, could not cope with the Dakota raids, even though they themselves acquired the horse and some of the traits of the horsenomads. The Teton harassed the traders who attempted to utilize the Missouri River; later they continued the sport with the wagon trains crossing the Plains. Peaceable contact with the Whites was mainly via French traders who established their posts along the riverine routes and took Indian women to wife.

To the traders, the Plains tribes were a source of supply and of profit. To travelers and others, they were a nuisance; being small in numbers, they hardly classed as major enemies of the state, but their mobility and hardihood made them difficult and expensive to control. For some time no one except their fellow Indians really wished to compete for the exploitation of the Plains. The White settlers bore an agricultural technique suited only to the eastern woodlands, with their high rainfall and tall trees. But then a set of inventions made the Plains seem suitable for settlement by Whites, and the age of the Plains Indians was doomed.

Toward the middle of the century, Samuel Colt refined the single shot pistol into the six-shooter, which was to become the ideal weapon for the mounted man. With repeating weapons Whites could defeat the raiding tactics of the Comanche and Dakota, whose wild encirclements had been designed to exploit the slowness of fire of the muzzleloading gun as compared to the rapidity, if meagre range, of the bow and arrow. The Indian trick had been to draw the fire of the defenders toward erratically moving targets staying at the maximum range of the firearm. The mounted Whites could now turn the tables by charging the Indians and relying on rapidity of fire at close range. But repeating weapons, especially rifles, had other uses as well, for they put the mounted man in a position superior to cattle and bison. Hunters armed with repeating weapons now invaded the Plains and engaged in a merciless and fantastic slaughter of the bison. The professionals were after the hides, but others were merely engaged in an orgy of bloodlust; usually the carcasses, and sometimes the entire animals, were left to rot. The nomadic Indian began to find his means of sustenance vanishing.

Meanwhile, in the Texas plains, there was evolving the cattle ranch: a blend of Mexican artistry in managing horse and lariat, of cattle from a variety of stocks (Spanish, French, and English), but acclimated to the plains, of the six-shooter as a weapon for the cowboy, and all within a mild climate whose grass lands were sheltered from gales and from Indian marauders. Before the Civil War, some cattle were already being driven to New Orleans and even Chicago. After the war, the business expanded rapidly, and cattle were driven northward to railheads at such points as Abilene, Kansas, for transportation eastward. Cattlemen now spread over that great sea of grass, the Great Plains, and for a brief time cattle, cowboy, lariat, and six-shooter dominated the area. The land was regarded as open, the grass was free, and water belonged to the first comer. The absence of wood made fencing prohibitively expensive, especially such fencing as might restrain cattle that were nearly wild in their temperament. However, in 1874, barbed wire was invented, and, in addition, the line of agricultural settlement was already reaching the Great Plains. The Homestead Act now made easy the acquiring of land title, and the Plains began to be enclosed. As water holes were preempted and farmers eyed the Plains, the drilled (artesian) well powered by windmill was introduced, facilitating both the development of agriculture and a wider range of area for cattle grazing. The nomadic Indian horseman was victim, and even the cattle rancher had to yield ground to settlers.

Cattle ranchers, homesteaders, travelers, railroad men, and even the settled Indians (such as the Civilized Tribes of Oklahoma) regarded the nomadic Indian as a menace. The federal government realized that they would be expensive to hunt down and control. In general, it preferred to negotiate and to utilize the older and more cautious Indian leadership in an effort to pacify the bands and concentrate them into reservation areas suitably far from areas of intensive White settlement or travel. The mechanism employed was the treaty, whereby the Indians surrendered their rights to vast areas of land in return for annuities in the form of rations. Since the Plains Indians were now suffering from a scarcity of food, owing to the slaughter of the bison, the prospect of rations must have been appealing. Besides, encounters with the U.S. army had been becoming less equitable. In 1854 the Oglalas, with the help of some Dakota bands, had wiped out Lt. Grattan and a band of 29 soldiers, but in the following year General Harney crushed a large encampment of the same Indians. In 1866–1867 a similar pattern was repeated, but with even worse effect, for the Army was now equipped with breech loading rifles, and Chief Red Cloud and his band suffered severe losses. Red Cloud thereafter became an advocate of peace and agreed to the treaty of 1868, by which the Teton were confined to the Great Sioux Reservation (the Missouri River forming the northern and eastern boundaries, and the areas of Kansas and Nebraska being free for settlement and travel). Undoubtedly the rations were swindled and poor, yet relationships were relatively quiet until 1874, when gold was discovered in the Black Hills; although the strike was to prove small, miners flooded into the area (which the treaty had closed to such invasion). Other Whites were settling (again in violation of the treaty) in the mountain valleys of Wyoming and Montana, and then complaining of harassment by the Sioux (i.e., Dakota).

To crown the matter, the Sioux warriors, who were being held in leash by their seniors and inhibited from massacring Whites, were continuing their customary practice of raiding other Indian tribes. Having also signed treaties, these other tribes were under the protection of the federal government and were settled near agencies and under the supervision of missionaries. Pressures were mounting upon the government and Army to seize more land and place the Sioux (Dakota) under tighter control. At that moment, bands of Sioux were hunting on the Powder River, having been given permission to do so because of the sorry state of the rations which were supposed to nourish them. When the Commissioner of Indian affairs issued the demand that the Sioux return to their agencies by January 31, 1876, or be deemed hostile, most of the hunters elected to stay where they were. The Army was sent to discipline them, and there ensued the spectacular defeat of Custer and annihilation of his force.

The Indians have usually proven to be losers in situations of this sort, regardless of the outcome of the battle. Public outcry over the defeat was used by those who had been seeking to erode the reservation area, and the Sioux who were now dependent upon rations, were in a poor position to bargain. There were successive surrenders of land until 1889, when the Great Sioux Reservation was dismantled into the smaller units of Pine Ridge, Rosebud, Standing Rock, and the like. While the treaties had promised a *quid pro quo* in the form of rations, and Congress had threatened suspension of rations if they failed to sign, there was in fact nothing automatic about the issuing of the food: it depended on annual Congressional appropriations and a chain of administrators who had abundant opportunity to misappropriate the monies to their own uses. Throughout the last quarter of the nineteenth century, the Sioux were generally starving and, owing to malnutrition, smitten with all manner of disease.

In 1889 word of the Ghost Dance reached the Teton. The revelation envisioned a millenialist transformation in which the Whites would be swept from the continent and the animal life restored. The Sioux participated with great energy in this chiliastic cult, and the agency personnel became terrified. The consequence was the Wounded Knee Massacre, in which green army troops succumbed to panic and hatred and gunned down not only the warriors, whose weapons proved pathetically inadequate, but women, children, and the aged.

Wounded Knee was not the only massacre by Whites of defenseless Indians, nor was Custer's Last Stand the only defeat by Indians of an Army unit; however, both involved a flamboyant and heroic people, and so have been remembered by Americans and added to their folklore.

Both events were also to be the last of their kind, not only for the Sioux, but for the Plains Indians; thereafter, the history of the peoples becomes a matter of reservation life under the aegis of the Indian Service.

THE MÉTIS

As the beaver were exhausted, the French *voyageurs* journeyed even further westward, up the St. Lawrence, across the Great Lakes, into the northern Plains. Bold and without racial arrogance, the French found the Indians sympathetic and their women attractive. Wherever they journeyed they established liaisons which ripened into marriages, and so was created a type of men who were bred by the fur trade and belonged to the trade and the company. As the trade moved westward, so did the men, and now the brides were no longer Huron but Cree and Chippewa (Salteaux). The hybrid offspring were sometimes known as Boise-Brulés (the people whose skill was like scorched wood) and sometimes as Métis (Mixedblood). Their patois was a French dialect out of Normandy and Picardy to which was added much Algonkian (Cree); the language grew more French as they dealt with outsiders and more Indian around the domestic fire. By the mid-eighteenth century they numbered about 30,000 and were neither Indian nor White, but exhibited the qualities of the hybrid. Not yet a people, a tribe, or a nationality, they shared a common status and an attachment to the fur trade. In the East and on the rivers, they used the canoe and traded in beaver; in the West and on the Great Plains, they hunted bison and developed the Red River Cart, on which they could haul hundreds of pounds of meat and hides. Many followed the Indian custom of having gardens along the river beds, and the European custom of running some livestock in a commons.

When they entered the northern Plains, they were invading land that had been granted in 1670 by the English Crown to "the Governor and Company of Adventurers of England Trading into Hudson's Bay." The terms of the charter made The Company "true and absolute lords and proprietors" of all the lands drained by the rivers flowing into The Bay, and so of a domain which (we now know) totaled a third of a million square miles. The Company was slow to exercise its privileges, and when the English and Scots came up the rivers from The Bay in order to establish trading posts, they found that their rival, working out of Montreal and relying upon the Métis, had matters better in hand. Thus outmaneuvered, the Company decided early in the nineteenth century to embark on a policy of settlement, the notion being to take Scots who had been displaced from their Highlands homes, and relocate them in this unsettled area south and west of Lake Winnipeg. This action initiated another one of those confrontations which distinguish American history, but this time those who opposed the land allotting, farming, and process of settlement were not Indian, but those cultural and racial hybrids—the Métis. In 1816, they organized sufficiently to drive the first group of settlers out of Fort Douglas. The colony was reestablished, but it became increasingly clear that The Hudson's Bay Company could not continue to rule as its private domain this vast area of land and its proud denizens, the Plains Indians and the Métis. Refusing to trade at Company prices in Company stores, they were trekking their pelts far southward (and so contributing to the establishment of the city of St. Paul). John Jacob Astor, lord of the American fur trade, resented the competition, and at his instigation the U.S. Congress tried to prohibit this trade across the border. Like their Indian relations, the Métis were indifferent to national boundaries or property lines recorded in governmental offices, and would just as soon smuggle.

The first Parliament of the new Dominion of Canada met in 1867. The Dominion at that time encompassed only what are now its eastern provinces, and not all of those. The question of the central area—the northern Plains—remained open, and there was fear and even likelihood that the United States would swallow them, just as they had swallowed Alaska. Acting swiftly, the Dominion managed to acquire from The Hudson's Bay Company the title to Rupert's Land, but was then startled to discover that the Métis were attempting to organize and challenge the results of the transaction. The result has been known as the "Red River Rebellion," but as Joseph Kinsey Howard points out, it was scarcely a rebellion, since the natives (Indians and Métis) had been ruled by an absentee and unrepresentative authority (The Hudson's Bay Company) which was not even a legally constituted government, and the transfer of status had taken place without their consent and without even formal notice. Those who organized to contest the transfer propelled forward into acting as their leader a young man who had acquired a seminary education in Quebec. Louis Riel tried to create a government for "the People of Rupert's Land and the Northwest," and to do so independently of Canada yet within the British Empire, but in the end the English–Canadians were better organized and his Provisional Government fled.

Had the issues been formally phrased, they might have focused on the vital questions of how the land was to be surveyed and which areas were to be private property and which common. The Canadians were to succeed in imposing the rectangular grid, just as it had been imposed south of their borders, regardless of terrain. Yet the Métis (like the early cattle ranchers) had alloted their property along the riverside, for without water they could not inhabit the land. Moreover, if they and their

Indian relatives were to secure their livelihood from hunting bison, vast areas of the Plains would have to be left open and common, just as they had always been, and only riparian rights could be left available for private ownership and transfer. In 1885 Métis tried again to oppose imposition of the rectangular grid, and a handful of fighters under Gabriel Dumont managed to discomfit the Mounted Police, but, like Plains Indians in similar straits, they were overwhelmed by repeating rifles, Gatling guns, and artillery. The Canadians imposed the rectangular grid, thereupon destroying the ecological position of the Métis. As the Canadian Plains were brought under the plow, those who had once been masters of the land were relegated to the lowest status.

INTERPRETIVE CONCLUSION

In this introductory chapter we have surveyed historically some of the interactions between various invading groups of Europeans (or Euroamericans) and representative bands of the native inhabitants of the Americas. From a negative perspective, I have tried to provide the background for debunking some of the mythic notions that have conventionally distorted the understanding of American Indians. For example, there is a natural tendency to read into history the present configuration of national boundaries, with the consequence that an artificial line is then imagined to have separated the natives of North America from their kinsmen in Central and South America. This misreading of history has the added misfortune of causing the student of North American Indians to ignore their historical interconnections with the high civilizations of the Mexican plateau and the Andean highlands. Another mythic notion which I have tried to undercut is that which pictures Indians as unchanging, as static in their cultures prior to the European invasions, and as unduly resistant to the changes and opportunities that were incident to these invasions. Correspondingly, the myths tend to show Whites as more cruel and aggressive than they always were, and as sharing more consensus than they did about the nature of morality, religion, or civilized life.

On the more positive side, I have tried to communicate a certain ecological understanding (in the classical sense of Park, 1936a,b, or Hughes and Hughes, 1952; or in the more contemporary sense of Bennett, 1969). We have witnessed not merely a process of military conquest and political hegemony, but, more fundamentally, a continual series of transformations in the adaptations of men to land and therefore of men to each other in relationship to the land.

Some of these ecological transformations—e.g., the rise of the horsenomads of the Great Plains—were pioneered by the Indians themselves; others—as among the Yaquis, the Six Nations, the Cherokees, and the Métis—represented a cultural alloying ("Melting Pot") or blending together of the elements of native and European cultures (a process stimulated and encouraged by missionization and intermarriage). Still other transformations—e.g., the cattle ranch of the open plains—were pioneered by the invaders and adapted to by the natives. In any case, they all illustrate how Indians—whether "Fullblood" or "Halfbreed" (Mestizo, Métis) —responded positively and aggressively to the opportunities presented by the interactions of peoples in the New World. Such distinctive and novel adaptations were associated with the emergence of new cultural forms, although in the end most of the adaptations were destroyed and the novel cultural forms rendered obsolete. In consequence, those who had maintained a distinct tribal identity became part of a lower caste, herded onto wastelands and administered by the agents of an alien government.

Such a fluid mingling of peoples and series of social and ecological adaptations cannot be brought under a simple system of conceptualizations. Rewording the schema of Milton M. Gordon (1964), we can speak of Hispano-Conformity as a principal ideology operative in Latin America, as we speak of Anglo-Conformity in the north. We can also observe that there has been considerable intermarriage, and a Melting Pot, especially in Latin America, with the emergence of a broad Ladino (or Mestizo) stratum in the population. Yet the overriding theme has been one of invasion and displacement—an ecological succession (Park, 1936a,b) which has sometimes been physical and sometimes sociocultural—as persons of European extraction came to dominate the land and to impose on its usage not only new technologies but also a new set of social and legal forms.

Finally, and most importantly, I have tried to show that "Indians" were not entities who were present in pre-Columbian times, but rather that this social identity emerged in relationship to the invasions of Euroropeans. This is especially clear in Latin America, where "Indio" is the correlative of "Ladino" and "Mestizo," but it is also true in the U.S. As we shall have occasion to discuss later in the book, part of "the Indian problem" is the problem of who are what kinds of Indians, and what should be their position or status in relationship to other persons and groups in North America.

SUGGESTED READINGS

Bennett, John W. 1969. *Northern Plainsmen: Adaptive Strategy and Agrarian Life*. Chicago: Aldine Publishing Company.

DeVoto, Bernard. 1962. *The Course of Empire.* Boston: Houghton Mifflin Company.

Gordon, Milton M. 1964. *Assimilation in American Life: The Role of Race, Religion, and National Origins.* New York: Oxford University Press, Inc.

Hagan, William T. 1961. *American Indians.* Chicago: University of Chicago Press.

Howard, Joseph Kinsey. 1952. *Strange Empire: A Narrative of the Northwest.* New York: William Morrow & Co., Inc.

Hughes, Everett Cherrington, and Helen MacGill Hughes. 1952. *Where Peoples Meet: Racial and Ethnic Frontiers.* New York: The Free Press.

Nash, Manning, ed. 1967. *Handbook of Middle American Indians,* ed. R. Wauchope; Vol. VI. *Social Anthropology.* Austin: University of Texas Press.

Oswalt, Wendell H. 1966. *This Land Was Theirs.* New York: John Wiley & Sons, Inc.

Park, Robert Ezra. 1936a. Human ecology. *American Journal of Sociology,* 42, 1–15. Reprinted: Park, 1952, pp. 145–158.

———. 1936b. Succession, An Ecological Concept. *American Sociological Review,* 1, 171–179. Reprinted: Park, 1952, pp. 223–232.

———. 1952. *Human Communities: The City and Human Ecology. Collected Papers of Robert Ezra Park,* Vol. II, ed. Everett Cherrington Hughes *et al.* New York: The Free Press.

Spencer, Robert F., Jesse D. Jennings, *et al.* 1965. *The Native Americans.* New York: Harper & Row, Publishers.

Spicer, Edward H. 1962. *Cycles of Conquest: The Impact of Spain, Mexico, and the United States on the Indians of the Southwest, 1533–1960.* Tucson: University of Arizona Press.

Stegner, Wallace. 1962. *Wolf Willow: A History, a Story and a Memory of the Last Plains Frontier.* New York: The Viking Press, Inc.

Underhill, Ruth M. 1953. *Red Man's America.* Chicago: University of Chicago Press.

Webb, Walter Prescott. 1931. *The Great Plains.* New York: Grosset & Dunlap, Inc. (Universal Library UL–29).

Wolf, Eric. 1959. *Sons of the Shaking Earth: The People of Mexico and Guatemala—Their Land, History and Culture.* Chicago: University of Chicago Press (Phoenix Book P90).

Estimates of the total aboriginal population of the Americas (North and South) have varied from as low as 9 million to as high as 100 million. Given the spread of agriculture, there must have been a pattern of increase in population, but, at the same time, and as had occurred in Europe, there would have been fluctuations in population size caused by variations in ecological factors, including drought and disease. (Europe in the centuries preceding settlement of the New World had experienced both a significant growth in population associated with technological innovation and the severe declines from the Black Death.) Density of population in the Americas would have varied from the sparse distributions of hunting and gathering peoples (e.g., the Eskimo) to the more concentrated settlements of the agriculturalists. Dobyns (1966, pp. 395–449), one of the scholars who believes that the total aboriginal population of the Americas in the fifteenth century was about 100 million, assigns 30 of those millions to the Andean civilizations and another 30 to the Mexican civilizations, while placing the North American figure at about 10 million. Other scholars, following the lead of A. L. Kroeber, have estimated these populations at about a tenth of Dobyn's figures, giving 1 million as the pre-Columbian population of North America.

Demography

SPANISH AMERICA

If estimating aboriginal population has its difficulties, the situation after the Spanish Conquest and settlement is also far from resolved, for the crucial issue now becomes that of defining "Indians" so that their numbers may be counted. As we have already indicated, the aboriginal population was composed of separate and distinct local groupings—a diversity of languages and a multitude of bands and tribes, as well as a number of larger political groupings. This heterogeneity was lumped together by the Spanish and classified as *Indio*. As the classification system developed, the term *Mestizo* was used to designate the individual who was actually a cultural and social hybrid, but who was regarded as if he were a biological hybrid, i.e., the offspring of the *Criollo* (*gente de razón*, or other label) with the *Indio*. The Mestizo spoke Spanish, wore European dress, practiced a form of Roman Catholicism, and did not maintain close ties to an enclaved Indian community. A label such as Criollo was reserved for the small and powerful elite who could defend their claim of pure Spanish ancestry. As a student of population, it is necessary to be cautious about the implications of the term "Indio." Certainly, insofar as biology is concerned, the Mestizo (or Ladino) population contained a large contribution from the aboriginal gene pool, and was in this sense more Indian than European. In terms of culture, there had been considerable interchange of traits between Indian natives and Spanish settlers, so that, for example, most Indian communities became at least nominally Catholic, and, conversely, many Indian traits, such as culinary habits, became widely diffused throughout the entire population. As a consequence, there has been considerable uncertainty as to how to delineate and measure the population of Indios. This has been accentuated by the disinterest of many Latin American nations in conducting exact censuses.

Some broad tendencies are clear. Pressures consequent upon the Spanish invasion resulted in drastic reductions in native population. Disease—sometimes even deliberately introduced—was a terrible factor, and the effect of diseases was magnified by the Spanish attempt to resettle the Indian bands in larger concentrations. The attempt to utilize Indians as slave labor (in mines and plantations) resulted in large numbers of deaths (the Spanish ultimately being moved to transport African slaves for the same purposes). In some areas, the Spanish elite regarded the hunting and gathering bands as species of game or vermin, and pursued them accordingly. As a result, substantial areas (e.g., the Caribbean Islands) of the New World were totally cleared of their aboriginal populations, and the Indian population may have decreased to as little as one-twentieth of its original figure. Catastrophic developments of this sort had grave effects upon native cultural patterns and social organization. For example, the native system of irrigated agriculture in areas now the U.S. Southwest and the Mexican North was abandoned; when agriculture was reintroduced there, it followed the European pattern. Lest the student think that decimation of the Indians was a phenomenon only of past centuries and confined to the Spanish, it might be remarked, first, that similar depopulations occurred in the Northern hemisphere (e.g., on the island of Newfoundland, whose aboriginal inhabitants, termed Beothuk, were aggressively hunted by French and English fishermen and so became extinct early in the nineteenth century), and, second, that the slaughter of Indians in such areas as Brazil has been continuing throughout recent decades (with attacks by machine gun and dynamite from airplanes and deliberate infestation with smallpox; cf. *The New York Times*, May 13, 1968).

In the Middle American states at the time of the separation from

Spain in 1821, the population of Indios has been estimated as from 40 to 75 per cent of the total population (see Table 2–1).

After independence, the problem of estimating Indian populations acquires further complexity because of lack of agreement on criteria for labeling individuals as Indian, differences among nations' census procedures, and varying efficiencies of national censuses. Generally, a linguistic criterion has been used, with an Indian defined as a person who is a

TABLE 2–1

INDIAN POPULATION OF
MIDDLE AMERICA AT NATIONAL
INDEPENDENCE (1821–1825)

Region	Total Population (Thousands)	Indians, % of Total
Mexico	6,800	54.4
Guatemala	661	73.6
El Salvador	250	42.8
Honduras	137	a
Nicaragua	207	40.0
British Honduras	—	—
Central America (minus Costa Rica)	1,600	55.0

SOURCES: Rosenblat (1954), Vol. I, Table 3; Baron Castro (1942), pp. 273, 554; Orellana (1950); Squier (1855), p. 52, as summarized and presented by Adams (1967), p. 471, Table 1.

a Not available.

TABLE 2–2

INDIAN POPULATION OF
MIDDLE AMERICA, 1956

Region	Total Population (Thousands)	Indian Population (Thousands)	Indian Population (%)
Mexico	30,538	795a	2.6
Guatemala	3,303	1,479	44.8
El Salvador	2,269	—	—
Honduras	1,711	80.7	4.7
Nicaragua	1,261	20.0a	1.6

SOURCE: *The Statistical Abstract of Latin America*, published by the Committee on Latin American Studies, University of California, Los Angeles, 2nd ed., as presented by Flores (1967), p. 20, Table 1.

a Monolinguals (speakers of Indian Language only); other figures include bilinguals.

native speaker of a local Indian language (see Table 2–2). However, as familiarity with Spanish has spread throughout the national populations, an increasing number of persons who are classified as Indian are bilingual. With the use of these criteria, the evidence indicates an increase in the total number of Indians but a decrease in their relative proportion of the national population. The figures (Table 2–3) for Mexico illustrate the general tendency. The figures from Mexico are also valuable for showing the detailed listing of languages and the proportions of each linguistic community which can be classified as monolingual (speaking only the Indian language) or as bilingual (also speaking Spanish); see Table 2–4.

If we explore further the nature of this linguistic definition of Indianness in Middle America, we find the following (cf. Van den Berghe, 1968). Those who are classified as Indians are participants in the ceremonial life of small local communities into which they have been born and where they have been raised. This ceremonial life is mediated through the native Indian language. The communal life makes severe social and economic demands on the participants, to the degree where the ceremonial system can be regarded as a social device that shares and levels the possessions of the adult males of the Indian community. Because the Indian communities are poor and lack land, individuals travel or migrate from them and settle elsewhere. While they may then find themselves near alien communities of Indians, they have no motivation to enter into the ceremonial and domestic lives of those who are not their kith and kin. Rather—for temporary periods or longer—the migrants tend to dissolve into the Mestizo (or Ladino) population, adopting the Spanish language as primary and the Spanish mode of dress,

TABLE 2–3

INDIAN POPULATION IN MEXICO

Date	Total Indians		Bilingual Indians, Number (Millions)
	Number (Millions)	% of Total	
1900	1.79	15.37	—
1910	1.69	12.98	—
1921	1.87	15.11	—
1930	2.25	16.05	—
1940	2.49	14.85	1.25
1950	2.45	11.30	1.65

SOURCES: Dávalos Hurtado and Marino Flores (1956); Marino Flores and Castro de la Fuente (1960); Mexico, *Dirección General de Estadística* (1960); Parra (1950); as summarized and presented by King (1967), p. 515, Table 1.

TABLE 2–4

MONOLINGUAL SPEAKERS OF
INDIAN LANGUAGES, MEXICO

Language	Total Speakers	Monolinguals	% of Monolinguals
Amuzgo	12,826	5,839	45.5
Cora	3,125	228	7.3
Chatino	13,446	8,259	61.4
Chinantec	35,654	15,702	44.0
Chol	31,139	18,898	60.7
Chontal	24,703	1,539	6.2
Huastec	66,646	17,276	25.9
Huichol	3,449	1,035	30.0
Kikapu	500	132	26.4
Maya	328,255	50,912	15.5
Mayo	31,053	2,509	8.1
Mazahua	84,125	16,254	19.3
Mazatec	77,530	47,167	60.8
Mixe	46,101	21,005	45.6
Mixtec	185,470	76,946	41.5
Nahuatl	641,334	212,813	30.1
Otomi	185,656	57,559	31.0
Popoloca	17,163	1,564	9.1
Tarahumara	18,421	9,796	22.2
Tarasco	44,102	8,166	44.3
Tepehuano	4,677	1,583	33.8
Tlapaneco	18,139	12,234	67.4
Totonac	106,696	54,333	50.9
Tzeltal	48,279	31,856	66.0
Tzotzil	74,827	44,103	58.9
Yaqui	2,640	199	7.5
Zapotec	226,995	60,680	26.7
Zoque	18,023	4,804	26.7
Others	139,935	11,678	—
Total	2,490,909	795,069	
Average			32.0

SOURCE: México, *Dirección General de Estadistica*
(1953), as presented by Flores (1967), p. 22, Table 3.

which is cheaper. Thus, transformations between Indio and Ladino
(Mestizo) are continually under way, as Indios leave their natal communities or return to them in response either to differential economic opportunity or a stage in their own life cycle. In Guatemala, as Van den
Berghe (1968) analyzes the process, there has been a drastic shift of Indians from their impoverished rural communities into the urban and
commercial agricultural areas, and the results can be seen in Table 2–5.

TABLE 2–5

ETHNIC COMPOSITION OF
GUATEMALAN POPULATION, 1774–1964

Year	% Indian	% Ladino
1774	78.4	21.6
1880	64.7	35.3
1921	64.8	35.2
1940	55.7	44.3
1950	53.6	46.4
1964	43.3	56.7

SOURCE: Van den Berghe,
1968, p. 515.

It is noteworthy that these migrants do not seem to cluster as visible and ethnically distinctive enclaves within their new environments, but instead dissolve into the lower class Ladino environment.

THE U.S.A.

General

We have indicated that the aboriginal population of the region which was to become the U.S.A. has been estimated as low as 1 million and as high as 10 million persons. We have also indicated that, with the White invasions and settlements, there arises the knotty question of designating or defining Indians for purposes of census. From a biological or genetic perspective, Indians made a significant contribution to the total gene pool of U.S. population, since much interbreeding occurred and many of the offspring merged into the non-Indian population, either as Whites, Negroes, or the small groups of "almost whites" that have dotted the southern landscape. Moreover, many of the Spanish-speaking peoples who migrated to the U.S. from Mexico were largely of Indian extraction.

If, however, we speak of Indian in the sense of socially distinct bands bearing a recognizably Indian culture, then the depopulation was catastrophic. By 1800 the native population was about 600,000, and 50 years later it was about 250,000. The causes were basically malnutrition and disease, with the former predisposing to the latter. The malnutrition was caused by the eroding of the ecological basis of Indian subsistence, while the diseases were consequent upon the White migrations, including especially smallpox and tuberculosis, but also influenza, mumps, and diphtheria. The decimation of the Plains Indian tribes is well documented. For example, a smallpox pandemic in 1837 reduced the Mandan from 1,600 to 31. In addition to starvation and disease, deliberate massacres were also a major factor. In a short span of years in California—it is believed—the miners eliminated nine-tenths of the original population.

As we note elsewhere, Indian administration in the era after the Civil War was rife with corruption, which meant that the tribes received less than the stipulated quantities of treaty goods and little in the way of health or welfare services. The plight of these peoples could not be hidden, and in time various reform associations took up the cause of the Indians. By the turn of the century there had begun some definite improvements. Correspondingly, the population of these tribes began to rise, so that in the half-century from 1910 to 1960 it has about doubled. Deliberate slaughter and debauchery had been ended, while more adequate diet, proper sanitation, and medical care have all contributed to positive growth of population.

As always, any figures on Indian population must be viewed in the context of the definition being used. For example, figures maintained by the Bureau of Indian Affairs (B.I.A.) issue out of its legal responsibilities as defined by law. While the B.I.A. inherited a custodial and even authoritarian role in relationship to Indian peoples, the legal basis for much of its operations has been its status as trustee for reservation lands, so that the peoples it is concerned with are those who qualify as owners and heirs to this land. Heirship, in turn, is determined by Anglo-Saxon principles of descent, rather than possession of cultural traits or participation in the life of an Indian community. Thus, in the strictest sense, the B.I.A. regards as an Indian any person who qualifies as an heir to reservation land, a qualification expressed in hereditary terms as "degree of Indian blood." In cases where a land base does not exist—as where Congress has allotted the reservation area in severalty and terminated federal responsibilities—the B.I.A. has small basis for action or responsibility. For example, the independent Cherokee Nation in northeastern Oklahoma was dissolved by act of Congress early in this century, its lands allotted in severalty, and its rolls of membership closed. Despite the fact that traditional Cherokee communities have continued to exist, maintaining the native language for domestic and ceremonial purposes, there was in 1969 neither an official roster of their population nor even any census of their numbers.

A different sort of estimate of Indian population derives from the operations of the U.S. Bureau of Census, but here too there have been great variations in procedures used and much leeway allowed to the census taker. Moreover, since there have been social and political disabilities connected with being classified as an Indian, many individuals of Indian ancestry have had considerable incentive to "pass" as non-

Indian. In principle, intermarriage, interbreeding, and adoption of Euroamerican traits (such as style of grooming and shearing the hair) was supposed to transform the Indian into the non-Indian, and many of those who underwent such transformations did not appear on public records as "Indian." It is arguable that if the U.S. counted a person as Indian in a manner parallel to that which counts him as Negro—i.e., some minimal degree of Indian ancestry, a drop of "Indian blood"—then the "Indian population" would number into the millions. In recent years there has been a considerable swing in this direction, inasmuch as a variety of advantages—economic, political, and even social—have begun to accrue to those classified as "Indian."

Most significantly, there has been passage of legislation and establishment of a special court of claims under which Indian tribes could sue the U.S. Government for such past violations of civil law as taking their land for insufficient compensation. When judgments are made for an Indian tribe as plaintiff, the proceeds are distributed on an heirship basis. While the mode of handling and distributing these awards has varied, it can happen that individuals share in them who are only marginally Indian in ancestry, and not at all so in their traits or social life. In like manner, there are some federal benefits, such as access to the Indian branch of the Public Health Service, which are available to individuals who can demonstrate that they have a quarter degree or more of Indian blood. Finally, claiming to be "Indian" now has a certain cachet in many circles, even though there are hotels, restaurants, and taverns in some Western towns which make a practice of denying service to clientele that is identifiably Indian.

After the 1950 census, some students of Indian affairs felt that it was likely that the Indian population in some geographic areas, especially urban, was being underrecorded. Accordingly, new procedures were adopted for the 1960 census so that "whereas formerly the classification was obtained in most cases by the enumerator's observation, in 1960 it was possible for members of the household to classify themselves" (U.S. Bureau of Census, 1960, Vol. I, pp. xli–xlii). And the specific question used was "Is this person White, Negro, American Indian, Japanese, Chinese, Filipino, . . . Aleut, Eskimo (etc.)?" The Census volume goes on to comment that

> In addition to fullblooded American Indians, persons of mixed white and Indian blood are included in this category if they are enrolled on an Indian tribal or agency roll or if they are regarded as Indians in the community. A common requirement for such enrollment at present is that the proportion of Indian blood should be at least one-fourth. Indians living in Indian territory or on reservations were not included in the official population count of the United States until 1890 [p. xlii].

The foregoing phraseology ("mixed white and Indian blood") avoids the issue of the interbreeding of other stocks, specifically Negro. The Census volume does go on to note that there are in the U.S. certain groups of mixed White, Negro, and Indian descent which have been variously classified, but which in 1960 were usually listed as "Indian." One consequence of including these intermixtures as "Indian" is that the Indian population of the U.S. appears to have undergone a population growth higher than might otherwise be attributed to it (46.5 per cent rather than 36.1 per cent). Note that the phraseology also chooses to distinguish "Eskimo" from "Indian"; this is a belated recognition of the differences among the native peoples of the Americas, but cannot be defended on the basis of a logical system of classification. The traditional Eskimo were no more unlike the traditional Sioux than the latter were unlike the traditional Papago, yet the latter two populations were lumped together as "Indian," whereas the former, because of their ecological isolation, were classed separately.

Distribution

Without further prolonging an already complex discussion, we may note that, as of 1960, census procedures show an Indian population for the U.S. of about a half-million persons, and Table 2–6 shows their distribution by region of the country and by state. It will be noted that the largest numbers of Indians are located in Arizona, Oklahoma, New Mexico, and California. Table 2–7, taken from the same authority, shows the distribution of Indian (and total U.S.) population by size of place. The most obvious disproportion is in the size of the population in urban areas: for the general population this is almost 70 per cent, whereas for Indians it is less than 30 per cent.

If we turn from discussions of overall Indian population to sizes of particular tribes, the situation is again made complex because the tribal identifications of the nineteenth and earlier centuries have in many cases broken down as a result of reservation settlement patterns, intermarriage, and acculturation. Thus, on the Fort Berthold Reservation of Montana, the Mandan, Gros Ventre, and Arickara have tended to merge, just as in western Oklahoma the various Plains Indians (Comanche, Apache, Kiowa-Apache, and Kiowa) have displayed the same inclination. Conversely, where a people has been divided by the process of reservation settlement, the tendency has been for differences between them to develop and become pronounced, as, for example, between the Apache located in Oklahoma and those in Arizona, or the Sioux scattered among the reservations of the northern plains (Dakotas, Montana, and Minnesota).

TABLE 2–6

INDIAN AND TOTAL POPULATION
BY REGIONS, DIVISIONS, AND STATES, 1960

Region, Division and State	Total Population	Indian Population	Region, Division and State	Total Population	Indian Population
United States	179,323,175	523,591	W.N. Central:		
			Minnesota	3,413,864	15,496
Regions:			Iowa	2,757,537	1,708
Northeast	44,677,819	26,356	Missouri	4,319,813	1,723
North Central	51,619,139	98,631	North Dakota	632,446	11,736
South	54,973,113	127,568	South Dakota	680,514	25,794
West	28,053,104	271,036	Nebraska	1,411,330	5,545
			Kansas	2,178,611	5,069
Northeast:			South Atlantic:		
New England	10,509,367	6,044	Delaware	446,292	597
Middle Atlantic	34,168,452	20,312	Maryland	3,100,689	1,538
			District of		
North Central:			Columbia	763,956	587
E.N. Central	36,225,024	31,560	Virginia	3,966,949	2,155
W.N. Central	15,394,115	67,071	West Virginia	1,860,421	181
			No. Carolina	4,556,155	38,129
			So. Carolina	2,382,594	1,098
South:			Georgia	3,943,116	749
South Atlantic	25,971,732	47,538	Florida	4,951,560	2,504
E.S. Central	12,050,126	5,424			
W.S. Central	16,951,255	74,606	E.S. Central:		
			Kentucky	3,038,156	391
West:			Tennessee	3,567,089	638
Mountain	6,855,060	188,004	Alabama	3,266,740	1,276
Pacific	21,198,044	83,032	Mississippi	2,178,141	3,119
			W.S. Central:		
New England:			Arkansas	1,786,272	580
Maine	969,265	1,879	Louisiana	3,257,022	3,587
New Hampshire	606,921	135	Oklahoma	2,328,284	64,689
Vermont	389,881	57	Texas	9,579,677	5,750
Massachusetts	5,148,578	2,118			
Rhode Island	859,488	932	Mountain:		
Connecticut	2,535,234	923	Montana	674,767	21,181
			Idaho	667,191	5,231
			Wyoming	330,066	4,020
Middle Atlantic:			Colorado	1,753,947	4,288
New York	16,782,304	16,491	New Mexico	951,023	56,255
New Jersey	6,066,782	1,699	Arizona	1,302,161	83,387
Pennsylvania	11,319,366	2,122	Utah	890,627	6,961
			Nevada	285,278	6,681
E.N. Central:			Pacific:		
Ohio	9,706,397	1,910	Washington	2,853,214	21,076
Indiana	4,662,498	948	Oregon	1,768,687	8,026
Illinois	10,081,158	4,704	California	15,717,204	39,014
Michigan	7,823,194	9,701	Alaska	226,167	14,444
Wisconsin	3,951,777	14,297	Hawaii	632,772	472

Source: U.S. Census of Population (1960), Vol. I, Table 56.

TABLE 2-7

LOCATION OF INDIAN AND TOTAL POPULATION IN THE UNITED STATES BY SIZE OF PLACE, 1960

	Total Population				Indian Population			
	Male	Female	Total	% Distribution	Male	Female	Total	% Distribution
Urban:								
Urbanized areas								
Central cities	27,927,624	30,047,508	57,975,132	32.3	31,615	32,563	64,178	12.3
Urban fringe	18,566,586	19,306,769	37,873,355	21.1	10,226	10,226	20,452	3.9
Total	46,494,210	49,354,277	95,848,487	53.5	41,841	42,789	84,630	16.2
Other urban								
Places of 10,000 or more	7,838,676	8,334,163	16,172,839	9.0	14,152	14,188	28,340	5.4
Places of 2,500 to 10,000	6,400,119	6,847,305	13,247,424	7.4	15,972	16,651	32,623	6.2
Total	14,238,795	15,181,468	29,420,263	16.4	30,124	30,839	60,963	11.6
Total Urban	60,733,005	64,535,745	125,268,750	69.9	71,965	73,628	145,593	27.8
Rural:								
Places of 1,000 to 2,500	3,149,869	3,346,919	6,496,788	3.6	10,849	11,495	22,344	4.3
Other rural	24,448,620	23,109,017	47,557,637	26.5	180,555	175,099	355,654	67.9
Total Rural	27,598,489	26,455,936	54,054,425	30.1	191,404	186,594	377,998	72.2
Grand total	88,331,494	90,991,681	179,323,175	100.0	263,369	260,222	523,591	100.0

SOURCE: U.S. Census of the Population (1960), Vol. I, Table 44.

Recognizing the foregoing qualifications, the largest and most unitary tribe are the Navajo, whose central base is a reservation largely in Arizona, but with portions in New Mexico and Utah. In 1960 the B.I.A. gave the Navajo population as about 74,000, but scholarly sources have advanced estimates as high as 100,000, and there are many distinctively Navajo persons who have migrated away from the reservation to other locations in the southwest. Because of their tribal size and, until recently, isolation in the deserts and mountains, the Navajo have not had a strong self-identification as "Indian." More than many other tribes, they see themselves as a distinct people, i.e., *Diné* (Navajo).

Another large tribal group are the Sioux, whose several reservation populations (Tax *et al.*, 1961) have been given as Pine Ridge, 10,648; Rosebud, 8,183; Standing Rock, 4,500; Cheyenne River, 4,307; Crow Creek, 1,132; Santee, 1,372; Lower Brule, 705; Fort Peck (Assiniboine and Sioux), 3,285; Yankton, 2,391; Sisseton Wahpeton, 3,542; and Pipestone, 582. Additional large numbers of Sioux are located in the cities and towns of the northern plains as well as in the major urban centers to which Indians have been relocated. A different large cluster of peoples are the Tribal Cherokee and Tribal Creek of eastern Oklahoma, whose numbers are difficult to count but may for present purposes be considered at about 10,000 each.

Throughout this century Indians have been migrating between their reservation homes and urban centers, but the movement assumed significant proportions and began to create significant new communities only with World War II. The process has continued, and by the late 1960's it was estimated that one-third of the total Indian population of the U.S. was located in urban places. Generally, people search for new homes reluctantly, usually because they are hungry or grossly oppressed. The push for the Indians has come because the resource base on their reservations is limited, while their population has expanded rapidly (largely a result of modern public health practices). The programed relocation of the B.I.A. has accelerated the process, but the economic need was there. As economically constituted, reservations cannot support the population which has been growing upon them. For example, it has been stated (Luebben, 1959, p. 6) that the Navajo Reservation can support at a minimal level only one-half of its estimated population of 75,000 "even under the best circumstances." Of course, a particular migrant may offer a variety of reasons for making the jump: "to be with relatives elsewhere," "to get a job," "to see life"; but the dominant influence is the simple search for survival. Given their low levels of skills, Indians have primarily been drawn to areas of rapidly expanding industry, especially those boomed by military contracts.

For the reasons discussed above, census data on Indians in cities have been especially inadequate, and only recently has there begun to accumulate even approximative data on many areas. Nevertheless, it is true that the Indian population of cities, especially in western states, has been increasing rapidly. During the decade 1950–1960, the Indian population of California increased 95 per cent; most of this was immigration to metropolitan areas. Los Angeles doubled in Indian population during that decade, and was estimated to contain 25,000, representing over 100 tribes and deriving from almost every state in the union. Three tribal clusters—Navajo, Sioux, and "Five Civilized Tribes"—constitute over half of the sample studied (Price, 1968). The figures for Minneapolis are smaller but showed a larger percentile gain during the same decade, from 426 to 2,077, and both numbers are taken to be underestimates. Experts in the Twin Cities area consider that the true figures are several times as great. For the sample studied, the tribal groups represented were Chippewa (Ojibway), 68 per cent; Sioux, 5 per cent; and Winnebago, 3 per cent (League of Women Voters, 1968). However imprecise, these figures suggest the strength of migration to the metropolis and the extent to which it becomes a tribal mixer. Other cities, such as Denver, Chicago, and Dallas, have also become the home of large numbers of Indians from a diversity of regions, cultures, and linguistic backgrounds. Thus the city becomes not only the frontier where Indian and White meet, but also where Cherokee, Sioux, Navajo, Chippewa, and many others are meeting, adjusting to each other, and helping to shape the identity of the American Indian.

CANADA

These northernmost territories of the Americas have been inhabited by hunting and gathering peoples who spent much of the year dispersed in small bands. Vast areas of land were characterized by low densities of Indian population. The major exception to this generalization was on the western coast, where the richness of marine and riverine life, and abundant wood, water, and other resources facilitated the development of an elaborate culture of near-civilized quality. The decline suffered by this Indian population may be seen in the fact that the coastal Indian population of British Columbia numbered nearly 50,000 in 1835, whereas by 1929 the number had sunk to 12,366. Since that time the population has again been increasing in absolute numbers, but the surrounding population of Whites has increased astronomically (LaViolette, 1961, pp. 98, 178).

For Canada as a whole, the population regulated by the Indian

Affairs Branch numbered about 100,000 at the turn of the century. By 1965, this population had more than doubled, and there were 551 bands and 2,267 reserves (including 72 Indian settlements not classified as reserves) which were administered by 87 agencies of the Branch (Hawthorn, 1966, p. 207). Of these bands, 42 per cent numbered less than 200 persons and 77 per cent numbered less than 500, while only 7 per cent had populations of above 1,000. This means that these bands have had little opportunity to acquire social or political power, and, since most of them are impoverished, were it not for their special governmental status, they have been a minority which could scarcely be called viable.

The configuration of Canadian laws and agencies has been quite different from that in the U.S., and we do not have space to enter here into the complexities. The Eskimo have been more isolated than the other American natives, and have been subjected to patterns of treatment different from what is offered to those labeled as Indian. In addition, the special hybrid group known as Métis (Slobodin, 1966), representing a union of French and Indian cultures, has also suffered various social problems and has sought special governmental status akin to that of the Indians.

SUGGESTED READINGS

Adams, Richard N. 1967. Nationalization, in *Handbook of Middle American Indians*, ed. R. Wauchope; Vol. VI: *Social Anthropology*, ed. M. Nash. Austin: University of Texas Press.

Barón Castro, Rodolfo. 1942. *La población de El Salvador*. Madrid: Instituto G. Fernández Oviedo.

Dávalos Hurtado, E., and A. Marino Flores. 1956. *Reflexiones acerca de la antropología mexicana*. Mexico City: Anales del Instituto Nacional de Antropología e Historia, 8, 163–209.

Dobyns, Henry F. 1966. Estimating Aboriginal American Population: An Appraisal of Techniques with a New Hemispheric Estimate. *Current Anthropology*, 7, 395–416 and seq.

Hawthorn, H. B., ed. 1966. *A Survey of the Contemporary Indians of Canada: A Report on Economic, Political, Educational Needs and Policies*; Vol. I. Ottawa: Indian Affairs Branch.

King, Arden R. 1967. Urbanization and Industrialization, in *Handbook of Middle American Indians*, ed. R. Wauchope; Vol. VI: *Social Anthropology*, ed. M. Nash. Austin: University of Texas Press.

LaViolette, Forrest E. 1961. *The Struggle for Survival: Indian Cultures and the Protestant Ethic in British Columbia*. Toronto: University of Toronto Press.

League of Women Voters of Minneapolis. 1968. *Indians in Minneapolis*. Minneapolis: League of Women Voters.

Luebben, Ralph A. 1959. The Navajo Dilemma—A Question of Necessity. *The American Indian*, 8, 2 (Winter), 6–16.

Marino Flores, Anselmo. 1967. Indian Population and Its Identification, in *Handbook of Middle American Indians*, ed. R. Wauchope; Vol. VI: *Social Anthropology*, ed. M. Nash, pp. 12–25. Austin: University of Texas Press.

————, and A. Castro de la Fuente. 1960. *La población agrícola y la educación en la República Mexicana*. Mexico City: Instituto Nacional de Antropología e Historia Pub. 4.

Orellana, G. R. A. 1950. *Estudios sobre aspectos técnicos del censo de población*. Univ. Autónoma de San Carlos de Guatemala.

Parra, Manuel Germán. 1950. *Densidad de la población de habla indígena en la República Mexicana*. Mexico City: Instituto Nacional Indigenista, Mem. # 1.

Price, John A. 1968. The Migration and Adaptation of American Indians to Los Angeles. *Human Organization*, 27, 2 (Summer), 168–175.

Rosenblat, Ángel. 1954. *La población indígena y el meslizaje en América. I, La poblacion indígena, 1492–1950; II, El mestizaje y las castas coloniales.* Buenos Aires: Editorial Nova. 2 vols.

Slobodin, Richard. 1966. *Métis of the Mackenzie District.* Ottawa: Saint-Paul University, Canadian Research Center for Anthropology.

Squier, Ephraim George. 1855. *Notes on Central America, Particularly on the States of Honduras and El Salvador: Their Geography, Topography, Climate, Population, etc., etc., and the Proposed Honduras Inter-oceanic Railway.* New York: Harper and Bros.

Tax, Sol, *et al.* 1961. *Map: The North American Indians, 1950 Distribution of the Descendants of the Aboriginal Population of Alaska, Canada, and the United States.* Chicago: University of Chicago, Department of Anthropology.

U.S. Bureau of Census. *Census of Population: 1960*; Vol. 1: *U.S. Summary.* Washington, D.C.: U.S. Government Printing Office.

Van den Berghe, Pierre L. 1968. Ethnic Membership and Cultural Change in Guatemala. *Social Forces*, 46, 4, 514–522.

CHAPTER THREE

THE EARLY PERIOD

Initial relations between the European invaders and the Indian natives were marked by much ignorance and ornamented on both sides by fantastic mythology. For a long time the invaders thought they were in or near "the Indies," and so they anticipated early discovery of a water route which would bring them swiftly into the familiar areas of Asia. The Europeans could not conceive that a continental land mass of the magnitude of the Americas had lain unbeknownst to themselves westward between Europe and Asia. Even after the voyages of global circumnavigation, scholars continued to visualize the Americas as modest land formations in a vast sea, and it was not until the nineteenth century, and particularly the Lewis and Clark Expedition, that they came to comprehend the geographic configuration of North America (including its great terrene mass).

Indian– White Relationships

Knowledge of the native peoples long remained in a similar confusion; the diversity of languages and cultures and the uncertainty of their relationships to geographic areas compounded the bewilderment. European scholars drew from their scanty knowledge and projected onto the image of the Indian their own vision of "man in a state of nature." Travelers' accounts ranged from accurate to fantastic and while seldom informed by intimate acquaintance, frequently expressed parochial bias if not vulgar sensationalism.

Two ideological conceptions anchored national policies. First, European statesmen anticipated that they would be dealing with political states akin to their own experience: kingdoms, sultanates, khanates, chiefdoms, and kindred systems organized with a central authority able to rely upon military force. The conquistadores had reported civilized societies of this sort (while portraying themselves in the conquering role of Julius Caesar or Pompey). In like manner, the Virginians regarded Powhatan as a "king"; James I crowned him by proxy, and Rolfe's marriage to his daughter was expected to consolidate an alliance with a minor power in a fashion familiar to continental diplomacy. Second, the invaders classified the natives as heathen and judged them as inferior on the scale of civilization. This status supplied the mandate for the European rulers and religious orders to convert, instruct, and thus elevate, so that the Indians might be incorporated into the system of Christianized national societies.

To these ideological conceptions was counterpointed a military reality. Some of the Indian tribes were ferocious in combat and, even though armed only with stone weapons (including bow and arrows), they could, when operating on familiar terrain, put to flight even well-equipped forces of Europeans. Late in the tenth century, the Icelanders had established a colony in Greenland, and, not long thereafter, had attempted to settle in an area which they called Vinland (cf. Jones, 1964). Wherever that area may have been (Newfoundland, Massachusetts), they found it inhospitable and were driven out by the attacks of the aboriginals whom they termed *Skraelings*. Since the old Scandinavians were notoriously able fighters armed with steel weapons, their withdrawal is testimony to the military vigor of the Indian natives.

The pattern described above was to be repeated throughout the European invasion and settlement of the Americas. Both sides possessed some bold and shrewd warriors; the Whites had a superior military technology, while the Indians had the advantage of operating as guerrillas on their home soil. The invaders were assured of victory only when they could recruit Indian allies to serve as their intelligence arm and prevent ambushes, and could press the campaign sufficiently to force a major engagement of forces, with the possibility of wrecking the native economy and capturing hostages. (Victories such as those of the Yaqui described earlier, or of the Sioux at Little Big Horn, are notable precisely because they violate the pattern of White superiority in formal conflict.)

The Spanish conquest of the Aztecs was deceptively easy, owing in part to some Indian mythological notions concerning the Whites, and in part to the political position of the Aztec state. When Cortéz landed in 1519, his army included 508 soldiers, 16 horses, and 14 pieces of artillery, together with a navy of 11 ships and 100 sailors. That he was able to conquer the capital city of Tenochtitlán within the space of two years is testimony less to his military power than to his diplomatic ingenuity. While the Aztec were ferocious fighters, they had also converted their subject tribes into bitter enemies, and Cortéz was able to place the Spanish in the vanguard of a native revolution. The Tlaxcaltec, Texocans, and other peoples became allied to the Spanish, furnished the bulk of their infantry, provided and prepared food supplies, maintained lines of communication to the coast, policed the conquered areas, and were indispensable to the Conquest.

The same Spanish people who could perform so brilliantly in set engagements found it impossible to hold the land against simple guerrillas. The Spanish fought for over two centuries with the Chichimecs living in what is now Querétaro and Guanajuato of northeastern Mexico, and the combat cost them far more in blood and material than the conquest of the Aztecs. Yet the Chichimecs, technologically among the most primitive peoples, were merely hunters and gatherers, had no houses, negligible clothing, and only bow and arrows as weapons. Just this simplicity of living made it almost impossible to destroy the basis of their guerrilla activity. Their willingness to die, rather than submit, meant that in formal combat they could inflict severe losses on any enemy company.

In military strength and political power most Indian peoples fell somewhere between the Aztec and the Chichimec. Thus, their amity was desired, if for no other reason than that their raids and guerrilla activities could have made large areas of terrain quite uninhabitable. The Indian peoples controlled significant resources, such as trade routes and exchange systems for furs, so it is not surprising that the various European powers placed a major emphasis of their policies toward new possessions upon stable and harmonious relations with them. In part, as we shall discuss more fully later, the desired state was to be achieved by bringing the heathen Indians into the light of Christian civilization, and therefore the various governments sponsored programs of missionization. Another part was to be accomplished by fair and cautious dealing, and so we have edicts from the British Crown that land for settlement must always be purchased from its native occupants, or from the Spanish Crown that baptized Indians are not to be enslaved for mine labor, or from the U.S. Government that traders are not to supply alcohol to the Indians.

After the French and Indian War, the English created two regional superintendencies of Indian affairs, with duties to observe, to negotiate treaties, and generally to preserve the peace between Indians and border settlers. We have noted in Chapter One that William Johnson, the northern superintendent, settled among the Mohawk and took one of their women to wife. Further to the south, two deputy commissioners, Alexander Cameron and John McDonald, were sent to the Cherokee in 1766, and both likewise intermarried. McDonald's daughter, Molly, married Donald Ross (a native of Scotland), and their son John—only one-eighth Indian by blood—was to become famous as Principal Chief of the Cherokee Nation. These patterns of intermarriage—between eminent men from among the Europeans and the daughters of eminent Indians—affirm the parity of relationship which many persons saw between the White nations and the Indian peoples. Moreover, those who intermarried and their descendants must have been highly influential in moving the Indian tribes toward a tighter and more formal political organization. Thus, in 1827, a Cherokee Nation was to appear in the southeast with an elective bicameral legislature and a National Superior Court; in 1848 a similar development was to occur among the Seneca of New York State.

We may summarize our characterization of this early phase of European-Indian relationships by noting that the European governments were inclined to treat the Indians as if they were minor states in the European pattern (e.g., Bohemia or Flanders), that they were confirmed in this orientation by the military effectiveness of Indians operating on their own terrain, and that the Indians responded to this treatment and to the advice of those who had intermarried among them by attempting to organize themselves in the form of republics following the European model. At the same time, the fact that the Indians at contact were heathen and (in North America) illiterate, and that some Indian peoples were technologically at the simplest hunting-and-gathering level of existence, provided the basis for an image of "the Indian" as "the savage" or "man in the state of nature," and thus for a rationalization of an authoritarian relationship which varied from the benevolently paternal to the destructively exploitative.

ECOLOGICAL SUCCESSION

The White "purchase" of Indian lands was based upon a mutual lack of comprehension. Whites saw the land in North America as a "wilderness," that is, as unoccupied; moreover, judged by their own techniques of exploitation, these lands were rich—in game, lumber, and fertility of soil. The Indians must have seen the invaders as both child-like (in their lack of skills required of every Indian adult for survival) and powerful (in their technology of metal); accordingly, the Indians would have tried to placate and steer gently these untutored but powerful men. The initial contacts were usually followed by pandemics of disease within the Indian community. Meanwhile, the White system of cultivation, accompanied by the activities of their hunters, soon reduced the once abundant game population; in addition, the game was driven off or made shy by the use of firearms, so that whatever remained was much more difficult to stalk. As the Whites multiplied, they intruded continually upon Indian lands, in most cases justifying themselves upon the moral grounds that the land was "a wilderness" (and so not utilized), and with the legal possession of charters and titles asserted and purveyed by the European governments. The ecological balance of Indian communities was destroyed, their traditional skills made irrelevant, and their societies deteriorated. Occasionally, the process led to violence in which one side slaughtered the other, or both sides slaughtered each other, but such incidents were more exciting than meaningful. Usually the Indians were slow to sense the danger, poorly organized for any sustained military campaign, and outnumbered locally by the inrushing Europeans. Where trade and intermarriage between European and Indian had begun very early, some Indian peoples (e.g., Iroquois, Cherokee) strengthened their inner organization to the point where they could resist the invasion of their lands. Such a conflict set the stage for direct military action by the Whites, and these Indian nations succumbed also, although their downfall was more spectacular than that of the peoples less well organized.

In dealing with the Indians and dislodging them from their lands, the British settlers wanted a free hand, except when the process led to open conflict, at which time they demanded military protection from the royal government. The latter, interested in securing its borders against its major rivals, usually preferred the friendship of those Indian peoples powerful enough to be of military assistance. We have already noted that difference of perspective on Indian matters had contributed to the Colonial American separation from England. The importance of the issue is demonstrated by the facts that one of the first acts of the Continental Congress was to declare its jurisdiction over Indian tribes, and that the commissioners it elected unanimously in 1775 to deal with Indians bordering on the mid-Atlantic States were Benjamin Franklin, Patrick Henry, and James Wilson. As the ex-colonies struggled to organize themselves, the Indian question remained amorphous, with the desire for friendship and alliance uppermost. The Delawares were offered the prospect of statehood in a treaty of 1778; the Congress issued a proclamation in 1783 warning against squatting upon Indian lands; a clause in a treaty of 1785 permitted the Cherokees to send a representative to the Congress. However, these actions proved without consequence. The Constitution of 1789 tended to avoid an explicit declaration on Indian matters, simply conferring (Art. I, Sec. 8) upon the Congress the power "to regulate commerce with the Indian tribes." The Constitution also endowed the federal government with the sole power to make treaties; since the government had already been making treaties with the Indian tribes, the presumption was that this was to be a continuing pattern, which would make the federal government preeminent in Indian affairs.

The War Department was established early in the first Congress, and its Secretary given the responsibility relative to Indian affairs. In 1790 the Congress began to license traders to deal with Indians, and attempted to regulate the sale of firearms and ban the sale of liquor (it is likely that neither provision was particularly effective). At that time, legislation began to use the term "Indian country," and in 1796 that area was explicitly defined.

Had Indian affairs been located in the State Department, the implication would have been that the Indian tribes were conceived as foreign and sovereign nations; locating them elsewhere (as the Commerce Department) would have implied that the Indians were totally within the domestic area. Their location within the War Department implied that, in the last analysis, the relations were those of control and subjugation of peoples outside of the frame of the Union. Among the earliest duties assigned to the Secretary in connection with Indian affairs was the negotiation of treaties, and Congress appropriated rather large sums for this purpose. This meant that the U.S. wished to move further into lands then being occupied by Indians, and was prepared to do so by a combination of force and persuasion.

In 1789, Henry Knox, Secretary of War, foresaw the future relationships of Indian and White (and therefore his own duties as the officer in charge of Indian affairs) in the following terms:

> Although the disposition of the people of the States, to emigrate into the Indian country, cannot be effectually prevented, it may be restrained and regulated.
>
> It may be restrained by postponing new purchases of Indian territory, and by prohibiting the citizens from intruding on the Indian lands.
>
> It may be regulated, by forming colonies, under the direction of Government, and by posting a body of troops to execute their orders.
>
> As population shall increase, and approach the Indian boundaries, game will be diminished, and new purchases may be made for small considerations. This has been, and probably will be, the inevitable consequence of cultivation.
>
> It is, however, painful to consider that all the Indian tribes, once existing in those states now the best cultivated and most populous, have become extinct. If the same continue, the same effects will happen; and, in a short period, the idea of an Indian on this side of the Mississippi will only be found in the pages of the historian [*American State Papers, Indian Affairs*, I, No. 4, p. 53, as cited in Pearce, 1967, p. 56].

THE MISSION TO THE SAVAGE

We have already noted that Catholic missionaries accompanied the Spanish penetration into Middle America; they were also associated with the fur trade carried on by the French along the riverine routes going westward from St. Lawrence. In 1669, a Jesuit mission was established at Green Bay (in what is now Wisconsin), and shortly thereafter Pere Marquette accompanied Jolliet in an exploration of the route of the Mississippi River.

Relatively speaking, the Protestants were slower and less adventurous in their missionizing. While the Jesuits preceded and accompanied the fur trade, journeying into the native villages, the English missionaries tended to work from the new settlements, and with some notable exceptions (such as Roger Williams and John Eliot) the process of colonization did not provide a basis of trust whereby the Gospel could be communicated. Many of the Puritan settlers of Massachusetts Bay regarded the Indians as agents of Satan, and justified their extermination (by gunfire or disease) as a blessing of Providence. It was not until after the American Revolution (when the power of even the Iroquois had been shattered) that a wave of missionary zeal swept the new nation and a large number of societies were founded for bringing the Christian message to the vanquished savages.

Since conversion to Protestantism required of the candidate that he read and accept the Bible, missionizing to such peoples as the North American Indians presented an intricate set of tasks. The Bible had to be brought to the Indians, which meant either that a script had to be devised for each native tongue, the people themselves made literate in it, and the Bible translated into it and duly printed, or, alternatively, that the people had to be made fluent and literate in English (or some other European language) and so brought to the Bible in one of its Protestant translations. The process of Christianizing thus became coincident with the process of educating or civilizing. Since the Indians were, by definition, "savages," Christianizing them meant destroying their Indianness and transforming them into Whites of darker hue. Under the circumstances, it would not have taken much reflection for the missionary to decide that it was more important that the Indians learn a civilized language—his—than that he devote the labor to learning their tongue. The most expeditious procedure would be for him to establish schools wherein the children could be properly instructed and restrained from cultivating the wicked habits of their elders. So the mission stations were rapidly transformed into educational systems; when securing regular attendance of the children proved difficult, as it usually did, the mission schools became further transformed into boarding schools. When maintaining the boarding school became a financial strain, the boarding school was further transformed into a work camp with educational trimmings, a process that could be rationalized on the grounds that the Indians required instruction in the moral virtues, especially those of honest toil. The volume of labor performed by the Indian youngsters in some of those manual labor schools is staggering to comprehend, and it is clear that little formal instruction could have been imparted in such circumstances.

We noted earlier that the Indian tribes of the eastern woodlands had practiced a mixed economy, in which the women engaged in a modest horticulture in the soil of the riverbottoms, while the men engaged in hunting, warfare, and ritual duties. Nevertheless, the missionaries categorized these Indian tribes as savage hunters, and it is hard to know whether this was because they scorned the native agriculture, or thought it unfitting that the women should labor while the men hunted, or because among the disorganized and defeated tribes where the missionaries operated the feminine agricultural patterns had been disrupted. In any case, the missionaries concentrated upon transforming the Indian men into dirt farmers diligent in their calling, and were not satisfied unless the Indians worked steadily all day and every day.

The missionaries preached the division of labor by sex as it had dedeveloped in European society: women were frail, men were sturdy. Women should devote themselves to house and children and maintain these according to the "gospel of soap," cleanliness being next to godliness. Man, being strong, should devote himself to the heavy labor of the fields. What the missionaries thereby demanded was complete reversal of the sex roles of traditional Indian society, and very few Indians were prepared to comply. In the same fashion, the missionaries' demand that each family be a self-sufficient and independent economic unit ran squarely athwart the native norms of generosity, hospitality, and communal interdependence. The Indian could comprehend the Christian plea for charity; he could not comprehend the moral value of "private property." Frustrated in their efforts to disrupt the native morality, the missionaries became advocates of allotting tribal land in severalty. They felt that once each Indian family had its own private plot of ground and was wholly dependent on that produce, then each member would be compelled to industry and so to put on the form of a godly life.

The missionaries utilized all manner of lures in an effort to induce the Indians to adopt the true path. The Quakers, for example, offered cash premiums for each bushel of wheat or rye the Seneca man grew and for each dozen yards of cloth that the woman spun from her own flax or wool. It was their thought that if they could acquaint the Indians with the correct habits, they would leave their savage ways. But the Indians conceived of these labors as favors which they were performing for the Quakers, and the premiums as just payment for activities which were otherwise so unrewarding. As the missionaries acquired this disillusioning insight, they discontinued the giving of premiums.

The missionaries were preaching an idealized version of their own cultural norms—the pattern of life as it appeared to the pious and virtuous farmers and middle class. Presumably they thought that, if the Indian adopted this path, he would dissolve into the community of Christians. But this did not prove to be so: when an Indian assimilated culturally, he did not gain social acceptance by the Whites, and he was not assimilated socially. The Indian—usually a Mixedblood already detached from the Indian community—who followed the preachments of the missionary found himself in the classical trap of the marginal man. To his more traditional Indian fellows he appeared as unmanly, ungenerous, and denying the obligations of tribal membership—he was a "White man." To the White community he remained an Indian and hence socially inferior, no matter how Christian were his morals. The Indian assimilate found that he was not allowed the privileges of citizenship; he could not vote, bring suit, testify in court, and so on.

TRADERS, AGENTS, AND OTHERS

The student reviewing the historical patterns of relationships between Indians and Whites is likely to overemphasize the role of the missionaries, if for no other reason than that they sometimes came to have formal authority over Indian areas (cf. the Catholic missions of New Spain, and President Grant's attempt to reform the reservation system in the U.S.) and left large volumes of papers detailing their labors and anguish. But from Hernán Cortéz, Nicolas Perrot, and John Cabot until the present day, Indians have dealt more with secular personnel than with those dedicated to religious orders and missions. However, the paper legacy of such men is slighter, as many of them could not write and, besides, they were not interested so much in describing the Indians as they were in learning how they could profit from them and their resources.

Since most of the explorers and early traders were single and virile men, they entered into sexual relationships with the Indian women, sometimes casually (prostitution) and sometimes in more permanent form (concubinage, marriage). Most of the native peoples of North America did not share the Euro-Christian morality about chastity and fornication, and sexual contacts between White and Indian were sometimes actually encouraged in the belief that the special virtues and powers of the invader would be transmitted to the host people. In any case, the more enduring the liaison, the greater the likelihood of mutual influence. Mixedblood families were often bilingual and often acted as channels of information and exchange between the Whites and the Indians (thus, the Dakota term for Mixedblood is also used to denote an "interpreter").

The traders also introduced the Indians of North America to distilled liquor. Very early they discovered that the Indians had no cultural resistance to the pleasures of rum or whiskey, and that these constituted the ideal means for lubricating the trade of furs or the sale of land. All that the Whites required, beyond the liquor, was caution (or a stout fort), for the drunken Indian men usually went on a wild emotional spree, fighting, shooting, and even killing. President Jefferson secured from Congress authority to prevent the sale of liquor to Indians, and 30 years later Congress passed further legislation to restrain this traffic. But, as with the later attempt at general Prohibition, the law was difficult to enforce; the Indian desire for liquor was too strong and the profit from conveying it to them was fantastic. The American Fur Company, the creature of John Jacob Astor, was repeatedly accused of violating liquor regulations and smuggling into Indian territory great quantities of whiskey and rum, which its agents then exchanged for furs at the most outrageous rates. The Indian agent at Camp Leavenworth estimated that from 1815 to 1830 the fur trade on the Missouri had totaled over $3 million, and that half of this was clear profit. About the same time, William B. Astor was acknowledging that the operation of the fur company was yielding even larger returns, namely $500,000 per year (Myers, 1909, Vol. I, p. 124).

Needless to say, the missionaries were gravely disturbed by the association between the Indian and Whites engaging in such un-Christian practices. It was bad enough that the Indians were being encouraged to hunt and trap, rather than to farm, but it was intolerable that they were being debauched with alcohol. Moreover, the Indians found an abundance of White companionship in their sociable activities. Traders, travelers, lumbermen, railroad men, ranchhands, and others of the less pious and less respectable among the Whites were happy to indulge with the Indians in such pastimes as whiskey drinking, card playing, breaking the Sabbath, enjoying the pleasures of the other sex, and being indolent. Before the Civil War, some missionaries believed that if the Indians could all be removed from the eastern part of the country, they could be sheltered in the West from contact with the worse sort of Whites. While this was a delusionary vision, it helped to provide a respectable sanction to drive for removal.

A form of corruption emerging in the Western territories was so distinctive that it became known as the "Indian ring." At minimum, it involved a triumvirate: a politician, an Indian agent, and a contractor.

The politician installed the agent, who selected the contractor, who shared among the three of them the funds which were supposed to be given out as Indian annuities (or rations). Since these transactions occurred in isolated areas, they were seldom subject to scrutiny by uncorrupted observers; the Indians, ignorant of the English language and of Anglo customs, and legally and jurally powerless, had no way in which they could seek redress for their miserable and abused condition. The governors of the Western territories were ex officio the Indian Superintendents, but since they were primarily concerned with development of the area for the benefit of Whites, they could scarcely be counted upon to protect Indian interests. Indeed, there was great temptation for them to participate or share in the operations of "the ring." Some honest men tried to resist and frustrate the operations of the local ring; there were also some persons who were real friends of the Indians and were shocked by their condition; but, given the climate of Western opinion, it was easier for the ring to enlist the power of the press and of the legal establishment rather than for the latter to crusade against the corruption of the law, and a number of critics of Western rings were dismissed or persecuted on fabricated charges. John Beeson, for example, settled in the Rogue River Valley of Oregon in 1853, and was appalled to observe how (despite treaties) his fellows were encroaching on Indian lands, thus provoking conflict, and then securing payment from the federal government for serving in troops which slaughtered the Indian owners. When he protested publicly, he was accused of being a traitor, and his narrative of events was savagely distorted in the press. In the end he had to flee for his life.

THE OBJECT OF REFORM

By the Civil War, the Indians of the U.S. had lost most of their military significance and a good portion of their numbers. For a brief period of time the Plains Indians were to remain spectacular phenomena, but within another generation they joined the ranks of the displaced, debauched, and undernourished. Even before their decline, as early as 1849, the Indian Service had been moved from the War Department to the newly established Home Department of the Interior.

As the Indians became militarily impotent, and their condition could no longer be concealed in a secluded wilderness, critics and reformers of Indian policy increased in numbers and energy. The Abolitionists had organized moral America for one crusade; now Indian affairs were to provide the focus for another. A congressional inquiry of 1865 documented the decline of population owing to disease, alcohol, war, and starvation. The Protestant missionary societies were thoroughly aroused, and their first effort at reforming the government led to the decision by President Grant to entrust the control of Indian affairs into their hands. The reservations were allocated among the interested denominations, and these latter were to provide Agency Superintendents who would be diligent, righteous, and above the corruption of their predecessors.

While this transfer ensured a more honest administration of the Indian Service, it did not resolve the basic issues. Without the likelihood of graft which would find its way into the pockets of their political supporters, the members of Congress were even less likely to appropriate sums of money to which the government was obligated as a result of the treaties. Western settlers were hostile to any policy which kept Indians alive and able to defend their lands against further intrusion. The missionaries were fixated on the notion of transforming the Indians into diligent and pious farmers, even when, as now became manifest, the lands on which the Indians were herded were agriculturally marginal. The Episcopalian Bishop of Minnesota, Harry B. Whipple, was inspired in his labors with the Santee Sioux, and stimulated much agricultural effort. Yet from 1871 to 1877, their crops at Lake Traverse were destroyed annually by drought and grasshoppers.

As the bison and other game were exterminated, the condition of the reservations became increasingly pathetic. Since Congress would not appropriate the requisite funds, the missionaries who were serving as Indian agents found themselves with an impossible task under intolerable circumstances: the agricultural equipment was insufficient, the school funds depleted, the agencies in debt, the employees underpaid and unskilled, and the Army being utilized to compel the Indians to starve peaceably. In this extremity, intense public interest was aroused by the plight of the Ponca, a peaceful horticultural people who were being removed from their ancestral homes along the Missouri in order to make way for another relocation of the Sioux. In typical American fashion, this event stimulated the growth of voluntary associations dedicated to assisting the Indian. When Helen Hunt Jackson published *A Century of Dishonor* in 1881, the muckrakers began to provide the compost for further organizational growth. By 1884, the Women's National Indian Association, founded in 1882, was beginning to operate a powerful lobby in Washington.

These reformers were not really knowledgeable about the Indian, or even interested in learning how the Indian thought or what he desired. They were motivated by an objective concern: that the Indian be dealt with honestly and fairly, and assisted in becoming a moral being exactly like themselves. Seeing that the reservation system as it was then established had not protected the Indians in their property or assisted them in becoming self-sufficient farmers, the reformers became advocates of a policy of allotment in severalty. They reasoned that if reservation lands were made into individual property rather than the congregate property of the tribe, their owners would share the rights and protections that Anglo-Saxon legal codes give to landholders. Moreover, they believed that if the lands were allotted to individual Indians as private property, then these persons would be motivated to cultivate the lands and progress in the status of civilized and Christian men. Western frontier associations and land speculators also desired land allotment and had tried to ram such bills through Congress, and the reformers were sage enough to see that there might be some problems attendant on allotment. Accordingly, they linked the allotment system with federal wardship, in which the land would be held inalienable for some period of time. The General Allotment Act (Dawes Act), passed in 1887, provided a compromise between the humanitarians and the land grabbers, but the latter were the more practical and far-sighted. Most of the reservation lands were western grass lands suitable for grazing rather than farming, and the Plains Indian men might then (as they did later) have easily made the transition from nomadic warriors to cowboys, but the allotments were too small for grazing lands. The Dawes Act was used to permit the final dismantling of the once vast reservations; it allowed the steady erosion of the best of the allotted lands, and it condemned the Indians to poverty.[1]

DEFENDERS OF THE
TRADITIONALLY INDIAN

Between 1887 and 1934, the Indians were separated from an estimated 86,000,000 of the 138,000,000 acres which still remained to them. The procedures used involved a variety of fraud and trickery that exploited Indian poverty, generosity, and impetuosity. Some of the maneuvers have been exposed and condemned publicly, while the disentanglement of others which are still hidden from view would require the combined services of attorneys, ethnohistorians, and criminal investigators. Even today the process is not ended.[2] In any event, most of the

[1] For the historical background to passage of the Dawes Act, see Fritz (1963), especially the final chapter. For a short summary of the Act see Brophy and Aberle (1966, pp. 18–20, and further discussion under allotments). For a detailed discussion by a great legal analyst, see Cohen (1945).

[2] The bald facts about the Indians' loss of lands have been frequently noted. Brophy and Aberle (1966, p. 219, Table 3) cite congressional figures to the effect that over 800,000 acres were lost during 1948–52 and 1,800,000 further acres lost during

land left in Indian possession by 1934 was semiarid or desert, not only worthless for farming but marginal even for ranching. The schemes of the reformers had failed, while the Indians found themselves in such a legal abyss that a U.S. Court of Claims could describe their legal status at the end of the century as "unknown to the common law or the civil law or to any system of municipal law. They were neither citizens nor aliens; they were neither persons nor slaves; they were wards of the nation, and yet . . . were little else than prisoners of war while war did not exist." The Indians could not then defend themselves, politically or jurally, but as described by a knowledgeable source in 1915, they were at the mercy of the Indian Superintendent, "a tsar within the territorial jurisdiction provided for him. He is *ex officio* both guardian and trustee. In both of these capacities he acts while deciding what is needed for the Indian and while dispensing funds" (McNickle, 1964, p. 52).

In this desperate situation of poverty, legal impotence, and utter misery, the Indians began to acquire a new type of ally. In the past there had been occasional scholars interested in the native customs of the Indians, but beginning in the latter quarter of the nineteenth century there were more of them, and they became organized as a distinct learned profession—ethnologists (or anthropologists). To these scholars it appeared that the distinctively Indian styles of life were rapidly disappearing, so it was incumbent to describe and record as much of them as possible. Traditional ceremonials which had been central to Indian life a century before had been abandoned, either because of the prohibitions of Indian agents or the inability of the people to stage the events in their altered conditions of life. The ethnologists thus acquired a vested interest in what so many of those with power in Indian affairs were trying to exterminate—that which was distinctively and traditionally *Indian*. Moreover, in their attempts to comprehend and describe these customs and rites, the ethnologists were forced to spend days, weeks, or months laboring sympathetically and intimately with the elderly and wise representatives of the traditional ways. What may have begun as an academic interest became in many cases a passionate emotional involvement.

The ethnological pioneers, Henry Rowe Schoolcraft and Lewis Henry Morgan, still saw the traditional ways as "savagery" and therefore as of only historical significance. But, especially with fighting liberals Franz Boas and his students, such as Robert H. Lowie, Paul Radin, and Alfred Kroeber, there was a basic respect for other peoples and their cus-

---

1953–57. Some of the techniques used earlier in this century in order to detach Indians from their lands are outlined by Hagan (1961, pp. 142–150). An eloquent denunciation of federal and state politics with regard to Indian lands will be found in Cahn (1969, Chap. 3).

toms—an attitude that came to be denominated as "cultural relativism."
These scholars sensed the moral and esthetic values of the traditional
Indian cultures, and could not help comparing them, invidiously, to the
parochial and arid values of the missionaries and Indian agents, who
were striving to exterminate what they could not appreciate, while their
charges lived in abject poverty.

It is scarcely coincidence that the political fight which developed
came to focus about the case of the Pueblos, for, of all the Indian peoples, these seemed outstanding in their maintenance of an independent
existence and preservation of so much of their indigenous heritage (a
heritage that actually bore significant traces of the early contact with the
Spanish and their missionaries). The battle was melodramatic and, for a
time, featured a classic "good guy," John Collier, against a "bad guy,"
Albert B. Fall, the Secretary of Interior who was to acquire such notoriety
in connection with Teapot Dome. Collier's account of events (1947, Chap.
13) is well worth reading. At the heart of the issue was ownership of lands
which traditionally had belonged to the Pueblos but were overrun by
trespassers who now sought to claim title. An earlier decision by the Su-
preme Court had favored the Whites, but in 1913 the Court reversed
itself on the issue. Meanwhile, the Pueblos had secured the services of an
attorney of distinction and were now making a real effort to reclaim their
lands. The squatters appealed to their Senator, and he, in conjunction
with Albert Fall, quietly introduced a bill which would have nullified
the Court's recent decision. When the threat was discovered, Collier
spearheaded the opposition and succeeded not only in mustering to his
side such a diverse aggregation as the artists' colonies of Santa Fe and
Taos, the General Federation of Women's Clubs, the American Indian
Defense Association, and many of the Indian tribes scattered over the
U.S., but also in uniting the Pueblos themselves for common action.

The Collier faction charged that the B.I.A. was maliciously hostile
to all elements of Indian culture and was failing radically in its assigned
mission of protecting Indian interests. In response to these charges, the
government in 1927 invited the Institute of Public Affairs (Brookings
Institution) to investigate. The resulting report (Merriam et al., 1928)
documented the failures of the government as trustee and mentor of the
Indians, and proposed a reformed and integrated program for Indian
administration, with a principal focus upon education. The recommenda-
tions were not so new in principle, but the report provided abundant
ammunition with which to arouse the interests of literate and conscientious members of the public. Even before Franklin D. Roosevelt assumed
office as President, he was the recipient of a petition signed by some of
the most distinguished citizens of the nation, urging him to reorganize

the federal system of Indian administration (Fey and McNickle, 1959, p. 94). Roosevelt appointed Harold Ickes as Secretary of the Interior and John Collier as Commissioner of Indian Affairs, and they instituted a complete reversal of federal policy.

Collier was a firm advocate of democracy at the local level, of local communities organizing themselves democratically to make their own decisions, and he saw in traditional Indian institutions the procedures whereby Indians had governed themselves and realized significant values. His goal was to assist Indian communities in organizing themselves as tribal governments in some compromise between traditional and modern forms, and to breathe economic life into the communities by increasing the land and capital base at their disposal. At the same time, the ruinous policies of his predecessors of allotting and alienating lands were to be stopped immediately. In this spirit, he immediately proposed drastic legislation to the Congress and, in somewhat compromised form, it was passed in 1934 as the Indian Reorganization (or Wheeler-Howard) Act.

To realize the goals of the Act, Collier had to utilize personnel who had accumulated within the Bureau and were protected by civil service regulations. In addition, he had to communicate to the Indian peoples that new rights, privileges, and opportunities might be theirs if they would but move to take them. In both endeavors he was only partially successful. His policies not only ran squarely counter to values which had become entrenched among Bureau personnel but, worse yet, undercut vested Bureau interests: if the Indians gained more control over their own affairs, where would that leave the Bureau employees? Likewise, many Indians had been so traumatized by the events of the past century that they feared any innovation and had become thoroughly convinced that all schemes proposed by Whites were, at bottom, designed to defraud them of whatever rights or possessions they yet retained. Hence, they were opposed to any change, no matter of what kind or by whom proposed, and the only Whites they knew enough to communicate with, even partially, were local employees of the Bureau. It was a triumph for Collier that 263 tribes did vote on the Act and, of those, 192 accepted it, which meant that at least these organized themselves to take advantage of its provisions.

CONCLUSION

In this chapter we have reviewed some of the major varieties of interaction between European invaders and native Indians over a period of several centuries during which the Indians declined in military, political, and economic power. As this decline continued, the Indians became the object of benevolent assistance, first by Christian missionaries and then by anthropologists and kindred liberal reformers.

Since our focus is upon patterns of interaction, there is no need for us to review in detail the history of relationships between the federal Indian agencies of the U.S. and the various tribes. Basically, there has been an extreme variability which can be accounted for by the fact of the Indians' powerlessness. The nature of policy made for Indians has depended on whether the significant pressures upon the federal government have been exercised by interests seeking to secure the resources in tribal hands or by benevolent groups seeking to confirm Indians in their traditional rights and claims. The Collier administration did serve to strengthen many of the tribes as distinct social and legal entities. The direction was reversed under the Eisenhower administration when Dillon S. Myer, the Commissioner, assisted by some powerful congressmen, pushed a program whose key slogans were "relocation" (movement of Indians from reservation to urban areas) and "termination" (of the special relationships between the federal government and the tribes, including trusteeship of Indian lands). The counterpressures became manifest when John F. Kennedy became President, as he appointed a commission to review federal policies on Indian affairs and selected as his Commissioner Philleo Nash, who held a doctorate in Anthropology but was also a successful businessman and politician (having been Lt. Governor of Wisconsin). By 1966, when Nash was forced to resign, strong pressures were building within Congress to terminate the basic programs of the B.I.A.

The consequence was a standoff involving little change in either direction. The Indians had become a symbol of great sentiment for both liberal and pious Americans, and such sentiment was a potential asset for any politician seeking a national audience. Prior to the presidential primaries of 1968, Robert F. Kennedy pioneered the creation of a Subcommittee on Indian Education within the U.S. Senate (Indian Affairs had previously been the concern solely of a committee of the House of Representatives). Kennedy used this committee to give publicity to the sorry conditions of Indian education, and thereby also consolidated his reputation as a liberal and a reformer. Given this "national Indian constituency" and the powerful politicians who were responsive to it, the situation of Indian tribes did not deteriorate in the 1960's as it had in the previous century. Moreover, of the federal monies expended in such programs as "The War on Poverty," a reasonable share has gone to impoverished Indian peoples. While the actualities of these programs have not attained the heights that their planners envisioned, nonetheless they have helped to keep people alive and their communities functioning.

The basic line of struggle has come to be bureaucratic: (1) Shall federal programs for Indians be channeled through a specifically Indian agency (such as the B.I.A.), or through general agencies which are designed to operate those kinds of programs (as Indian health agencies are now operated by the Public Health Service)? (2) In either case, how shall Indian tribes or communities maintain some degree of control over these programs? Looking, for example, at schools—since education is one of the largest and costliest units within the B.I.A.—should these continue to be operated by the B.I.A., or by a special agency of the U.S. Office of Education, or should they be turned over to local communities? If their operation remains within the government, should there be some equivalent to school boards elected by Indians, and, if so, how shall these be chosen, at what levels should they function, and how much authority should they have? If the schools are turned over to local control, must and should they be integrated, and how can steps be taken to ensure that the Indian community is represented on the school board rather than kept subordinated and voiceless by locally dominant Whites? Some of these educational questions will be considered further when we come to discuss Indian education, but the fundamental issues of ethnic and political relationships are more general. In any case, it may be noted that during the 1960's there was a proposal to place federal schools within the operations of the U.S. Office of Education, but that this was countered by the actions of the National Congress of American Indians and other national Indian groups which feared that it might be a new step toward "termination."

In summary, we have witnessed in this chapter the dialectical interplay among several of the major ideologies of race and ethnic relations within the U.S. There was the early pluralistic notion of separate Indian nations, and also the Melting Pot nation of intermarriage which, while it invariably involved White male and Indian female, nonetheless allowed the couple to establish their home in either society. Simultaneously, there was the operation of the ideology of genocide (extermination). An effective counter to this latter ideology was that of missionization, although the Anglo Protestants were slower and less efficient in this effort than the Latin Catholics had been. Missionization may be regarded as having been designed in practice to achieve "cultural (rather than biological) extermination." Powerful as this ideology became in rallying popular support "to help Indians," it was too inflexible to affect the Indian deeply or to cause many of them to assimilate, and it was insufficient to force the Congress to appropriate monies to honor federal treaties. Moreover, it seemed as if the very compromises effected by the mission agencies left the Indians vulnerable to those who would seize their lands

and bring about their extermination. At this juncture, the emergence of
American anthropology, with its focus upon the native peoples of this
hemisphere, gave a formidable boost to the ideology of Cultural Pluralism.
Anthropological exponents of this creed managed to capture important
seats within the federal administration, and while they failed to achieve
idealistic goals, their organizations have become one of the new forces
in Indian affairs and their ideology has helped to reshape federal Indian
policies.

SUGGESTED READINGS

Berkhofer, Robert F., Jr. 1965. *Salvation and the Savage: An Analysis of
Protestant Missions and American Indian Response, 1787–1862.* Lexington:
University of Kentucky Press.

Brophy, William A., and Sophie D. Aberle, compilers. 1966. *The Indian:
America's Unfinished Business.* Norman: University of Oklahoma Press.

Cahn, Edgar S., ed. 1969. *Our Brother's Keeper: The Indian in White America.*
New York: New Community Press.

Cohen, Felix S. 1945. *Handbook of Federal Indian Law.* Washington, D.C.:
U.S. Government Printing Office (Department of the Interior, Office of
the Solicitor).

Collier, John. 1947. *Indians of the Americas.* New York: New American Library
(Mentor MD 171).

DeVoto, Bernard. 1962. *The Course of Empire.* Boston: Houghton Mifflin
Company (Sentry SE 15).

Driver, Harold, ed. 1964. *The Americas on the Eve of Discovery.* Englewood
Cliffs, N.J.: Prentice-Hall, Inc. (Spectrum S 93).

Fey, Harold E., and D'Arcy McNickle. 1959. *Indians and Other Americans.*
New York: Harper & Row, Publishers.

Fritz, Henry E. 1963. *The Movement for Indian Assimilation, 1860–1890.*
Philadelphia: University of Pennsylvania Press.

Hagan, William T. 1961. *American Indians.* Chicago: University of Chicago
Press.

Jackson, Helen Hunt. 1881. *A Century of Dishonor.* Boston: Roberts Bros.

Jones, Gwyn. 1964. *The Norse Atlantic Saga.* New York: Oxford University
Press, Inc.

McNickle, D'Arcy. 1964. *The Indian Tribes of the United States: Ethnic and
Cultural Survival.* London: Oxford University Press (Institute of Race
Relations).

Meriam, Lewis, *et al.* 1928. *The Problem of Indian Administration.* Baltimore:
The Johns Hopkins Press.

Myers, Gustavus. 1909. *History of the Great American Fortunes.* 2 vols. Chicago: Charles H. Kerr.

Pearce, Roy Harvey. 1967. *Savagism and Civilization: A Study of the Indian and the American Mind.* Baltimore: The Johns Hopkins Press (Paperback JH–29).

Wolf, Eric. 1962. *Sons of the Shaking Earth.* Chicago: University of Chicago Press (Phoenix Books P 90).

CONTEMPORARY UNITED STATES
TRIBAL COMMUNITIES

Part Two

CHAPTER FOUR

LEGAL BACKGROUND

Historically a reservation was a region of the country which was reserved by treaty for an Indian people so as to eliminate their presence from other areas that Whites were beginning to exploit. To control and "civilize" the Indians, the reservation was placed under the jurisdiction of an Indian Agent representing the authority, and supposedly the interests, of the U.S. Government. Having at his disposal both military and judicial powers, as well as control of rations, the Agent was a petty tyrant who might be benevolent but was often self-serving. Over the years, the authority of the Agent has been limited, reduced, and clarified, as his duties and powers have been more clearly defined by statute and tested in the courts. Today the Agent is the highest local representative of the B.I.A., and the authority of that agency is now generally interpreted as being based upon Anglo-Saxon conceptions of trusteeship. In other words, the land (and sometimes the money) of many Indian persons is held in trust for them by the U.S. Government.

Contemporary Plains Reservation Communities

Older conceptions of the status of Indians and Indian reservations are slow to disappear. Once there were notions that Indians were "wards of the federal government"—incompetent like minor children or the feeble-minded. There were also beliefs that Indians "did not pay taxes," or could not purchase alcoholic beverages, or were confined to their reservations (and might not leave without official permission). It would be wise for the reader to discard these notions as historical relics. Legally speaking, Indians today are citizens of the United States, as well as of the particular state wherein they reside, and are entitled to all of the privileges and rights, and subject to all the duties and responsibilities, of other citizens, including taxes, service in the Armed Forces, and obedience to pertinent federal and state laws. Certain kinds of taxes cannot be assessed on Indian lands, but this is because they are held in trust by the federal government, not because they belong to Indians; if the land is removed from its trust status, it automatically becomes subject to ordi-

65

nary taxation. The sale of alcoholic beverages is forbidden in some reservation areas, but at the present time the prohibition is by area, not ethnicity, and its source is a specific, locally enacted statute. Indians are the targets of special federal programs, as we shall be noting, and they do in some areas suffer the special disabilities of the impoverished and the uneducated, but these are socially based and not juridically grounded.

Generally speaking, the legal status of the Indian tribes has been thorny. The tribes were regarded historically as separate nations, and treaties were concluded between them and the United States, or between them and state governments, or even earlier between them and the Colonial English Government (and acknowledged by the U.S. in its capacity as subsequent sovereign). From their position as separate and autonomous nations, the tribes became classed as "domestic dependent nations" and for a long time preserved some of the corresponding legislative and judicial powers. Yet at the same time the federal Congress assumed the power to legislate on tribal affairs and to abrogate treaties whensoever it suited. To sum up a tangled situation, we can note that the recent tendency of the courts and Congress has been to erode still further the remaining Indian rights established under treaties (note, for example, that the courts did not sustain the rights of the Tuscarora against the Power Authority of New York State when the latter proposed to preempt and flood lands which had been guaranteed by treaties of great authority). The result of these processes has been to leave to tribal governments a set of powers somewhat similar to a reduced and subordinated version of state government, or, alternatively viewed, an enlarged version of county government. So far as federal programs are concerned, residual rights and privileges tend to be rationalized more on the grounds that Indians are impoverished than that they are entitled to special considerations by virtue of the particular provisions of specific historical treaties.

In the discussion that follows, we shall be outlining the general nature of reservation communities of Plains Indians in such Western states as the Dakotas. By keeping the description general rather than particular, we shall be free of the hazard of seeming to characterize critically the officials and peoples of a particular area. Within this generality, however, we shall focus on the characteristics of the larger kind of reservation community, since only this kind of situation presents easily visible evidence of the persistence of some unique traits of a tribal culture (as, for example, the native language) and of the solidarity of tribal society. By contrast, in the smaller communities—especially on the eastern seaboard of the U.S.—Indian communities have been transformed into a kind of rural proletariat, not dissimilar to rural Negroes or Mountain Whites, so that their culture is generalized lower class and not significantly "Indian."

ECOLOGY AND ECONOMY

The central problem of most reservation communities is economic. In an era when the U.S. is becoming more urbanized and industrialized, and when marginal agricultural lands are becoming depopulated, the Indian reservations find their economic foundations ever less satisfactory. It is worth remembering that the lands reserved for Indians were selected because they were away from the main natural routes of travel, inhospitable for agriculture, and lacking in other visible resources (such as mineral wealth). Accordingly, most reservations have not had an adequate ecological basis for their existence as self-sufficient communities. From their inception, the reservations have required subsidization of some sort. In the earliest days this took the form of rations; today that process continues as "surplus commodities." To be sure, hopes have often been expressed that Indians would become self-sufficient through their adoption of agriculture, but a glance at any map will show that the majority of lands included in reservations are far from the prosperous agricultural areas of North America. Moreover, where Indians were intensively engaging in agriculture—as the Papago, Pima, and Pueblo peoples of the Southwest—their activities have been jeopardized or reduced through preemption of water resources. Reservation lands throughout much of the U.S. have been turned to cattle (or sheep) ranching as the optimal usage of lands unsuited by their low rainfall, lack of irrigation, and uneven topography for any intensive cultivation. Unfortunately, cattle ranching requires a low density of human laborers per acre, and in recent times even this figure has been further reduced through modern technology. The consequence is that most reservations are characterized by a chronic condition of unemployment: as in many Asiatic countries, the land is populated by more people than are needed for efficient utilization of labor power. A very few tribes, notably the Osage and Southern Ute, have been fortunate in that the mineral wealth of their lands was discovered in a political context when it could be retained for them rather than seized or swindled outright. While tales of tribal Indians inundated with great wealth have been colorful, more significant in the long run have been the cases of more modest assets—such as those of the Navajo—which have provided the economic basis for a variety of tribal developmental programs and afforded some stability and power to tribal governance.

In judging tribal economic status, it is important to note the tribal traditions as to division of labor by sex and proper and honorable roles for men. Except in the Southwest (and among the Indians of Middle America), agricultural labor has been regarded by Indians as unsuitable for men; instead, they have seen their roles as those of hunter, warrior, and gambler. The acme of manhood were deeds of daring, fortitude, and brilliant swiftness, while patient drudgery was the lot of womenfolk. In consequence, it has been difficult to institute family farming among the peoples of Plains reservations, although in some instances it is conceivable that an intensive skilled agriculture, relying on irrigation and shrewd usage of natural resources, might have been successful (always presuming that water rights could have been defended against White settlers). Difficult as is the practice of agriculture in the Plains, groups such as the Hutterites—strongly knit by a religious ideology and possessed of ingenious traditions of agricultural practice—have made surprisingly successful adaptations. Some idealistic reformers, such as the coterie associated with the late John Collier, have argued that if the Indian tribes had been encouraged to elaborate native traditions of sharing and cooperative activity, rather than having these assaulted by missionaries and governmental agents, they might have evolved a successful agricultural adaptation. Some demonstration projects, such as the one at Red Shirt Table in the Pine Ridge Reservation, South Dakota, during the 1930's, became thriving enterprises so long as there was support and guidance from within the Indian Service; when that was withdrawn the project collapsed. In retrospect, an intriguing feature of Red Shirt history was that the people themselves had moved to integrate a strong and demanding form of Christianity (Seventh Day Adventist) into their communal existence, but that neither the federal agents nor the Adventist missionaries were sufficiently flexible and insightful to utilize this in assisting the community toward the kind of organization that is characteristic of successful contemporary agricultural communes (e.g., Hutterites, Israeli Kibbutzim).

Especially since the inception of "The War on Poverty" under the administration of John F. Kennedy, a number of programs have attempted to improve the economic structure of reservation communities. Most cases have involved the attempt to induce industries to establish plants there. However, since reservation areas are usually lacking in natural resources, the only assets that may be offered the industrialist are cheap and docile labor (the Indians) and low taxes, so industrialization of the reservation has been only superficial. Moreover, given the difficulties of transportation and communication, the major types of industries which can profitably be situated on reservations are those whose products are light in weight and sturdy enough to endure long haulage.

Another variety of program for reservation areas has been the attempt to capitalize on the image of Indians as "colorful" and "historical" by attracting tourists. Here the isolation of the reservation region can be regarded as a partial advantage, since there are large tracts of land which can be developed for outdoor recreation and entertainment. The most successful of such enterprises has been associated with the Eastern Cherokee; however, they have enjoyed the asset of a location adjacent to a great natural recreational area, The Smoky Mountains, and yet reasonably close to the large eastern centers of population. While entrepreneurs associated with other tribes and reservations have attempted to inaugurate tourist programs, including pageants, rodeos, and dancing contests, these seldom have achieved the kind of success that significantly improves the lot of the tribal Indians. Moreover, it requires a special type of person to tolerate exposing himself and his family life to the gaze of tourists who are often boorish and sometimes offensively condescending in their attitudes. Where Indian crafts have been maintained or can be reinstituted, items can sometimes be produced whose sale brings a bit of cash, but most tourists prefer to purchase the kind of small, cheap item that can easily be machinemade. It is difficult to establish markets and price scales which bring reasonable returns to skilled Indian craftsmen. It has been estimated that, given the labor involved, women who produce fine Navajo rugs secure only a few cents per hour.

The consequence of the reservation economic situation is that the cash incomes of large numbers of Indian families are miniscule and large numbers of Indian adults are unemployed. As a concrete case, we can review the summary figures for the State of South Dakota, where Indians constitute about 6 per cent of a total 1968 population of 698,000 persons. If poverty is defined as receiving a cash income of below $3,000 annually, then almost a third of the total state population is poor. Indians are disproportionately represented among these poor, for almost 80 per cent of Indian families are in this classification. Among Fullblood[1] families situated on Indian reservations, the situation is extreme. For example, on the Pine Ridge Reservation, 40 per cent of Fullblood families had incomes below $1,000 per year (Kent and Johnson, 1969, pp. 29 f.; U.S. Public Health Service, June 1968).

[1]Terms like Indian, Negro, White, Black, Ladino, Mestizo, Métis, Fullblood, Mixedblood, or Mixedbreed designate social statuses (and relationships) rather than either biological (racial) lines or cultural traits. (In this respect, these terms are like those which designate the subcastes—*jatis*—of India, which are sometimes labeled occupationally [e.g., Potter, Washerman, Sweeper] even when most of the members of the jati do not follow that trade.) Since they are correlatives, rather than descriptive nouns (real persons are not colored white, black, or red), they should all be treated typographically alike, and, since most of them are properly regarded as proper nouns to be printed with an initial capital letter, that practice has tended increasingly to be followed in the current literature on Indian affairs, and will be followed in this book.

Unemployment figures are correspondingly high. Among reservation men, only about one-third report permanent employment and about one-quarter report temporary employment, so that over 40 per cent have not even temporary employment. Women report a significantly higher rate of employment, with over 40 per cent being permanently employed, 35 per cent temporarily employed, and the remainder unemployed (Kent and Johnson, 1969, pp. 20 f.). The Indian pattern repeats the experiences of other depressed minority groups, where declining opportunities for unskilled manual labor have afforded greater opportunities to women.

The principal source of reservation employment is the government —almost half of the Indian working force is employed by government agencies. In a sense the principal industry of the reservation is caring for the Indians. This statement may sound extreme, since chief among the government agencies is the educational system, which would be present in any community. But it remains true that "the government is the economy," as in a region where a major military base is located. Not only does the government provide employment, it also provides income or its equivalent in goods and services, i.e., food (surplus commodities), health care (Public Health Service), welfare (Aid to Families with Dependent Children), and so on. There is a paradox here (as will be analyzed shortly) in that the greater proportion of agency expenditures does not reach the Indian families directly, and we can estimate that "a maximum of 20 per cent of the total grant for many governmental programs ever reaches the reservations" (Kent and Johnson, 1969, p. 112). Enough public and general assistance monies flow toward reservations to total almost $500 annually per household, but clearly little of that reaches the individual family, or else the family income figures would not be as they have been reported. On the other hand, monies flowing into the region, state, and reservation do provide a general economic support and stimulation that is of considerable significance.

Since jobs are scarce and federal employment is compensated according to national scales, access to federal jobs becomes a valuable prize. Competition is intense, and intrigue flourishes; to know where a program will be established or where a job opening will materialize becomes a valuable piece of information. Those who are already established in the reservation bureaucracies and are attuned to official gossip occupy a privileged position as compared to the tribal folk located on the prairies. Good jobs tend to be the prerogative of those whom the rural folk label "Mixedbloods" (whom we shall shortly be describing as a kind of local or reservation elite).

Given the poverty of the Indian residents, their thin density per acre, and the lack of resources in the reservation area, the development of transportation and communication has tended to remain slow. Until a generation ago, many reservations lacked any system of paved roads, telephone service was erratic, and news was disseminated via "the moccasin telegraph" (i.e., by word of mouth from the traveler on foot or horseback). If there were schools, children either were boarded or arrived there after a lengthy daily trip via foot or horseback. The introduction of consolidated schools and the curtailment of boarding schools necessitated a system of bussing, which in turn initiated a drive for major improvements in roads. Most reservations now have at least a primary system of paved roads linking the agency towns and the schools. The secondary grid, linking the paved road to the Indian residence, may still be dirt and subject to the vagaries of weather.

Indians have been moving in increasing numbers from reservations to urban areas. Sociologically, their movement is an instance of the world-wide migrations over the past several centuries which have brought great volumes of peoples from rural to urban areas. The push is lack of land and decreasing need for agricultural manpower at home, while the pull is the prospect of economic opportunity in the cities. Many Indians have made their first moves to urban locales under the sponsorship of "relocation programs" operated by the federal government. Such programs have often appeared to be failures because many of the migrants returned home. But, whether under federal programs or their own resources, Indians have been migrating, and a period of life in urban locations has become a feature of that migration. The consequence for the reservation area is that it has tended to become the haven for those too young, too old, or too incapacitated to participate in the migrations; the youthful, the strong, and the males predominate among the out-migrants. The reservation has thus been transformed into a center for child-rearing, social welfare, and ethnic sentiment. Indians return there to visit their families, renew emotional and ethnic ties, and deposit children for the privileges of federal schools and welfare programs.

It has been proposed by reformers that a program of industrial development would improve reservation life by providing jobs and the amenities of modern life. As we have already noted, the handicaps to industrial development are numerous, including far distances of transportation, lack of resources, and undereducated labor force. To these we must add absence of a stable labor force. The young, old, and incapacitated do not constitute a satisfactory basis for development. It could now be argued that the impact of development might be to attract back to the reservation the working element of the population, who would otherwise be adapting to urban life. The issue is arguable, but certainly some of the rhetoric of "industrial development" seems parallel to that about the "shiftless and idle poor," in that it is a response to the costs of welfare services and—in the face of the facts—it tries to reassure critics and taxpayers that some scheme could reduce these costs.

Industrial and commercial development of reservations might have a salutary influence upon the vocational aspirations of the Indian youngsters being reared there. At present, the vocational models available to them are the employees of the B.I.A. and the Public Health Service. The Indian children do not seem to perceive the vocational possibilities of other kinds of enterprises (stores, banks, motels, and so on). Considering the heavy out-migrations of rural and small town populations, it may be that the Indians are right, and local nonfederal employment is simply not attainable. Moreover, critics have argued that "industrial development" is more of a rhetoric than an actuality, because there is no organized and funded program for development of reservation areas. Perhaps this is just as well, for economic enterprise can only be successfully undertaken by persons thoroughly familiar with the assets and liabilities of the particular locale, population, and trade.

SOCIOPOLITICAL ORGANIZATION

A basic issue that perturbs many reservation communities concerns who is to be regarded as a tribal member, entitled to the prerogatives and privileges thereof. As the bands were historically organized, the issue could scarcely arise, since membership was basically a matter of participation and kinship: those born into a band and participating in its life were its members, and those who might (rarely) leave and join (usually marry into) another band were members of that second band. But as the U.S. assumed control over the destinies of the tribes, it imposed Anglo-Saxon conventions of heirship in regard to tribal resources, and thereby in regard to legal membership in the tribe. Indianness consequently became not a matter of participation in communal life, but a question of the "degree of Indian blood," the latter being denoted by such fractions as half, then quarter, then eighth, sixteenth, and even thirty-second!

Cultural anthropologists who studied Indian peoples did not resolve these matters, since their interests led them to regard Indianness as a matter of possession of traits which could be classed as traditionally Indian. By this standard, those who spoke the native language, knew the traditional myths and rites, and employed traditional implements were somehow truly Indians, whereas others (who might be their grandchildren and participants in the same household or community) were not. Thus, alongside of the previous continuum, ranking people from Fullblood Indian to varieties of Mixedblood, now appeared the analogous continuum of "culturally Fullblood" or "culturally Mixedblood."

There has been no agreement, either among federal agencies, tribal governments, or programs of benevolent associations, as to how to define an Indian or specify a member of a tribal grouping. Some parties utilize a descent principle in the form of "degree of blood"; others use a residence principle, i.e., whether the person is resident on or born to residents upon the tribal reservation; others use a combination of the two. For many federal programs, a quarter degree of blood is sufficient qualification, although, strictly speaking, that is a small degree of "Indianness." Yet the rationale for this loose specification is excellent from a welfare point of view, since many persons of such small degrees of Indian blood are impoverished, poorly educated, and members of a rural proletariat which could well utilize assistance; moreover, some of these folks are participants in what deserve to be labeled as "Indian communities."

Application of these Anglo-Saxon hereditary principles to define the "Indian" has had several significant consequences. First, among most tribes, it has served to create a substantial population which has a vested interest in the dismantling and per capita distribution of any tribal estate. Some tribes include substantial numbers of people who are not "Indian" or are only minimally "Indian" in any social or cultural sense, but who are by law entitled to a share in any tribal properties. Whenever then the issue of terminating the reservation is presented—i.e., allotting the lands, or selling the tribal resources and distributing the proceeds in per capita payments—and the matter is brought to a vote, this population has a vested interest in termination, and, depending upon how the electorate is specified, may be able to outvote those who, being more Indian in a social and cultural sense, would prefer to maintain the system as it has become. Thus, "being Indian" becomes a classification with privileges but without concomitant responsibilities, and this, it may be argued, is quite different from the aboriginal situation wherein membership in a band involved duties and responsibilities as well as privileges.

What has happened is that Indian communities which were once culturally homogeneous and knit together into a tightly cooperative social fabric have been subjected to intensive pressures from a highly diversified aggregate of missionaries, traders, soldiers, and governmental administrators. In consequence, most reservations are remarkably heterogeneous in terms of religious composition, educational backgrounds, income, and occupation, as well as style of identification with Indianness. A reservation containing an Indian population of 10,000 may include elderly men wearing braids, living in primitive cabins, and speaking little or no English, together with younger men wearing conventional urban business dress and holding college degrees. The population may perform religious rites representing a diversity of creeds: Roman Catholic, Methodist, Seventh Day Adventist, Church of the Latterday Saints, Native American Church (peyote), as well as a highly modified Plains Sun Dance and native shamanism. Educational levels may vary from almost none to postgraduate study, and cash incomes may vary likewise. Besides this range within the populace which claims to be or is acknowledged as "Indian," there may be a parallel diversity among the "non-Indians": missionaries, government agents, anthropologists, physicians, welfare workers, educators—of a wide range of ethnicities and trainings, although a surprisingly large proportion are of rural origin and from the local area—themselves displaced by the urbanizing and industrializing processes of American life. In their ethnic and religious heterogeneity, Indian reservations are microurban environments, even though their geographic situation and poverty serves to place most of the Indians in the condition of rural proletarians or colonized natives.

Given the foregoing, most tribal governments have a difficult time existing and maintaining sufficient communal support to transact business. As in most communities, there are strong tendencies to regard the local government as a source of benefits for organized factions and interest associations; very few regard it as an instrumentality for community developments and changes benefiting the general populace. Most of the local folk derogate the tribal government and its politicians except when they can extract some favor—a job, a loan, or a place in some special program—via its officers, and most of them regard election to office as a reward to be bestowed upon senior men, friends, and kin rather than as a choice among competent men with competitive policies. In these, as in many other respects, tribal reservations and their governments are not too different from national and local governments elsewhere, but since reformers and federal programmers have sought to use the tribal governments as vehicles for radical change and development, they sometimes become frustrated and critical when their well meant programs are despoiled and distorted.

By contrast with such federal agencies as the B.I.A., the tribal government suffers from having a lower budget, less savvy in securing federal funds, less continuity of personnel, and generally less sophistication. In addition, the varieties of graft and favoritism that afflict human enterprises are more blatant and more exposed to public gaze among the tribal officers than among those of the federal bureaucracy.

BANDS AND STRATA

When the Indians were confined to reservations, most settled themselves as local bands in relationship to the resources of the area—the water courses, trading posts, agency headquarters, and routes of travel. These bands were composed of kinsmen who recognized obligations to each other, including the sharing of certain kinds of property, and the joint organization of rituals and festivities. As we have discussed earlier, such bands lacked a coercive authoritarian structure, although they were often associated with wise men or spiritual leaders (priests). When the reservations were coming into existence, many persons associated themselves with war chiefs whose authority was sometimes reinforced by a tactical alliance with the Indian agent, who then proceeded to distribute rations through the mediation of the chief. Yet for most bands there was no recognized system of authoritarian leadership; action emerged out of group discussion and consensus.

The bands tended to be egalitarian, especially in relationship to the necessities of life. Band members shared food and assisted each other as they might. Some ritual ceremonials, as at death, might involve massive distributions of household property, so there was little opportunity for one man or one family to accumulate and maintain stores of property for any significant length of time. But this style of sharing did not reach far outside the band; if it did, it went only to particular bands with whom a pattern of reciprocation had been established.

While to an outsider the reservation might seem equivalent to a single society or "nation" composed of a single Indian people, speaking a common language and sharing many traits, to the inhabitants themselves there is no such unity, since they are first and foremost members of bands of kith and kin. In contrast, the Indian Agent and his associates have been charged with administering the reservation as a whole, so they have had to introduce reservation-wide institutions. Correspondingly, when the federal government stimulated development of tribal governments, these were established on a reservation-wide or even multireservation basis. Traditional Indians have meanwhile continued to maintain their participation in, and allegiance to, their local band communities. Wax, Wax, and Dumont (1964) have referred to these participants as "Country Indians," preferring this designation to such terms as "Fullblood" or "cultural Fullblood," which emphasize the heredity or traits of the *individual*, rather than the *social* nature of the band. The significance does not lie in the individual's possession of particular *cultural* traits (e.g., dialect, dress, habitation), but in his *social* participation in the life of the local band. If the primary domestic and ceremonial language of the band is a native Indian tongue, an Indian will be gravely handicapped unless he is fluent in it, but the fluency in itself is not the crucial item, since an individual (e.g., an administrator) may speak the language and reside close to the band and yet not be a participant member.

Many reformers and administrators have regarded the traditional band patterns of interdependence and sharing with severe criticism. In their view, these patterns simply reflected irresponsibility and freeloading: Indian tribes had a plentiful supply of loafers who, seeing that one of their tribesmen had accumulated a small store of food or cash, would descend upon him like vultures until all his substance was exhausted. Under these circumstances there could be no motivation for individual achievement or industrious labor and forethoughtful husbandry. Accordingly, these reformers have elaborated many institutional devices to inhibit or thwart the native patterns of sharing. From their ethnocentric perspective, there is only one social unit where sharing should occur, and only one social unit which is fundamental to any society, and that is the nuclear family. A man should share with his wife and children, but scarcely further than that, unless it be a tithe to his church.

In the face of these institutional assaults by reformers, and in the context of the bitter poverty of Indians and their dependence upon governmental and missionary rations, it is perhaps amazing that the band organization should have survived to the present day. But the fact is that it is the strength of the band organization—its vitality, tenacity, and flexibility—which has enabled Indian communities to survive at all. These patterns of sharing, voluntary cooperation, equality, and solidarity have sustained these communities under condition which would otherwise have destroyed their membership.

Partly as a result of reformer pressures and partly other factors (including intermarriage, travel, and so on), a stratum of Indians has emerged in reservations that is socially and culturally quite distinct from the Country Indians. Historically, this group is descended from the early intermarriages between Indian women and white trappers, traders, and soldiers; the children of these unions, called "Halfbreeds" (or simply "Breeds"), now more commonly termed "Mixedbloods," were men marginal to both White and Indian societies, often playing the role of cultural and linguistic interpreters. While the Country Indians exist as local bands of kith and kin, those who are socially Mixedblood exist as an elite stratum that is reservation-wide. (There is even a national stratum of social Mixedbloods whose existence is linked educationally and occupationally with the federal Indian Service—the B.I.A., the Indian Public Health Service, and other administrative and benevolent agencies.) By background and training, this stratum is strategically located to serve as mediators between the Country Indians and agencies of the exterior society. They often secure the staff positions or other good jobs in the agencies established on the reservation, be these schools, churches, clinics, or welfare organizations. Outsiders find them congenial for purposes of negotiation, because they can speak for themselves (without having to worry about representing the thought of their bands) and because they can visualize the situation and needs of the reservation as a whole or of Indian peoples as a whole. Insofar as the Country Indian remains loyal to a local band of kith and kin, he is subject to the charge of favoritism and petty graft; outsiders see the Country Indian as "selfishly" interested in the well-being of his relatives and indifferent to the needs of the reservation and the possible contributions of the agency program (cf. Gans, 1962, Chap. 9; Whyte, 1943, Chap. 6). In contrast, the social Mixedblood shows that he understands the goals of agency programs and seemingly can act to implement that program over the reservation as a whole.

When middle class urbanites sense a community need, they meet together, organize themselves formally (with constitution and bylaws), elect officers, and deliberate on specific courses of action. Some reformers have tried to apply these patterns to Indian bands, and have been distressed at their failure. They speak of a lack of leadership in Indian communities, of apathy, or disorganization; they also speak of teaching democracy to the Indians. Yet, as we have noted, the Indian band communities are already well organized in an extremely tenacious, if loose and informal, fashion. Only when prolonged discussion results in a unanimous decision that something should be done is there felt a need for further organization. At this point the community pushes forward as its spokesmen (not leaders, although they may be accorded that title) those individuals whom the members assess as best able to present their case or coordinate the activity. Since the band community is egalitarian, no one is a leader in a bureaucratic or political sense; some individuals judged to be wise may be relied upon for advice and judgment, and some who are thought to understand the workings of particular external agencies, such as a governmental office, may be selected as spokesmen to deal with that office. But traditionally, and even today, life in a Plains Indian band is without formal coercion, although encompassed with a multitude of informal pressures.

SOCIAL CLASS AND GEOGRAPHY

Town versus countryside seems to epitomize life on an Indian reservation, town being the symbol of the intruding national society, and the countryside the home of the retiring Indian. His are the tents and cabins scattered over the prairie and clustering along the hillsides overlooking the creeks, while to the national society belong the miniature areas of urban subdivision housing, complete with lawns and paved streets, centering about complexes of federal buildings, schools, hospitals, and stores.

The outsiders—Whites, Blacks, Spanish-Americans, Indians of alien tribes—tend to be concentrated in the town, and it is easy to think of the town as the locus of the non-Indian and the Mixedblood. But the town has its share of urban slums, the inhabitants of which are as likely to be Indian in blood quanta as any of the rural folk. Many of the town-dwelling Indians have lost their lands or retain so little land that they cannot garner a living from it; their poverty is testimony to that aspect of their Indian heritage which left them (or their elders) easy victims to fraud or too naive in their handling of familial allotments. Nonetheless, towndwelling does provide a certain sophistication; as compared to Country Indians, towndwellers are more likely to be fluent in English, to have greater cleverness in handling bureaucrats, and to be more conscious of the institutional dynamics of the greater society. Accordingly, the town-dweller is likely to refer to his country cousins as "old-fashioned," "backward," or "residual" Indians; if he is a Mixedblood, he may sometimes merely gesture outward from the town and refer to "them"! However, if at one moment the townsman derogates the country people, at the next he is likely to give them the accolade of being "real Indians" or "real Fullbloods." He may scorn the Country Indians for being shy, dumb, or old-fashioned, reluctant to use the modern medical facilities of the Public Health Clinic, or dressing in styles that are out of date, but he will also praise them for being the most skillful at traditional arts and crafts, such as singing, dancing, beadwork, or leathercraft, or for having the greatest store of traditional wisdom.

The town–country relationship is relative, not absolute. Indians living in the big agency towns will relate in this fashion to those who live in modest communities scattered about a school, trading post, and church, who will, in turn, so relate to those who live out in the countryside far away even from the trading post.

In comprehending these relationships, it is well to realize that the traditions of the Country Indians may not be distinctively "Indian," but may in fact have been acquired from missionaries, traders, or Indian Agents of a half-century ago. For example, among the Country Sioux, traditional women wear high-necked, long-sleeved, shapeless dresses such as they were instructed to make by missionaries of the Victorian era. Even when they wear buckskin (real or synthetic) as dance costumes, they follow the same fashion, and doubtless would be quite startled at the relative nudity of their ancestors of the early nineteenth century.

THE USES OF MONEY

While it is tempting to think of the traditional Indian as having dwelt in a subsistence economy, in actuality much of what is now considered (by both Indians and Whites) as characteristic of traditional Indian culture developed in relationship to trade with the Whites. The colorful, dramatic culture of the horsenomadic tribes of the Great Plains involved regular periods of trade in which the Indian would exchange buffalo pelts and furs for guns, ammunition, whiskey, or other articles of civilized manufacture. When the Indians were confined to reservations, the goal of the missionaries was to convert them into Christian farmers diligent in their calling. No vocational conversion was necessary among the Papago, Pima, and Pueblo of the Southwest, as these tribes had already evolved agricultural techniques superbly tailored to their difficult locale. But elsewhere the Indian men had the ethos of hunters and warriors, and regarded farming as the work of drudges, such as women. Moreover, the western prairies lacked the moisture of the eastern farmlands, and conventional techniques of farming led to a high ratio of crop failure as well as to duststorms. In many of the western reservations, the land has been converted to ranching, usually of cattle, but sometimes of sheep (Navajo).

Indian men were initially enthusiastic participants in ranching, since the transition from horsenomad to mounted cowboy was not great, especially in the days when the range was open and cattle had to be driven. Many of the Sioux made excellent adaptations to this role, just as the Navajo had to being sheepherders. But during World War I, when the demand for beef was high, the Sioux were encouraged to sell their herds in the name of patriotism and profit. Since that time, cattle ranching on most reservations has come into the hands of professional ranchers who operate as skillful businessmen, using large quantities of capital and modern equipment to handle great herds of purebred cattle, and who need to lease large areas of land. Being partly Indian by blood, these ranchers secure legal preference for leasing large blocks of reservation land (via the B.I.A. in its capacity as trustee for the land). The Indian landowner seldom works his land, since he owns too little and lacks the capital and skills. He often resides on a small portion of it, and through the lease gains some sort of income, ranging from a few dollars to several hundred annually.

The typical reservation offers the ordinary Indian little opportunity for agricultural or industrial enterprise or for employment. As we noted earlier, unemployment rates are high and cash incomes low. Given the vast numbers of families who secure so little in the way of cash income, it is important to ask how they survive. The fundamental social answer is that Indians survive through an intricate but informal process of mutual assistance and cooperation. The unit of survival is neither the nuclear family of man, wife, and children, nor even the extended family that includes grandparents. Some families do attempt to exist on a nuclear basis, but unless they are part of the Mixedblood stratum and have government jobs, they are in deep trouble. The real survival unit is a complex of families, most often situated quite close to each other. Such a cluster of families will share transportation facilities, cash income from odd jobs, food, and whatever else is available. Unfortunately, most of the welfare reports from reservation areas fail to specify these units, and instead concentrate on such issues as whether or not a child is living with its natural parents. In consequence there are few adequate descriptions in the sociological literature of just how Indian families manage to survive.

Somewhat like an enlisted man's life in a military camp, Indian life in a reservation allows for survival with minimal use of money. The majority of people are living on land for which they do not have to pay rent (because it belongs to themselves or their kin). Health services are provided through the U.S. Public Health Service (its clinic, hospital, visiting nurses, and so on). Some food is available from the federal government because it has been categorized as "surplus commodities." Children who attend school secure one nourishing meal a day at noon; children in boarding school secure all their meals (a comparative analysis would probably show that children of poor Indian families have much better records of attendance than do children of urban slum dwellers). Wood is available for the effort of cutting and hauling; water is also available for the hauling. Life in a modest cabin on the reservation prairie is far from elegant and requires continual effort and a store of ingenious skills, but it can be endured. In some respects, the style of living is more like that of the frontiersmen of a century ago than it is like urban living, and from this viewpoint, it is not a bad life. Indeed, some of the difficulties of this way of life derive from its social circumstances. It is one thing to live on the prairie in a cabin without electricity, running water, or other amenities, if one's neighbors live under the same circumstances; it is quite another to live in this fashion and send children to school or adults to work, in neat and clean clothes, at fixed hours of the day. If the children have to walk a considerable distance in bitter cold weather in order to reach a bus stop, if the employee in the family has to rely on an automobile whose vital organs are in poor repair, or if the household includes sick and elderly people, then life has a tendency to deteriorate into a continual round of crises.

Since the Indian economy operates to such considerable extent without the use of money—but on a basis of barter and reciprocity and provision of goods and services by specialized agencies—cash itself becomes a peculiar thing, used for special and luxury purposes. The reader may be reminded of the way in which cash is handled by enlisted men, sailors, lumberjacks, ranchhands, or other groups whose daily necessities are furnished by an employer. The Indian uses cash for securing those special items that cannot be obtained within the reservation world, especially to satisfy the wants of children: for sweets, clothes, and toys. But it can also be used to make possible the lengthy trip to visit relatives situated far away, or to purchase a newer car or to pay for repairs to an older one. The pattern of this usage is often distressing to welfare workers or other reformers who themselves live as a nuclear family on a definite and scheduled cash income. To these persons, Indian usage of cash appears irresponsible and haphazard. Perhaps the most sensible criticism derives from economists of a classical turn, who feel that the governmental agencies established to provide services thought to be good or necessary for Indians deprive the Indians of the liberty enjoyed by other Americans of making their own adjustments of wants and incomes. Thus, Indians are currently being urged out of their prairie cabins into suburban type housing, despite the fact that the reservation economy shows little evidence of providing the stable employment and income necessary for the mass of Indians to afford the mortgage payments and utilities charges required by the fancier housing. Economists have also criticized the pattern of governmental expenditure as being devoted too much to provision of consumer services and too little to capital development (cf. Eicher, 1961).

Evolving in symbiotic relationship to the reservations has been a cluster of agencies which consume large quantities of the monies designated as being "for Indians," and which in turn provide or impose upon Indians a variety of services. The eldest of these agencies is the Indian Service and its heir, the B.I.A., which provides such services as land management, education, and trusteeship of lands. In time there appeared the Public Health Service and, under President Kennedy, the Office of Economic Opportunity. Especially in the later case, universities have become involved as regional middlemen or brokers to these federal programs: they receive large quantities of federal funds, recruit a professional staff to coordinate and operate, and provide small quantities of in-house research. Many otherwise modest institutions of higher education (e.g., University of South Dakota, Black Hills State Teachers College, Arizona State University) have become participants in these enterprises and recipients of hundreds of thousands of federal dollars. In a sense, the universities have inherited the social role played in the nineteenth century by missionary groups who came to control the reservations because the federal operations could not be kept free of the taint of political corruption. But, just as the missionaries, the universities are insulated from the influence of local Indian communities, and organize their programs according to ideologies, professional codes, and bureaucratic procedures that exclude any control by the relatively uneducated Indians. As the universities build staffs and operate programs, they become increasingly dependent upon these monies, and constitute a vested interest of some potency in maintaining reservations in a subordinated state. Indian communities seeking to gain greater control of their own destinies find that instead of having real control of the funds presumably allocated for their benefit, they must deal with professional welfare entrepreneurs.

EDUCATION AS PANACEA

Contemplating the depressed position of the Indians in contemporary life, many reformers have felt that education was the answer. By "education" they really mean acculturation and assimilation, so that in all significant respects Indians would become like Whites—or, rather, like the "better sort" of Whites. These reformers selectively ignored an important aspect of U.S. history (illustrated in the Indian case by the Six Nations, the Cherokees, and even the Métis): cultural assimilation does not necessarily bring structural assimilation. People who assimilate culturally and become potent economic competitors may thereby provoke political assaults, such as were suffered by the Japanese-Americans during World War II.

Regardless of the above, the federal government and the various mission organizations have stressed education in their dealings with Indians, and school compounds are one of the most distinctive features of the landscape on today's reservations (while within the B.I.A. the Branch of Education requires the most funds and handles the most people). The visitor may drive for miles on a reservation, scarcely noticing the small Indian dwellings nestling among the hills. Then there suddenly appears a school compound containing several large classroom buildings and perhaps a boarding hall, together with a large quantity of residential housing, much of it looking as if it had been lifted straight out of contemporary mass-produced suburbia. The whole, or at least parts of it, may be surrounded by fencing, and the residential housing may be graced with the only lawns to be seen for miles. The ecological contrast between Indian residential communities and school compounds is profound and is diagnostic of the relationship between Indian pupils and the educational establishment. The situation almost appears colonial, or at the least caste-like: between Indian community and schools there is a strong social barrier, typified by the fences which surround the compound. Parents rarely visit the schools; teachers rarely visit the homes; each side finds interaction with the other uncomfortable.

The consquence of this barrier is that by the intermediate grades Indian children have begun to develop a closed and solidary peer society within the walls of the school. The more the children are culturally distinct from the educators, and the deeper the social gulf between their community and that of the educators, the easier it is for them to organize themselves. In situations where their community retains an Indian language as the primary tongue, the children have available a secret means of communication which excludes most of the educators (as well as other outsiders). Thus, within the classroom the children can practice an active and intensely preoccupying social life, without the interference or even the awareness of the teacher. The children are not so much hostile to the teacher or to his scholastic procedures as they are set apart from it, so that the teacher stands outside vainly struggling to secure the attention of children who necessarily appear to him as indifferent, apathetic, childish, or stupid. The parents, familiar with the ways of their children, might be able to diagnose for the teacher what is occurring within the classroom and assist him in dealing with the peer society. But most teachers think of their isolation from the parents as a blessing, and compare their undisturbed situation in Indian schools with the special pleadings and connivings of parents in the typical nonreservation school. The teachers will remark that elsewhere parents are continually interfering with classroom discipline, or complaining about the treatment accorded their children, or protesting the grading of their children's performances. In pleasant contrast, the reservation school is freed of these harassments, and teachers conceive of themselves as able to go about their business without the interference of critical, ignorant, and partisan laymen.

In the intermediate grades, where the peer society is just beginning to become solidary, the classroom may be the scene of considerable confusion. The pupils may behave in ways that the teacher perceives as exhibiting "shyness": reading in a voice too soft to be heard, writing on the chalkboard in letters too small to be read, or hiding the face behind a book when called upon. As a counterpoint, there may be much activity sub rosa—taunts among the children in the native language, hair pullings, pummelings, kickings, exchange of comic books, and so on—which occurs only on the margins of the teacher's awareness. By the upper elementary grades, when the pupils are in their mid or late teens, a profound order may have established itself within the classrooms. A quiet prevails that is imposed by the students as a way of sheltering their own lives from the intrusive efforts of the educators. An observer can sit for hours in such classrooms without hearing any voice but that of the teacher, although in fact an intense interaction is occurring among the pupils.

Meanwhile, on the level of scholastic achievement as measured by nationally standardized tests, the relative performance of Indian children shows a steady decline with advancement in grade. Whereas in the early grades—and despite major cultural and linguistic handicaps—Indian pupils are much on a par with children elsewhere, by the upper elementary grades there has been a sizable dropoff (cf. Wax, Wax, and Dumont, 1964, Chap. 2). Some observers have attributed this to a "going back to the blanket." More recent observers of a psychiatric turn of mind (e.g., Bernard Spilka, John Bryde) have contended that the Indian child becomes alienated from both the society of his parents and that of the school, and this phenomenon is associated with loss of inner confidence and decline in motivation. Other observers, of an educational bent, have criticized the program and curriculum of the Indian schools, contending that little provision has been made for the oral teaching of English as a second language. The result is that, regardless of motivation, Indian children of the advanced grades simply lack the linguistic facility—in speaking, reading, comprehending—to deal with the formal classwork required of them. Our own account, here and elsewhere (Wax, Wax, and Dumont, 1964; Wax and Wax, 1964, 1968; R. Wax, 1967), has given heavy emphasis to the rise of the peer society and the failure of educators to harness that society to the performance of educational tasks.

Agreement on the significance of the peer society for the life of Plains Indian youth is forthcoming from both ethnohistorians as well as contemporary students of Indian life. Robert A. White, whose study of Sioux life in Rapid City is summarized briefly in Chapter Seven, agrees on the significance of the peer society, and argues that the maladjustment of the lower class ("Camp Sioux") men to the contemporary environment is a consequence of an overly active involvement with the peer society at the expense of the nuclear family. Accordingly, he, as some other reformers, has advocated programs which would reduce the attachment of the young Plains Indian person to the society of his peers. However, it is clear that disrupting the peer society is a negative tactic bound to heighten the personal disorganization of Indians, whether as pupils or as adults. If the peer society provides the main social focus, if it provides the Indian with his sense of identity and self, then to destroy the society is to destroy him as a person and leave someone who, rather than being liberated, has been deracinated and deprived of any sense of security or worth.

An alternative procedure to combating the peer society is for educators to work with it and so guide it that some of its formidable energies are directed towards scholastic tasks. As a simple example, it has frequently been observed that Indian pupils hesitate to engage in an individual performance before the public gaze, especially where they sense competitive assessment against their peers. Indian children do not wish to be exposed as inadequate before their peers, and equally do not wish to demonstrate by their individual superiority the inferiority of their peers. On the other hand, where performance is socially defined as benefiting the peer society, Indians become excellent competitors (as witness their success in team athletics). When principles utilizing this perception are skillfully introduced into the school and classroom, the educator of sensibilities can stimulate eager and productive efforts among his students, sometimes from as simple a device as contests that pit boys against girls in spelling bees or arithmetic races (cf. Dumont and Wax, 1969).

In disregard of the foregoing analyses of educational difficulties among Indian children, the most recent reformative programs aimed at Indian reservations have been preschools of the Head Start variety. The rationale for these programs has been that the unsatisfactory scholastic performance of adolescent Indian pupils has been due to deficiencies in their early childhood experiences. Lacking access to the mass media (especially television) and residing in homes with few reading materials and perhaps little conversational English, Indian children enter school deprived of the rich cultural experiences enjoyed by middle class children. Accordingly, a special preschool situation is necessary wherein young children will be stimulated and their horizons enlarged by special kinds of materials and experiences. Given the bitter poverty of most Indian households and the difficulties elders have in feeding and providing health care for their children, it is hard to be critical of a program, such as Head Start, in which children are fed, provided with medical and dental care, and sheltered from the elements. Nonetheless, it should be said that the concept of "cultural deprivation" works both ways, and there are a multitude of experiences enriching the lives of Indian children—even on an impoverished reservation—of which middle class urban children are deprived. Children on a Plains Indian reservation are exposed to singing and dancing of a high esthetic quality and become early participants in these activities; they have a great natural area to roam within and to explore, and become familiar with the ways of life of numerous domesticated and wild animals and plants; they generally encounter social life on a scale which is visible and comprehensible to a young child. Finally, it should be noted that while Head Start Programs may prepare a child better for conformity in school—and perhaps for scholastic achievement—they may not assist him toward developing into a stable adult able to cope with the actualities of his environment.

Effecting reforms of the educational system for Indian children has proven as difficult as reforming education in metropolitan areas. While much of the monies devoted to Indian education are distributed via the U.S. Office of Education—and in recent years have totaled as high as $60 million—they are diverted into a multiplicity of local school systems in a fashion that inhibits any surveillance of their expenditure. The federal agencies have not had either the independence or the resources to monitor expenditures at the local level, while the Indians, whose children are supposedly the beneficiaries of these sums, have lacked the organization, knowhow, and influence to perform this role. Within the B.I.A. there is an Assistant Commissioner of Education, but he lacks authority even over the federal schools, because the local principals report to the Area Directors (of the half-dozen area offices of the B.I.A.), and each such Director is more responsive to the pressures of local interest groups and congressmen than to advisory statements issued from the Washington office. While the federally operated reservation schools concentrate their operations on Indian children, the numerous local schools tend to regard the monies for Indian children as part of their general operating expenditures, and it is often dubious whether Indian children derive any benefits from the monies presumably allocated for them. (Appendix B contains further data on patterns of schooling of Indian children.)

SUGGESTED READINGS

Dumont, Robert V., Jr., and Murray L. Wax. 1969. The Cherokee School Society and the Intercultural Classroom. *Human Organization*, 28, 217–26.
Eicher, Carl K. 1961. An Approach to Income Improvement on the Rosebud Sioux Indian Reservation. *Human Organization* 20, 191–202.

Gans, Herbert J. 1962. *The Urban Villagers.* New York: The Free Press.

Kent, Calvin A., and Jerry W. Johnson. 1969. *Indian Poverty in South Dakota.* Bulletin #99. Vermillion: Business Research Bureau, School of Business, University of South Dakota.

Thomas, Robert K. 1966. Colonialism: Classic and Internal. *New University Thought,* 4, 37–43.

U.S. Public Health Service. *Pine Ridge Research Bulletin.* Serial, issued irregularly.

Wax, Murray L., and Rosalie H. Wax. 1964. Cultural Deprivation as an Educational Ideology. *Journal of American Indian Education,* 3, 15–18.

———. 1968. The Enemies of the People, in *Institutions and the Person,* ed. Howard S. Becker *et al.* Chicago: Aldine Publishing Company.

———, and Robert V. Dumont, Jr. 1964. Formal Education in an American Indian Community. Monograph #1, The Society for the Study of Social Problems (Supplement, *Social Problems,* 11, No. 4).

Wax, Rosalie H. 1967. The Warrior Dropouts. *TRANS-action,* 4, 40–46.

———, and Murray L. Wax. 1965. American Indian Education for What? *Midcontinent American Studies Journal,* 6, 164–170.

Whyte, William Foote. 1943. *Street Corner Society.* Chicago: University of Chicago Press (2nd ed., 1955).

BACKGROUND

This chapter will focus upon a particular Indian people who have not participated in the reservation system, but who are nevertheless of some considerable size and more than usual historical interest. In trying to communicate the nature of a nonreservation yet tribal Indian population, we are forced to be more specific than in the previous chapter, where we could describe in general terms a typical reservation situation. The people selected for description are the Tribal Cherokee of Oklahoma, and my familiarity with them is firsthand, since in 1966–1967 I led a research team that studied their educational and general social situation, and have thereafter been interested and occasionally involved with their affairs.

A Tribal Nonreservation People: The Oklahoma Cherokee

During the seventeenth and eighteenth centuries, the Cherokees resided in the Southeast (now Georgia, the Carolinas, and Tennessee), but in response to the pressures of settlers and speculators seeking lands, some Cherokee had begun to move westward toward what is now Oklahoma. The major movement was during the Presidency of Andrew Jackson (1829–1837), for at that time the great mass of the tribe were rounded up and forcibly removed from their homes. The forced migration westward has come to be known as "The Trail of Tears," because it wrenched the tribe from its ancestral home and the conditions of the journey were such that many died enroute. (A small portion of the tribe, living in the mountains or other places difficult of access—and therefore of negligible interest to Whites seeking land—managed to evade the process of removal. These folk were the progenitors of what is now the Eastern Band of Cherokee, which has its reservation adjoining the Great Smokey National Park. For further details on the contemporary condition of the Eastern Cherokee see Gulick [1960] or Kupferer [1966].)

During the century immediately prior to the removal, the Cherokee Nation had evolved from a loose federation of villages toward a nation state organized along republican lines, complete with bicameral legislature and appellate judiciary (Gearing, 1962). While the evolution was stimulated by the intercourse with Whites and the presence of Whites intermarried within the tribe, it reached deeply among the people. Sequoyah, an indigenous genius—who did not speak or write English or any other European language—devised a *syllabary* for the printed representation of the Cherokee language. So ingenious was his invention that in a short time its use had spread widely among the Cherokee (who may well have reached a higher rate of literacy than the frontier settlers dwelling nearby). The new nation issued its own newspaper, printed both in English and in Cherokee, and its overall level of accomplishment was such that, together with neighboring southeastern Indians, it was spoken of as a "Civilized Tribe."

After removal to the west, the Cherokee again organized themselves as a republic, and despite bitter internal factionalism associated with the removal and aggravated by the Civil War, the new state managed a successful reintegration and adaptation to the new environment. The commitment to education was deep, and during the last quarter of the nineteenth century the Nation was said to have had the finest school system west of the Mississippi.

But neither the Cherokee nor the other tribes of the Plains could defend themselves against frontiersmen seeking land. The Constitution of the Cherokee Nation specified that all lands were held in common, with usage rights allocated to communities and families according to custom, and the Cherokee refused to "open" these lands to settlement by Whites or to convert them into merchandisable real estate that could be bought and sold. Pressures were organized within the Congress of the U.S. to achieve by legislation what could not be accomplished by the individual White settler or land speculator. After prolonged struggles, legislation was enacted in 1906 that dissolved the Cherokee Nation and allotted its lands in severalty among its citizens. The process was bitterly resisted by the Fullblood (rural traditionalist) elements among the Cherokee population, and many refused to register for their allotments, thinking that their refusal to participate would prevent the process from moving to completion. Meanwhile, White intruders upon the Cherokee domain insinuated their way onto the membership rolls and thus secured allotments. The resistance of the Fullbloods proved futile, and the Cherokee republic was destroyed, its lands allotted, its printing plant disassembled, and its schools transferred to exterior control. Bereft of organized and responsible national leadership, and unfamiliar with Anglo-Saxon laws of private property, the Cherokee Fullbloods lost most of their land allotments to the invaders. During the succeeding years, most of the Mixedblood elements of the Cherokee people integrated themselves into the social fabric of the state of Oklahoma, while the communities of *Tribal Cherokee* maintained social integrity and isolation in the hills of northeastern Oklahoma. But while they could maintain their language and religious practices, they lost their prosperity; whereas they had once been self-sufficient and comparable economically to their White neighbors of Arkansas and Kansas, now they dwelt in rural slums (Debo, 1951).

In order to expedite the allotting of lands and the dissolving of the Cherokee republic (against the resistance of its people), the U.S. Congress had granted to the President power to appoint a "Principal Chief" (as the chief executive office of the Cherokee Nation had been denominated). In itself this appears to be a strange piece of legislation, since the President has not the comparable power to appoint governors of states, or mayors of cities, or executives of corporations. However, in the decades after allotment, various presidents utilized this power in order to appoint a congenial person to pose as the representative of "The Cherokee" in the conduct of official business. These appointed Principal Chiefs were in no sense (except the name) comparable to their predecessors, for the latter had been directly elected and could not have ruled without enlisting the active support of large numbers of the Cherokee, including the numerous and powerful groups of Fullbloods. Now, however, a great deal of the business of the appointed chiefs was occurring outside of the awareness of the Tribal Cherokee, as there were neither elections nor official organs of publication and dissemination. Besides, most of the business was conducted in the English language and in locales far removed from northeastern Oklahoma.

As of 1970, the Principal Chief of the Cherokee Nation was a man about one-eighth degree Indian by blood, appointed to his post in 1949 by President Truman.[1] In the years since appointment, he had risen to the highest ranking position of one of America's largest industrial corporations. Under his direction, the official "Cherokee Nation" became a sizable enterprise, since it won in the name of the Cherokee a large sum of money via the Indian Claims Commission in compensation for some of the lands which the Cherokee had been forced to yield during the nineteenth century. Thus the "Cherokee Nation" emerged as a million-

---

[1]For a critical appraisal of the Principal Chief, see the testimony and statement of Mildred Parks Ballenger in the *Hearings* Before the Subcommittee on Indian Education, Part 2, February 19, 1968, Twin Oaks, Okla., pp. 547–562. The *Hearings* also contain the statements of the Chief and his associates, as well as much other interesting information.

dollar enterprise, and it had excellent prospects of acquiring further capital from similar suits filed before the Indian Claims Commission.

With the foregoing as brief historical and political background, we turn to examine the situation of the Tribal Cherokee as of the late 1960's. Our discussion is organized in two major parts. The first is a review of the economic and ecological position of the Tribal Cherokee; the second is an analysis of the relationship of their children to the local rural public schools.

ECOLOGY AND ECONOMY

Judged as data, much of the economic and demographic information about the Tribal Cherokee is less than satisfactory. Since the Nation was dissolved in 1906, there has been no central source of basic research and data about the Cherokee: no tribal roster has been maintained on a regular basis, and no censuses have been conducted of their numbers and their economic and social condition. However, combining materials from several different sources makes it possible to gain a fairly accurate picture of the numbers and situation of the Tribal Cherokee. As the reader will perceive, a review of these procedures is itself highly instructive.

Region and Peoples

Compared to the arid plains spreading westward in Oklahoma and southward in Texas, northeastern Oklahoma is green and forested. The initial lumbering of the area brought a brief explosion of population and towns, and the continual regrowth of the forest now provides a basis for some modest industry based on wood and a setting congenial to tourism and outdoor recreation. The climate and cheap labor also make it a suitable region for raising botanical nursery stock, and one of the nation's largest wholesalers is located in Cherokee County. Yet the native soils are neither rich nor easy to till. In their original period of settlement during the nineteenth century, the Cherokee attempted to introduce a stable and permanent agricultural adaptation. Yet today family-based agriculture has all but disappeared, and the major agricultural use of the land is cattle ranching, with some dairy farming and poultry raising. During the past generation the area has been open to outside communication by means of paved roads, and, in addition, the Army Corps of Engineers has been busily damming the rivers. The effect on the region has been profound: ancient Cherokee communities have been flooded out, while the forests and artificial lakes have attracted sportsmen, tourists, and vacationers.

What was the principal region of settlement of the Cherokee Nation is now politically structured within Oklahoma as five counties: Adair, Cherokee, Delaware, Mayes, and Sequoyah. The Cherokee Republic, when it existed, claimed sovereignty over a far larger area; Cherokee families were settled during the nineteenth century not only in (what is now) Georgia and the Carolinas, but also in Tennessee, Arkansas, Oklahoma, Texas, and elsewhere. Nonetheless, the Five County Region, as we shall be referring to this part of Oklahoma, remains the major geographic concentration of the Cherokee people (the Eastern Cherokee in the Carolinas are about half as numerous).

This Region embraces numerous ambiguities as to the definition of who is what kind of Cherokee. Under the proper circumstances, a very large proportion of the population will claim to be "of Indian blood," "Cherokee lineage," or "Indian," and since the persons involved vary considerably in their social position and way of life, some distinctions for purposes of clarity are essential. The most distinctively Cherokee groups are the communities scattered along the hollows of the rural countryside (a map of the settlements is given in the 1968 *Current Anthropology* version of Wahrhaftig's essay, 1965). Many of these settlements are quite old and can trace their histories back to the original Nation. Most are located near and oriented toward such distinctively Cherokee institutions as a Nighthawk Ceremonial Ground ("stomp ground") or a Cherokee Baptist Church. The members of these communities recognize those of other communities as being real Cherokees. Each such community has a distinctive Cherokee name, and its members usually speak Cherokee as their primary domestic and religious language. Given the location and agricultural origin of these communities, they might be distinguished, as did Cullum (1953), by the label "Rural Cherokee." However, although they are still rural, they are far less so than in the past; their basis in subsistence agriculture has disappeared, and many of the persons attached to them have employment, or even temporary residences, elsewhere in more urbanized areas. Wahrhaftig has employed the term "Tribal Cherokee," and we have been following his usage, although the word "tribe" may wrongly connote to some readers that these communities are linked together in some overarching political framework.

In sharp contrast to the persons who participate in such Tribal Cherokee communities are those who are "of Cherokee lineage" but whose lives are otherwise scarcely distinct from those of their White neighbors. Many of them bear the traces of their genetic heritage in the hue of their skin and the cast of their features; they are visibly part "Indian" to those who are knowledgeable in such matters. Some pride themselves upon their descent from the leading families of the Cherokee Nation, and this descent offers an entree into certain elite associations of Oklahoma as well as the privilege to speak (or be responsible) for the impoverished and uneducated folk who are also known as Cherokee or Indian. On the other hand, they are quite detached from the lives of the Tribal Cherokee; they neither speak the language nor attend the local ceremonials, except as occasional spectators. Being Cherokee is expressed through participation in benevolent, cultural, or political associations which are concerned with Cherokee history, or through assisting those whom most consider to be backward and ignorant Indians. Some of these associations have the quality of the Daughters of the American Revolution in that membership is restricted by birth to a selected elite. A few of these persons have taken their identification as Cherokee as a responsibility to be borne honestly, devotedly, and courageously, but for many others it has simply provided an opportunity to engage in a regional struggle for social status and political power.

For many years, persons have been emigrating from the communities of rural Cherokee. Some communities have been dislocated by dams; others have lost members as a result of economic pushes and pulls; an increasing number of women seem to be lost through intermarriage or concubinage with Whites. In these ways, some people have lost their affiliation and participation with Tribal Cherokee communities and appear as deracinated or detribalized proletarians. They may have enough "Indian blood" to qualify for some federal and benevolent programs, but such benefits accrue to them as individuals rather than as members of a functioning community. This population may be further subdivided into the stable working class, who are relatively permanent residents of the urbanized areas of Oklahoma, and the free-floating proletarians who migrate from area to area in search of opportunities.

Some persons may emigrate from Tribal Cherokee communities and yet preserve a strong linkage with them. They will journey home many times per year in order to participate in ceremonials or assist in familial crises, and while they seem to have an urban residence elsewhere, their social allegiance may remain in northeastern Oklahoma. Some observers may presume that such emigrants must eventually assimilate, but this is not necessarily so (Wahrhaftig, 1969). We must differentiate carefully between the kinds of persons described in the preceding paragraph and those being described here. We should also note that some Cherokee migrants have reestablished communities in new environments, including the urban, thus emerging as enclaves centered about a ceremonial center, such as a church.

Whites who settled in northeastern Oklahoma found themselves subordinated socially and economically to the Mixedblood families who constituted the elite of the Cherokee Nation. It is still true that there is a social advantage in this area to being "of Cherokee lineage," and that those who lack that cachet thereby acknowledge that their families are more recent immigrants. A few of these immigrants have become economically successful, but most Whites have remained poor, and in recent years have been migrating from these rural areas. Since the rate of out-migration by Whites is higher than that of Cherokee, the region is becoming slightly more Indian (Wahrhaftig, 1965b). Meanwhile, successful Whites have been intermarrying with descendants of the Cherokee elite, while the poorer Whites have been marrying or establishing liaisons with the Tribal Cherokee; in neither case should this be presumed to signify assimilation or dissolution of the ethnic group.

In addition to Indian and White, the region contains a very small number of Negroes. Some, possibly all, are descended from the slaves who accompanied the Mixedblood Cherokee elite in their move from the Southeast, and as such were awarded by the federal government most of the same rights as the native Cherokee at the dissolution of the Cherokee Nation. In any case, the proletarianization of the Tribal Cherokee has left little room for a darker companion, since it is the Tribal Cherokee in this region who perform the underpaid, difficult, and degrading labor which is reserved for the Negro in the Deep South and the Chicanos in the Southwest.

Demography and Poverty

The federal Census of 1960 reported a population for the Five County Region of about 82 thousand, with the individual counties ranging from 13 to 20 thousand in population (see Table 5–1). Of this total population, about 15 per cent were classified as "Indian," with the range from 23 per cent for Adair County to less than 7 per cent for Sequoyah. While the 1960 procedures whereby the Census enumerated Indians left something to be desired, there is generally a strong agreement between these figures and those which Albert Wahrhaftig estimated for the Tribal Cherokee of the five counties. He found that something over 12 per cent of the regional population were members of Tribal Cherokee communities, and the difference of 3 per cent can easily be accounted for by Indians outside those communities. If anything, the agreement between Wahrhaftig and the Census is too good, since it allows insufficient numbers for those who might classify as Indian but are not members of Tribal Cherokee communities. This discordance leads to the surmise that Census

TABLE 5–1

PEOPLES AND REGION (1960),
BY COUNTIES

	Adair		Cherokee		Delaware	
	No.	%	No.	%	No.	%
Population						
Total	13,112	100.0	17,762	100.0	13,198	100.0
Non-White	3,057	23.3	3,456	19.4	2,097	15.9
Negro	1	—	281	1.6	2	—
Indian	3,055	23.3	3,159	17.8	2,093	15.8
Migration (net loss or gain through civilian migration, 1950–1960)	−3,717		−3,420		−2,554	
Urban places			Tahlequah 5,840			

	Mayes		Sequoyah		Total	
	No.	%	No.	%	No.	%
Population						
Total	20,073	100.0	18,001	100.0	82,146	100.0
Non-White	1,799	9.0	2,042	11.3	12,451	15.2
Negro	105	0.5	841	4.7	1,298	1.6
Indian	1,682	8.4	1,195	6.6	11,184	13.6
Migration (net loss or gain through civilian migration, 1950–1960)	−1,825		−4,156		−15,672	
Urban places	Pryor Creek 6,476		Salisaw 3,351			

SOURCE: U.S. Bureau of the Census, 1963b, Tables 2, A2.

procedures have worked to list as Indian mostly those persons who were either Tribal Cherokees or otherwise impoverished, lower caste, or non-participants in middle class society.

The poverty of the region is visible in its substantial out-migration (see Table 5–1). Between 1940 and 1960 the five counties lost almost 18 per cent of their total population. The decline has been most significant among the rural populace, with some townships, such as Long and McKey for Sequoyah and Chance and Christie of Adair, losing 40 to 50 per cent of their population. These out-migrations are somewhat disguised by the modest growth of such urban places as Tahlequah (the site of Northeastern State College in Cherokee County), Pryor (Mayes County), and Sallisaw (Sequoyah County), as well as by other transformations.

TABLE 5–2

FAMILY INCOME IN 1959, BY COUNTIES

	Adair		Cherokee		Delaware		Mayes		Sequoyah		Total	
	No.	%	No.	%	No.	%	No.	%	No.	%	No.	%
All families	3,369 =	100	4,348 =	100	3,612 =	100	5,312 =	100	4,532 =	100	21,173 =	100
Annual income												
Under $1,000	725	21.5	560	12.9	581	16.1	572	10.8	940	20.7	3,378	16.0
$ 1,000–$ 1,999	1,044	31.0	1,130	26.0	983	27.2	1,031	19.4	970	21.4	5,158	24.4
$ 2,000–$ 2,999	566	16.8	737	17.0	687	19.0	758	14.3	724	16.0	3,472	16.4
$ 3,000–$ 3,999	384	11.4	576	13.2	460	12.7	631	11.9	593	13.1	2,644	12.5
$ 4,000–$ 4,999	228	6.8	331	7.6	285	7.9	544	10.2	361	8.0	1,749	8.3
$ 5,000–$ 5,999	186	5.5	331	7.6	163	4.5	540	10.2	331	7.3	1,551	7.3
$ 6,000–$ 6,999	72	2.1	201	4.6	128	3.5	367	6.9	205	4.5	973	4.6
$ 7,000–$ 7,999	61	1.8	95	2.2	100	2.8	227	4.3	118	2.6	601	2.8
$ 8,000–$ 8,999	34	1.0	89	2.0	79	2.2	197	3.7	93	2.0	492	2.3
$ 9,000–$ 9,999	19	0.6	77	1.8	42	1.2	137	2.6	50	1.1	325	1.5
$10,000–$14,999	20	0.6	148	3.4	80	2.2	210	4.0	120	2.6	578	2.7
$15,000–$24,999	26	0.8	35	0.8	20	0.6	82	1.5	15	0.3	178	0.8
$25,000 and over	4	0.1	38	0.9	4	0.1	16	0.3	12	0.3	74	0.3
Median income												
Families	$1,919		$2,657		$2,352		$3,468		$2,492			
Families and unrelated individuals	$1,732		$1,793		$2,998		$2,854		$2,114			

SOURCE: U.S. Bureau of the Census, 1963a, Table 86.

More direct measurements of the poverty of the region are the statistics of family income (see Table 5–2). Among all the counties of Oklahoma, Adair had the *lowest* median figure in 1960, $1,919, and three of the other counties, Cherokee, Delaware, and Sequoyah, are also below a median level of $3,000, with only Mayes County, which has the fewest Indians, rising higher. For purposes of comparison, we might note that the median family income (1960) within the State of Oklahoma was $4,620, while within the U.S. as a whole it was $5,660. Accordingly, the five counties constitute a very depressed region within a state which is itself relatively depressed (Table 5–3). Moreover, if we convert family income into per capita income, by estimating a median family size as about four, the median for the four lowest counties comes to less than $700 annually.

The levels of educational achievement confirm the portrait of a depressed population (see Table 5–4). In 1960, for the population aged 25 years or over, the median number of school years completed was somewhat over eight. This represented a deficiency of two years as compared to the medians for either the state or the nation. The deficiency is more drastic if we investigate the portion of the adult population who have completed less than five years of school: for Adair County the figure is almost one-quarter, for Mayes County 10 per cent, and the other counties range from 14 to 20 per cent. These figures may be compared with a figure of somewhat over 8 per cent for the nation and for the state.

The Tribal Cherokee

Since the question of who is what kind of Cherokee—or who is what kind of Indian in northwestern Oklahoma—permits several types of answers, and would thus require several different approaches for performing a demographic tally, we shall simply note here an approach recently employed by Wahrhaftig, with the resultant estimate of population.

If a Tribal Cherokee is one who participates in Cherokee ceremonial activities, then an estimate of population can be derived from a census of the ceremonial institutions. As of 1963 there were 42 churches in the Cherokee Indian Baptist Association, 9 Cherokee Methodist Churches, 5 Cherokee-Creek Baptist Churches, 3 other Cherokee Churches, and 6 Nighthawk Stomp Grounds. Estimating an average of 34 households per church and 50 households per stomp ground, and estimating further an average of 4.9 persons per household, a population of 11,694 results (Wahrhaftig, 1965b, p. 9 [1968, p. 513]). Thus, we might

TABLE 5-3

FAMILY INCOME AND PUBLIC ASSISTANCE, BY COUNTIES

	Adair		Cherokee		Delaware		Mayes		Sequoyah		State of Oklahoma	
	No.	%	No.	%	No.	%	No.	%	No.	%	No.	%
A. Income in 1959 of families, 1960												
Median income, $	$1,919		$2,657		$2,352		$3,468		$2,492		$4,620	
Under $3000		69.3		55.8		62.3		44.4		58.1		31.0
$10,000 and over		1.5		5.1		2.9		5.8		3.2		10.1
B. No. of family units, 1960	3,369	100.0	4,348	100.0	3,612	100.0	5,312	100.0	4,352	100.0	612,790	100.0
Aid to families with dependent children, 1964–1965	460	13.6	469	10.8	322	8.9	291	5.5	533	12.2	24,716	4.0
C. Amount of welfare assistance returned to county per sales tax dollar collected	19.28		9.31		17.56		6.37		14.99		2.70	
D. Total assistance payments ($1,000)	1,880		1,826		1,668		1,578		2,394		122,573	

SOURCES: A. U.S. Bureau of the Census, 1963a, Table 86, 1963b, Table 2; B. Oklahoma Public Welfare Commission, 1965, Table 35; C. Oklahoma Public Welfare Commission, 1965, Table 2; D. Oklahoma Public Welfare Commission, 1965, Table 3.

safely estimate the population of Tribal Cherokee as being approximately ten thousand. We know that the residential population of Tribal Cherokees is periodically supplemented by emigrants who return, sometimes briefly for ceremonial occasions, sometimes more prolongedly as the opportunity arises or necessity requires. However, since the rest of our statistics in this section will concern those who were locally resident at the time of surveys, we can for the moment disregard the commuting participants in Tribal Cherokee society.

Dealing with a population of this sort, whose boundaries are not strictly visible to the outside observer and whose economy tends to fluctuate about the subsistence level, the researcher finds it difficult to assemble meaningful statistics about income. Nevertheless, it is clear to any impartial observer that, by the standards of the greater society, the Tribal Cherokee are economically depressed. Their homes are usually cabins built of logs or crude lumber and sheathed with cardboard or other cheap and readily available materials. There is usually no running water, although electricity may be present, at least for light. Yet many of the non-Indians of this region are also poor, and if we focus on housing, we find that only a third of the housing units in Adair County in 1960 were "sound and with all plumbing facilities" (U.S. Bureau of the Census, 1963).

Welfare statistics tend to disclose the comparative economic disadvantage of the Indians (see Table 5–5). Thus, in Adair County, where somewhat less than one-quarter of the population is classed as Indian, almost half of the families on Aid to Families with Dependent Children (A.F.D.C.) are Indian. Considering the Five County Region as a whole, almost 35 per cent of the families on A.F.D.C. are classed as Indian. Relative to their proportion in the population, Indians are overrepresented by factors of from two to three.

On more direct measures of income, the comparative disadvantage of the Tribal Cherokee is clear (Table 5–6 compared with Table 5–2). Median annual family income in 1960 ranged from $1,293 in Sequoyah county to $1,941 in Cherokee. We have noted that White income in this region is very low, but Indian ("Non-White" in Table 5–6) income in Sequoyah and Mayes Counties has a median level half that of the Whites, and the level in the other counties is numerically equally low, if comparatively less disadvantaged to the total population. In any case, it is clear that considerably over half of the families had incomes below $2,000 for the year, and estimating family size as four to five persons means a per capita income of $400 to $500 for the year. Confronted with such stark figures, there is little need for discussion. The Tribal Cherokee exist on the verge of destitution.

TABLE 5–4

EDUCATIONAL ACHIEVEMENT OF
REGIONAL POPULATION, BY COUNTIES

	Adair	Chero-kee	Dela-ware	Mayes	Sequoyah	State of Oklahoma
A. Population, 25 years old and over (1960)						
Median school years completed	8.2	8.6	8.5	8.8	8.2	10.4
Completed less than 5 years of school (%)	22.6	16.3	14.0	10.4	20.2	8.6
Completed high school or more (%)	18.3	26.4	22.9	29.9	18.0	40.5
B. Rural population						
Median school years completed	8.0	8.3	8.5	8.7	8.2	8.8
Rural non-White population, median school years completed	5.8	7.7	6.3	6.9	7.1	7.8

SOURCES: A. U.S. Bureau of the Census, 1963b, Table 2; B. U.S. Bureau of the Census, 1963a, Tables 87, 91.

Casual observation confirms these bald statistics. Housewives in the region are accustomed to paying Indian women $3 per day for what is termed "baby-sitting," but amounts to laborious domestic work and caring for young children. During 1965–1966, we observed Cherokee adults eager to secure work in the local (botanical) nursery, chicken packing plants, and strawberry fields for wages as low as $4 to $6 per day. We were not in a position to investigate the influence of recent federal provisions on minimum wages; however, we would guess that their effect has not been great and that most rates have remained subpar, since the Cherokee believe that they have a choice between low wages or no wages at all. Indeed, many Cherokee adults are unemployed or underemployed. Cherokee once engaged principally in family agriculture, but they have lost much of their lands and whatever land remains is of poor agricultural quality. Even in 1953 only about a quarter of the households surveyed by Cullum were classed as "self-employed, i.e., farmers," and having a corresponding cash income from the sale of agricultural products; a decade later, Wahrhaftig classified almost none of the households as having this economic adjustment. Correlatively, Cullum found that of every ten heads of households, three were not in the labor market, and an equal proportion rated only as unskilled laborers who earned less

TABLE 5–5

PUBLIC ASSISTANCE TO INDIANS
OF THE REGION, 1964–1965, BY COUNTIES

	Adair		Cherokee		Delaware		Mayes		Sequoyah		Total	
	No.	%	No.	%	No.	%	No.	%	No.	%	No.	%
Old Age Assistance												
Total	1,199	100.0	1,131	100.0	1,114	100.0	1,189	100.0	1,504	100.0	6,137	100.0
White	894	74.6	892	78.9	923	81.0	1,044	87.8	1,282	85.2	5,035	82.1
Indian	262	21.8	223	19.7	191	16.8	135	11.4	137	9.1	948	15.4
Aid to Families with Dependent Children												
Total families	460	100.0	469	100.0	322	100.0	291	100.0	533	100.0	2,075	100.0
White families	232	50.4	258	55.0	180	55.9	200	68.7	405	76.0	1,275	61.4
Indian families	227	49.3	187	39.9	142	44.1	90	30.9	122	22.9	768	37.0
Aid to the Blind												
Total	36	100.0	20	100.0	21	100.0	20	100.0	55	100.0	152	100.0
White	27	75.0	14	70.0	16	76.2	14	70.0	41	74.5	112	73.7
Indian	8	22.2	6	30.9	5	23.8	5	25.0	12	21.8	36	23.7
Aid to Disabled												
Total	242	100.0	253	100.0	266	100.0	267	100.0	359	100.0	1,387	100.0
White	163	67.4	187	73.9	202	75.9	222	83.1	303	84.4	1,077	77.6
Indian	79	32.6	58	22.9	64	24.1	44	16.5	32	8.9	280	20.2

SOURCE: Oklahoma Public Welfare Commission, 1965.

TABLE 5-6

FAMILY INCOME OF NON-WHITES IN 1959, BY COUNTIES

	Adair		Cherokee		Delaware		Mayes		Sequoyah		Total	
	No.	%	No.	%	No.	%	No.	%	No.	%	No.	%
All families	674 =	100	676 =	100	412 =	100	358 =	100	421 =	100	2541 =	100
Annual income:												
Under $1,000	196	29.1	130	19.2	129	31.3	102	28.5	180	42.8	737	29.0
$ 1,000—$ 1,999	266	39.5	221	32.7	118	28.6	99	27.7	104	24.7	808	32.8
$ 2,000—$ 2,999	112	16.6	91	13.5	79	19.2	80	22.3	84	20.0	446	17.6
$ 3,000—$ 3,999	46	6.8	85	12.6	36	8.7	15	4.2	25	5.9	207	8.1
$ 4,000—$ 4,999	13	1.9	38	5.6	16	3.9	24	6.7	14	3.3	105	4.1
$ 5,000—$ 5,999	14	2.1	40	5.9	—	—	26	7.3	8	1.9	88	3.5
$ 6,000—$ 6,999	14	2.1	40	5.9	3	0.7	4	1.1	6	1.4	67	2.6
$ 7,000—$ 7,999	5	0.8	9	1.3	4	1.0	—	—	—	—	18	0.7
$ 8,000—$ 8,999	—	—	14	2.1	12	2.9	3	0.8	—	—	29	1.1
$ 9,000—$ 9,999	—	—	—	—	4	1.0	—	—	—	—	4	0.2
$10,000 and over	8	1.2	8	1.2	11	2.7	5	1.4	—	—	32	1.3
Median income:												
Families	$1,530		$1,941		$1,653		$1,778		$1,293			
Families and unrelated individuals	$1,458		$1,123		$1,550		$1,727		$ 953			

SOURCE: U.S. Bureau of the Census, 1968a, Table 88.

than $1,000 per year. Wahrhaftig's figures were even more dispiriting. Almost half of the Tribal Cherokee households are now dependent upon transfer payments, such as A.F.D.C., pension, social security, and Old Age Assistance.

Under the circumstances, it is reasonable to inquire how the Tribal Cherokee manage to survive. Where do they obtain the resources, not only to maintain themselves as a stable population, but even to furnish a certain amount of surplus which becomes added to the general non-Indian population? As Wahrhaftig has pointed out, the answer is two-fold: efficiency and cooperation. The Cherokee survive because they coexist as kin groups and communities in a network of exchange of goods and services. The nuclear household is almost meaningless when compared to this overarching network. People reside in clusters which share such matters as tending the young, cooking the food, transporting to town for work and shopping, and owning and occupying the land. This intricate division of labor, which is highly efficient in its use of local resources, talents, employment, and cash, is combined with an emphasis upon subsistence and flexibility of adaptation. Since the Cherokee live mainly upon land which is held in trust for them, they pay either no rent or only a modest charge (exacted by the B.I.A. for its services). Dwellings are built of scrap lumber or local timber with the assistance of skilled laborers within the community. Men hunt and fish as the opportunity provides (although opening the area by means of roads and transforming it into a sportsman's vacation ground has been undermining this possibility). Overall, the situation reminds the observer of the remark that for $4,000 annually a family can starve in Manhattan, but for considerably less, it can live in modest comfort in a rural area. The Cherokee have far, far less, but they survive.

Caste and Poverty

The Tribal Cherokee are an administered people: impoverished, relatively powerless, and socially degraded. With patience and forbearance, the outsider can elicit from Tribal Cherokee and their friends a variety of tales of abuse and trickery that reveal persistent violations of the spirit and letter of the law.

One class of complaints will be familiar in principle, if not in detail, to those knowledgeable about life in the urban ghetto. There is widespread fear that welfare workers will remove Indian children from their kinfolk and send them to a boarding school (e.g., Sequoyah High School, operated by the B.I.A.). While such institutions are not designed as reformatories, they can be so used through the medium of court orders (or informal coercion by judges) reinforced by threats of severing an individual or family group from the welfare rolls. In an economy so perilously close to bare existence, this threat has a paralyzing power, and there has been no redress. The issue is not whether the welfare workers throughout the five counties are well qualified, well motivated, and well informed—they are most likely underpaid, overworked, and themselves victimized by more powerful forces within the region—but that from the viewpoint of the Tribal Cherokee family, they represent an awful and irresponsible power. Moreover, the threat of their activities is especially grave, inasmuch as the welfare workers must, according to official policy, orient their services about a nuclear family in an autonomous household unit, whereas the Tribal Cherokee have only been able to survive as extended kin groupings and interdependent residential units within a community.

In another similarity to the slums, the Tribal Cherokee are sometimes victimized by local storekeepers. The local folk are induced to shop in the local store by the availability of credit, the difficulties of transportation to the business sections of the county seat, and the suspicion and derogation that they may encounter in some of the city stores. Nonetheless, they are often overcharged in the rural stores, and local observers will speak of regular prices and Indian prices, the latter being considerably higher. Insofar as credit is given and the storeowner maintains the records, there is opportunity for self-serving error—a frequent temptation for persons with this power—and whether or not such "errors" are indeed customary, the Cherokee believe them to be so. In addition, most of these rural stores also serve as local post offices and receive the mail for their rural clientele. It has been contended that some storekeepers make a regular practice of monitoring the mail of clients who are in debt to them, and of so handling the welfare or other checks that they maintain complete financial control over their clients' affairs.

Where Cherokees have had land, it has sometimes been swindled from them through adroit and aggressive measures. Oklahoma state laws recognize the acquisition of rights through adverse possession, and one device by which the bold have been able to enlarge their own domains has been the building of fences which enclose substantial parts of their neighbor's lands. Combating such piracy requires an attorney, funds, and bravery in facing officials of the greater society. A more devious tactic for legalized theft of land requires that the assessor levy taxes on land which has been allotted but is being held in trust by the government, and is supposedly nontaxable. The owner may not be notified of the sums being assessed, although, even if notified, he could neither pay the sum nor fight the case in court. After a certain number of years of supposed tax delinquency, county action puts the land up for sale.[2] From one perspective, it does not matter whether the alleged frauds occur frequently, seldom, or never. The fact is that they are believed to occur, and the belief testifies to the powerlessness and anxieties of the Tribal Cherokee.

Educational Achievement

We have already noted that the levels of educational achievement for the total population of the Five County Region are considerably below national and state norms. The median levels for the Indian population of the region are considerably lower. In evaluating these figures for the Indians, we must bear in mind two circumstances which have the effect of diminishing even further the effects of the schooling reported. First, upon their entry into school, most Cherokee children have been ignorant, or almost ignorant, of English, so their first few years in the classroom are devoted to learning to speak and read English. Second, most of these schools have been small rural enterprises, operating on a relatively short school year and with a predominantly Cherokee population, so the opportunity to speak or utilize English is limited.

A survey was conducted by Cullum in 1952 under the sponsorship of the B.I.A. and the State of Oklahoma. His data were reported fully, and calculation of medians shows a level of educational achievement of 4.6 years for adult men and 5.3 years for women (see Table 5–7).[3] The

---

[2]After a few years of possession, the Oklahoma statute of limitations protects the purchaser of land bought at such sales from any reversal of this process of acquisition. Other devices by which Indians have lost their lands include the following: (1) In order to secure welfare benefits, Indians have been required to divest themselves of all assets, including land which is supposedly restricted and being held in trust. Especially since the Great Depression of the 1930's, much land has been lost in this fashion. (2) When land has been held in trust for a long period of time, and several generations of owners have died without leaving wills, there may finally be many persons who have some claim to the land. According to Oklahoma law, any one of these heirs may file a legal action which requires that the land be divided in kind, or that it be assessed and the value distributed among the heirs. Since many of the heirs are penniless, this partitioning of an estate will usually force a sale. Since intermarriage between Indians and Whites has been frequent, a substantial number of sales have been initiated by Whites, or persons only minutely Indian in blood, but who nonetheless have an heirship claim to restricted lands.

[3]Cullum miscalculated these medians, as is clear from inspection of his data, and his report stated the figures as being a year too much. Since the crucial figures are given in Table 5–7, the reader can verify the medians himself, if he should wish. Wahrhaftig (1965a, p. 36) has argued that they are likely to have been additionally exaggerated because, on the basis of Cullum's description of this sample, roughly one-fifth would have been functionally White, and if these persons had been reared

TABLE 5–7

EDUCATIONAL ACHIEVEMENT OF TRIBAL CHEROKEE,
1952 (PERSONS 18 YEARS OR OLDER)

	Males		Females		Total	
	No.	%	No.	%	No.	%
Highest School Grade Completed						
None	43	7.9	46	8.4	89	8.2
One	46	8.5	37	6.8	83	7.6
Two	32	5.9	23	4.2	55	5.0
Three	57	10.5	41	7.5	98	9.0
Four	60	11.0	56	10.2	116	10.6
Five	58	10.7	53	9.7	111	10.2
Six	45	8.3	58	10.6	103	9.4
Seven	35	6.4	38	6.9	73	6.7
Eight	88	16.2	88	16.1	176	16.1
Nine	22	4.0	24	4.4	46	4.2
Ten	20	3.7	17	3.1	37	3.4
Eleven	12	2.2	16	2.9	28	2.6
Twelve	21	3.8	32	5.9	53	4.9
Entered college	5	0.9	18	3.3	23	2.1
Total persons	544	100.0	547	100.0	1,091	100.0
Median school grade completed	4.6		5.3		4.9	

SOURCE: Cullum, 1953, medians corrected.

survey conducted in 1963 by the Carnegie Cross-Cultural Educational Project yielded median figures for adult Cherokee only one-half grade higher for education achievement: 5.3 grades for adult men and 5.8 for women. Considering the different bases on which the surveys were conducted, these small differences are not likely to be meaningful (Tables 5–8 and 5–9).

While the U.S. Census has not printed data for Indians in this region, it has for non-Whites (Tables 5–10 and 5–11), and the medians of educational achievement range from 5.8 grades in Adair to 7.7 in Cherokee, with Mayes County, usually among the highest in economic

according to typical White patterns, their median figure for school years completed would have been seven. However, it is necessary to be cautious on this matter, for it is possible that the Whites classed by Cullum's interviewers as being "Indian" might well have been very low on the scale of educational achievement and could conceivably have depressed the population median rather than raised it. Fortunately, the issue is not crucial, and the medians from Cullum's data (when properly computed) are in near agreement with those of the Carnegie survey, when corresponding age groups are compared and allowance is made for the passing of a decade.

conditions, providing a 6.9. Considering the defects in the Census handling of Indians, I believe we would be justified in accepting the results of the Carnegie survey and taking the median figure for completed schooling among adult Tribal Cherokee as being below six years. Accepting this means that, on the average, Cherokees have two to three years less schooling than their White neighbors of the region, and four to five years less schooling than other residents of Oklahoma. Should a Cherokee move to one of the cities of Oklahoma, he would encounter a population whose median level of school completion was six or more years beyond his own (e.g., Oklahoma City, 11.9; Tulsa, 12.2—median school years completed among population aged 20 or older, 1960). Economically, the Tribal Cherokee is in a bind; since he occupies the most impoverished status in an economically depressed region, there is no possibility of his improving himself locally. If he emigrates to an urban

TABLE 5–8

MEDIAN SCHOOL LEVEL OF
LOCAL COMMUNITY OF ADULT
TRIBAL CHEROKEE, 1963

Community	Males	Females	Total
Hulbert	6.5	5.6	6.0
Cherry Tree	7.0	7.8	7.5
Marble City	4.0	6.0	6.0
Bull Hollow	5.5	5.0	5.0
Total	5.3	5.8	5.5

SOURCE: Wahrhaftig, 1965a, Table 10.

TABLE 5–9

FUNCTIONAL ILLITERACY
AMONG ADULT TRIBAL CHEROKEE:
PERCENTAGE WHO COMPLETED
GRADE 4 OR LESS

Community	Males	Females	Total
Hulbert	48	25	37
Cherry Tree	29	28	28
Marble City	48	25	37
Bull Hollow	47	47	47
Total	42	38	40

SOURCE: Wahrhaftig, 1965a, Table 13.

TABLE 5–10

NON-WHITE POPULATION, 1960:
YEARS OF SCHOOL COMPLETED, BY COUNTIES

	Adair	Cherokee	Delaware	Mayes	Sequoyah	Total
Persons 25 years old and over	1342	1404	902	775	930	6695
No. school years completed	197	187	51	73	119	627
Elementary						
1–4	387	276	278	185	185	1311
5 & 6	210	157	182	137	148	834
7	101	114	80	78	104	477
8	211	220	136	158	197	922
High School						
1–3	103	158	106	57	107	531
4	98	169	54	49	44	414
College						
1–3	13	66	15	26	12	132
4 or more	22	57	—	12	14	105
Median school years completed	5.8	7.7	6.3	6.9	7.1	

SOURCE: U.S. Bureau of the Census, 1963a, Table 87.

TABLE 5–11

NON-WHITE POPULATION, 1960:
SCHOOL ENROLLMENT, BY COUNTIES

	Adair	Cherokee	Delaware	Mayes	Sequoyah	Total
Total enrolled, 5–34 years old	796	1313	604	570	651	3934
Kindergarten	10	—	—	—	—	10
Public	10	—	—	—	—	10
Elementary (1–8 years)	625	828	496	459	493	2901
Public	625	729	496	459	493	2802
High School (1–4 years)	157	354	108	111	158	888
Public	157	162	108	111	158	696
College	4	131	—	—	—	135

SOURCE: U.S. Bureau of the Census, 1963a, Table 87.

area in search of employment, he finds himself at the very bottom of the labor pool. With less than six years of formal education in a rural school and a foreign language, he is unlikely to be fluent in anything but the most basic English; he can scarcely read; and, while he can perform simple arithmetical computations, he is unable to interpret the verbal and cultural contexts of most numerical problems. He may be a shrewd judge of human character, be strong, loyal, reliable, and willing to work, but he will be lucky if he gains even the most menial and poorly paying employment.

TRIBAL CHEROKEE AND
RURAL PUBLIC SCHOOLS

The Research Project

The previous section reviews the kind of publicly available data (much of it derived from the U.S. Census) which indicate the condition of the descendants of what was once known as a "Civilized Tribe" operating a school system finer than anything west of the Mississippi. Reviewing these data, our research team decided to investigate the social life of the Tribal Cherokee and the nature of their encounters with public schools. There has been much debate over whether Indian children should attend federal schools, which are in effect segregated establishments serving Indians almost exclusively, or be "integrated" into local public schools. The tendency has been away from the federal and toward the local public schools (as of 1970 less than a third of Indian children were attending federal schools). The case of the Oklahoma Cherokee seemed to offer valuable comparative data, as their children have been served predominantly by local public schools since 1906. An additional motive for investigation was the possibility of comparison between a reservation and a nonreservation people. Over the years there has been much argument about the merits and demerits of reservations as a locus for Indian life. Since the Cherokee had never been subjected to reservation conditions, they constituted a fine case for comparison with the Oglala Sioux, among whom our research team had worked in 1962–1963. Besides, reservation peoples such as the Sioux have been the subject of many research projects—to the point where they sometimes have felt "over-researched"—whereas the Oklahoma Cherokee had largely been ignored by academic investigators.

Accordingly, we designed a project to study the relationship between the Tribal Cherokee and the local public schools of northeastern Oklahoma, and we secured financial support from the U.S. Office of Education via the University of Kansas. But, as in many situations, it is far easier to design a research project than to conduct one. We found the language barrier insuperable: Tribal Cherokee adults could not be satisfactorily interviewed in English, and the conditions of the project made it difficult for the staff to learn sufficient Cherokee for conducting interviews. Interpreters were essential, and fortunately we were able to recruit several bilingual Cherokee matrons who embraced the project with enthusiasm. Additional problems were created by the fact that some persons associated with the regional power structure felt threatened by this kind of investigation and did their best to thwart it. Earlier in this chapter we reviewed some of the sociopolitical divisions of northeastern Oklahoma; toward the end of it we will turn to the topic of the encounter between the regional establishment and university projects for research and betterment. At the moment, it is sufficient to remark that the Cherokee matrons recruited as project field researchers perceived the value of the inquiry and persisted in their endeavors, despite all manner of harassment. The difficulties experienced by the professional staff of the project made it impossible to provide constant intensive supervision to the Cherokee researchers, and the latter often proceeded on their own. While their research procedures and English phrasing are sometimes original, the resultant portrait of conditions is most eloquent. As a result of their perseverence, we are able to present information— previously impossible to obtain—concerning the attitudes of the Cherokee toward school and vocation, and to place these attitudes within their unique view of the world and of the place of man within that world. First, however, we turn to a brief presentation of the language difficulties of the Cherokee child.

English as a Second Language

As already indicated, the primary domestic and ceremonial language of the Tribal Cherokee continues to be Cherokee. Not only at the Nighthawk (Stomp Ground) ceremonials and at the churches of the Cherokee Baptist Association, but at other ceremonial and political gatherings, Cherokee is *the medium* of discourse, and English is seldom utilized. An individual can participate in these communities only if he speaks Cherokee fluently, whereas his opportunity to acquire fluent English derives only from experience outside his domestic community (e.g., time served in the armed services).

On leaving a Tribal Cherokee household and entering first grade, few children have any command of English. In response to a question addressed to parents about the language(s) spoken by their children at time of entry into school, less than one-tenth reported to our Cherokee researchers that their children were monolingual speakers of English, and only one-quarter reported them as bilingual. The personal experiences of the project associates would lead us to be skeptical of claims for genuine competency in both Cherokee and English, as the spoken English of persons whose native language is Cherokee impressed us as barely serviceable in most of the cases we observed. This judgment might have been anticipated, given their lack of education and isolated mode of life. Accordingly, it is reasonable to assert that two-thirds of the children in question were entering school with "a little bit of English" or none at all.

Aspirations and Realities

In the discussions that follow, we will try to enter a social reality which is difficult for the researcher to comprehend and to communicate to a total outsider. The cultural world of a tribal people—economically depressed, socially degraded, linguistically isolated, politically victimized—resists entrance by a comfortably situated alien. We scarcely know how to frame questions concerning schools, vocations, and aspirations that will be meaningful to and deserve the attention of these people.

The Tribal Cherokee do communicate the ambivalence of their hopes and cautions about the educational process (Table 5–12). The principal value of an education is seen as economic: if a person were able to finish school he would get a job—a better job, a job secured more easily, an easy job, indeed, *any* job. With a job he would no longer be dependent on welfare and subject to its vagaries and demands; he would also have "an easier life." Associated with these basically economic orientations are such notions as the general utility of knowing English and therefore being able to negotiate for a job or otherwise deal with Whites. Finally, there is the notion that education offers a path

TABLE 5–12

"WHAT IS THE MAIN REASON, IN YOUR OPINION, WHY A PERSON SHOULD GET AN EDUCATION?"

Reasons	Respondents	
	158 =	100%
Economic		
Job: to have a job, better job; job opportunity; easy job	138	87
Independence: self-support, make own living	57	36
Betterment: easy life	46	29
Self-improvement		
They are better if they have an education; she won't grow up like I did; could help older people	32	20
Communication		
To understand English; to translate	24	15
Negative (value doubtful)		
No jobs for the educated; Cherokee Indians have good education but still they have no jobs	27	17
No response	9	6
Total responses (multiple)	333	

SOURCE: K.U. Household Survey, 1966.

to improvement of the self as a responsible social being. In none of these positive responses is there a conception of the value of abstract knowledge, but rather of education brought into the service of some pragmatic goal.[4]

A small but significant group (17 per cent) respond quite differently:

> Interviewer: In your opinion what is the main reason a person should get an education?

> Respondent: I guess they would be ready to go working at the Chicken plant and baby-sitting. That's all they do. I know a lot of educated people among the Cherokee who didn't get a job; they couldn't find one.

The respondent thinks education is useless, without hedging or qualification. The answer instructs us of economic conditions in the region and suggests the web of poverty and discrimination which ensnares the Cherokee eager for maturity and independence. "Education for what?" recurs throughout the responses of the survey, "to process chickens and to baby-sit? The child might as well remain home!" We do not contend that most Tribal Cherokee are this disenchanted with the ability of the school to act as a vocational preparatory ground. However, an attitude of this sort, already apparent among a significant minority, may be crucially influential among the young people when they are struggling with the trials of school life and look beyond the classroom walls to see those who might be models unable to employ their skills.

At the moment, those who perceive schooling as an enforced process of assimilation (as does the respondent below) tend to believe in the economic payoff. If they should come to realize that there is no payoff, but only continued poverty, they might have excellent reason to withhold their children from the schools.

> Well, I think it just fade away, this Indians before long. All the white people live in Oklahoma—is the way I see. Also I think they are trying to get rid of this Indian—to forget their own language. And so they could find an easy job and be easy to talk English where they could listen when they ask a job, and the white people will understand what this Indian want, when they are educated enough. [I think that Indians are disappearing and that soon Oklahoma will be completely White. I think they are trying to destroy the Indians, beginning with the eliminating of their language, and instructing them in English so that they can easily find employment and better understand what is being asked of them and tell Whites what they want.]

[4]The quotations reproduced in the following pages are taken from interviews reported in "The Household Survey" by Robert V. Dumont, Jr., and M. L. Wax, included as Chapter 3 of Part II of the research report by Wax, *et al.*, 1969.

Either way lies bitter despair; either education is useless, leading nowhere but to the occasional menial labor of working in the chicken processing plant, or to the forgetting of one's language, one's ethnic identity, and one's self.

Yet the Tribal Cherokee have not abandoned faith in the educational pathway. There is in the following remarks an almost messianic hope for an educated Cherokee who would help his people, even if there is also covert recognition that such a redeemer is practically an inconceivable paradox, inasmuch as the educational process turns him against his own:

> I'll say they could have an easy job and an easy life for their own good, and also they could help their own people who don't understand English. They can translate English and Cherokee both. There is a lot of Cherokee Indians in our country who don't talk or understand English, and the white people were cheating on the Cherokee just because they couldn't understand the English, or whatever the Whiteman said.
>
> They will do whatever the White man says, even if they don't understand. They tell you, sign your name and the old Cherokee will sign X in his signature. That was it. And the White man will get what he wants from the Cherokee Indians with the signature.
>
> I know. It has happen a lot of times. I wish we could have Cherokee who could have a good education, who could help his people. But it sure is hard to find one that can help his people when he has a good education. It is hard for him to be on his own nationality side. He would just be against his people.

Hopes and Costs

> I sure do like to see my grandchildren to get graduate in high school, if I can afford it for their clothes. The clothes is so high priced—even shoes, and the schools—they wear high priced clothes and shoes when they were in high school. They get ashamed when they were in high school.

The aspiration is toward white collar jobs and careers, even the professions; rarely is technical or vocational training mentioned. Since the respondents are themselves poorly educated and only marginally literate in English, the aspirations are so high as to be classified as illusionary. And since the Cherokees are thoroughly practical, they themselves provide the bitter comment that deflates:

> They just give up—lack of clothing, just hard to find better clothes for schooling. That's what happened to me. I guess we Cherokee are wishing too much when we are in school, but unable to get a thing we wanted, and the White people get what they want because they are rich people, and we Cherokee are not. Just wishing, that's all.

The issue of clothing becomes swollen when rural Indians are transferred to a town high school. On this alien ground they confront children who have decisive superiority, whether in scholastic performance, school politics and influence, or knowledge about the life of the town and city. An Indian pupil who might have been performing reasonably well scholastically—judged by the standards of the rural school and compared to his peers—now becomes keenly aware that his English fluency and scholastic preparation are inadequate. In difficulties with his academic subjects, derogated by school administrators, and generally degraded in the social hierarchies of the school, he responds to the exhortations of his elders by blaming the deficiencies of his clothes. The young ladies in particular, struggling to construct a social identity for themselves and to present to their audience a self that is attractive, find the lack of parental funds and absence of sophistication in the elder generation to be grave handicaps in the competitive state of mid-adolescence.

Even more significant in these arenas where persons of different physical types are mingling is the derogation of Indian traits. The girl who is dark of skin and otherwise branded as "Indian" finds these are ineradicable markers of her inadequacy. She can only give voice to her lack of clothes, while her parents, anxious that she remain in school, strive to scrounge funds, materials, and garments. When Cherokee parents are asked how much schooling they would like their children to obtain (Table 5–13), about half say that they would like the children to finish college. The remainder say they would like the children to finish high school. But the parents immediately add that they know that their hopes are vain, for "we cannot afford it" (Table 5–14):

> If I could support her, I would like to send her through college, but we have failed the oldest of our children. But we finally made it for Anne,

TABLE 5–13

"HOW MANY YEARS OF SCHOOLING WOULD YOU LIKE YOUR CHILDREN TO GET?"

Years of Schooling Mentioned	No.	%
	158 =	100%
Tenth grade	1	1
Complete high school	53	34
Some college, other post high-school	76	48
As much as they can get	15	9
Other, no answer	13	8

SOURCE: K.U. Household Survey, 1966.

TABLE 5–14

FACTORS AFFECTING ACHIEVING
EDUCATIONAL GOAL

	Complete High School		Complete College		Total	
	No.	%	No.	%	No.	%
	53 =	100%	76 =	100%	129 =	100%
Expense: if we could afford it	26	49	47	62	73	57
Self: if they wanted to; if they could learn	9	17	13	17	22	17
Other: Dad is in poor health	12	23	14	18	26	20

SOURCE: K.U. Household Survey, 1966.

she is in Haskell. If I could afford them, I wish they would get through four years in college.

Less than a fifth of these respondents mention the desires, abilities to withstand school pressures, and so on, of the children themselves. These parents remind us of the autonomy of the child in traditional Cherokee values, and also direct our attention to his plight within the school system. Despite these qualifications, the startling fact is that almost all of the Cherokee have high educational aspirations for their children. For a people so impoverished, whose children experience such difficulties in the school system, this pattern of responses is phenomenal. At the present time, few of the children endure throughout the high school trials, and almost no one completes college. The hope for education is almost religious.

Language and the School

It is a truism to note that there must be communication between teacher and pupils; without dialogue there can be no education. Yet the language of the teacher and of the curriculum is English, and the primary language of most of the children entering school is Cherokee. Clearly, if educational progress is to be made with these young children, either the teachers must acquire some fluency in Cherokee, and corresponding curricular materials developed, or the children must be given an intensive program in learning English as a second language. Ideally, both developments would coexist, since the problems encountered by a Cherokee trying to develop fluency in English can be comprehended most easily by someone familiar with the phonetics and syntax of both languages. A few such programs have been developed elsewhere in the U.S., involving other non-English speaking groups: in Dade County, Florida, there is now a school evenly balanced in curriculum and student body between Spanish and English speakers. But by and large, U.S. educators have a long tradition against according recognition to the alien language of a subordinated people. (Throughout much of the Southwest [Arizona, California, New Mexico, Texas], large numbers of children have entered the schools with Spanish as their primary language, and the schools have responded by regarding the speaking of Spanish as an offense to be punished; not surprisingly, the Spanish speaking children then proved to be educational problems and were judged incapable of academic achievement. In New York City during the 1950's and early 1960's there was the frequent anomaly of Puerto Rican and other Latin American children being "taught Spanish" by a teacher whose fluency in that language was so poor that she could not understand them when they spoke Spanish among themselves. Although educated persons with a native fluency in Spanish were available, they could not secure positions in the school system because they had traces of native accent in their English speech, and therefore could not pass the requirements for entry into the school system [Wasserman, 1970, p. 69].)

Until recently, the schools and educators of northeastern Oklahoma acted as if the language problem were entirely the responsibility or concern of the Cherokee parents. If only the parents would give up this backward habit of "talking Indian," their children would make progress in the schools. This is not to say that individual educators were not personally troubled by the situation, or that some of them did not labor as best they could in a difficult situation, but rather to emphasize that institutionally there were neither training, curriculum, facilities, nor programs for assisting Cherokee speaking pupils. Since the pupils (and their parents) could not stop communicating with each other in the only language they knew well, and since neither the educators nor the institutions which trained and certified them were doing anything about either using Cherokee as a scholastic resource or teaching English as a foreign language, communication between teacher and Cherokee pupils in the classroom continued to be difficult and painful (cf. Dumont, 1971; Dumont and Wax, 1969).

In their response to the survey, the Cherokee parents themselves show that they understand clearly the situation of their children on entering school, and a number of them suggest appropriate changes in the educational arrangements:

> We would like to have a better teacher in the school. One who can do better teaching for the Cherokee Indians. Some Cherokee Indian is hard to learn to talk English—some are hard headed and they couldn't catch it right away, how to read, write and speak. Cherokee are not all the same—some were easy for it.

> We would like to have Cherokee teacher in each school where the little ones start in the first year of school, because the little ones some of them, they don't talk English. In our school, here, it is alright where George goes. Also we would like to have a Cherokee book teacher.

In default of action by the schools, the issue of language devolves upon the Cherokee parents, and it is plain from their responses that many of them have considered the matter and deliberately attempted to affect the language learning of the child. Most elders tend to feel that the child must learn to speak Cherokee as his primary language within the domestic circle, whereas English he will acquire in the course of his schooling. As one parent remarks: "No they don't speak English when the children entered school—they took it up after they started school. The father doesn't allow children to speak English at home till they can speak good Cherokee." Another parent states: "No, I think the best way for Cherokee kids is to learn Indian first, then English afterwards, so they can talk both." There is considerable logic to this position, as without fluency in Cherokee the child will be alienated from many of his senior relatives, and would be unable to participate in the ceremonial activities of his local community.

On the other hand, Cherokee elders are knowledgeable about the hardships suffered by those children who enter school with no knowledge of English whatsoever, and it is plausible that most of the families who say that their children knew "a little bit of English"—and a considerable proportion of those who said their children were bilingual—had in fact encouraged this acquisition of English. The amount of English signified by these statements can easily be overestimated, and "a little bit" can be very, very little, "Jane knew a little bit—her name, how old she was, and what her mother's name was." "Roy had just a few words he could understand in English and the youngest one was all right, because the oldest teach them when they were little." The pattern of the older children, enrolled in school, drilling the younger in the basic responses required during his first week of school seems frequent.

In a variety of ways, Cherokee adults and children, knowing little English of poor quality, attempt to instruct the younger generation in some basic English phrases. It would be a grave misinterpretation to assume that this activity represents a wish for assimilation of the child or a desire that he cease to be a Cherokee; it would be equally erroneous to conceive that the Cherokee wishes to assist the school in accomplishment of its tasks. The older generation knows that the child entering school without English will often encounter awkward and sometimes traumatic or even brutal experiences. Teaching the child some rudiments of English protects him from embarrassment and from the wrath of teachers who do not comprehend his plight. Paradoxically, knowledge of English strengthens the child in his Cherokeeness, for it enables him to cope with the demands of alien authorities.

The older generation of Cherokee are willing, even eager, that their children acquire fluency in English, for such knowledge will ease their way in school and facilitate their acquisition of good jobs. However classroom observations made it apparent that, even in the upper elementary grades of the rural school, proficiency in English was minimal and in some cases nonexistent, while at any grade level the lack of comprehension was sufficient to impede classwork, if not bring it to a halt. These classrooms could typically be characterized as a small aggregate of English speaking pupils in continual discourse with the teachers, while about them was a silent group of Cherokee. It is true that the Cherokee children are often more reticent in class than their White counterparts, but the linguistic handicap in this case is plainly visible.

The Harmony Ethic in the Classroom

The teacher who steps before a room of Tribal Cherokee pupils is separated from them by a difference in moral norms as well as by language. Native Whites of the region share a strong individualism and an emphasis upon aggrandizement of the self. Indeed, the local rural schools have often been expressions of such individual enterprise, inasmuch as they constitute a device by which an enterprising individual can secure a living through claiming monies from governmental agencies for handling Indian pupils. The native White morality stands in marked contrast to the Harmony Ethic which governs the conduct of the good Cherokee. Following Robert K. Thomas, Gulick has characterized the ethic in these terms (1960, pp. 137, 139):

> In living from day to day according to the Harmony Ethic the Conservative Cherokee tries to avoid giving offense to others and in so doing, he must always "wait and see what the other's likes and dislikes are, and . . . perceive what demands are likely to be made of him." Thomas characterizes this demeanor as being particularly sensitive to subliminal cues in overt behavior. . . . Whereas one actively maintains Harmony by giving of one's time and goods, one can passively maintain it by "minding one's own business." If everyone consistently minds his own business, it is clear why the recognition of the needs of others (calling for active generosity) can only be achieved by acute sensitivity to the cues of others.

In this fashion, Tribal Cherokee counterbalance respect for the autonomy of the individual with active concern for harmonious and peaceable relationships. Since children are accorded a similar degree of autonomy, the adult dealing with them must be sensible of their needs and wishes, and avoid an authoritarian intrusiveness. He must allow children to mind their own business, but he must be prepared to assist them as they encounter difficulties. This should not be an impossible task for most teachers, even those reared in Oklahoma Whiteman's culture, but it would require much more restraint than they have customarily exercised, and more respect for the young than they would normally allow White children of corresponding age.

To the foregoing is added a crucial addition (Gulick, 1960, p. 139):

> Self assertiveness, which is probably a concomitant of self realization, appears to be quite foreign to the Conservative [Tribal Cherokee] personality, presumably as an ego-ideal, and most certainly as a form of social behavior. The assertive individual is offensive in terms of the Harmony Ethic. This applies not only to aggressive behavior but to any form of drawing attention to oneself.

Yet most techniques of classwork require assertion of self, and demand that a child expose himself before his peers either in excellence or failure. Typically, the teacher singles out a particular child for attention and conducts with him an intensive interaction, while the remainder of the class constitutes a watchful audience. For Tribal Cherokee, it is exactly such individuated interaction—with its emphasis upon the self of the student—that is morally most troublesome. Only when the self becomes subordinated, as when the individual is the representative of a band of his fellows, can the child comfortably perform in solo fashion before an audience. In the arithmetic race between two teams of pupils, where members of each team work successively at the board in competition with the other to complete the problem most rapidly, Cherokee derive great satisfaction. Victory manifests the competency of the team, and the individual performs for the service of the group. In contrast, during normal classwork, individual Cherokee go most reluctantly to the board to work alone and before the observant gaze of their fellows. Even by the eighth grade, Cherokee students find this display and exposure of self distasteful; unless they can restructure the situation according to their own norms, they will be highly uncomfortable and may remain silent and passively resist the attentions of the teachers.

Manifestation of these Cherokee norms in the classroom is highly visible in contrast with the conduct of students of Oklahoma White background. After a short time the observer can close his eyes even within a strange classroom and, merely by timbre and loudness of voice, distinguish Cherokee from White among the students. Without even hearing, he can observe the distinctions between the two groups in their responses to a question addressed to the class as a whole. White students compete for the attention of the teacher, and the raised hands soon become frantically waving signals of the desire for public attention. The

Cherokee students wait, and, although they raise their hands, rarely wave them. Among their youngest members, there is sometimes an obvious impulse to wave—for these little ones the care of the teacher is much desired—but restraint is predominant among the older ones. The difference in ethos sometimes leads to intriguing divisions of labor between the two ethnicities. In one class of primary grade pupils, a Cherokee girl wanted a box of crayons that was located in the back of the room, where the observer was seated. Cautiously and deliberately, she estimated the motions and exposures that would be required to secure the box. The teacher, who was working with another group within the classroom, had instructed them not to move. So the Cherokee girl bargained with the White girl seated beside her, and the latter moved boldly and with a somewhat flaunting expression to the rear of the room and secured the desired box.

How Teachers Relate to Cherokee Pupils

The meeting of the teacher and the Cherokee children is rife with opportunities for trouble. Failure to communicate exacerbates the culturally different approaches to teaching and learning, so the classroom becomes an area of social conflict that is especially severe when the children are youngest. The tension that has developed in the primary grades does not lessen as the child ages and acquires more fluency in English and more familiarity with the ways of teachers. Rather, it goes undercover; the child learns to defer to the teacher and to comply superficially with his demands. The classroom becomes an intricate study in varieties of silence, representing not only the pupils' lack of fluency, but their defense against the intrusiveness and authoritarianism of the teacher. Although the latter has no problem in securing the appearance of order—there is almost never the challenge to his authority by noise and commotion created by boisterous White children—he cannot utilize that order as the basis for educational achievement. Armored by their silence, the spirits of the children elude the networks of curricular programs.

Many of the teachers are from the local area and have been raised all their lives among Cherokee. But the acquaintance which they have so acquired is similar to that of many Whites of the Deep South in relation to Negroes: it is a ritual of caste and not a comprehension of humanity. To the average White of northeastern Oklahoma, the Indians are not so much members of a culturally (and linguistically) distinct community as they are simply inferior—culturally, socially, and economically; acknowledging their uniqueness would be to challenge the social order.

The experience and training of the teacher have therefore left him without genuine comprehension of his Cherokee neighbors, and with no awareness that there is knowledge to be acquired or that there would be any utility to its acquisition.

Roughly speaking, educators respond in three different ways to these intercultural difficulties. Many find the educational task beyond their capacities while their social isolation permits them to relax into a comfortable lethargy. They resort to traditional devices of busywork, minimal direction, and dismissing class whenever there is a plausible reason; occasionally they will give forth with a spiritless monolog. Little more need be said, except that the children and parents experience this teacher as "nice," but—and this may be startling to those who think of the Cherokee as indifferent to education—they do not overlook the neglect of learning. Knowing that the Cherokee are reluctant to criticize publicly, the following is a strong statement: "The teacher treat this child nice and [but] she don't teach like she should. The teacher don't teach nothing. She don't care if they learn nothing!"

A second group of educators responds aggressively to the situation. Unable to comprehend the reality of cultural differences or the handicap of the pupil struggling with an alien tongue, they transfer to the classroom attitudes they would assume toward White pupils deficient in performance. Implicitly, they regard the Cherokee children as either stupid, incompetent, idle, or malingering. They must teach and the pupils must learn, and the starkness of this confrontation generates a classroom atmosphere crackling with anxiety. In the seventh and eighth grade classroom of one rural school, Dumont observed a teacher who was well aware that what she was doing was but a pretense of teaching. Each day she attacked anew, and each day her ire was aroused as the students seemingly would not permit her to achieve what she had to do; her experience was traumatic. She might have been an excellent educator among the English-speaking pupils for whom she was prepared, but her determination to teach could not be gratified, as it was linked with a determination to conquer, and so she could not pause to analyze the real nature of her daily catastrophe.

A corollary to the foregoing responses by educators is the educational surrender: keep them in school until the eighth grade and then turn them loose. This was the advice of a professor of education on the faculty of a regional college primarily oriented toward producing teachers. He agreed that the local and informal rural school was important to the children of the Tribal Cherokee, and that consolidation to the larger and impersonalized town school would undercut an educational achievement that was of some modest significance. For him, this analysis was not pessimistic, but a realistic assessment of the potentialities of the Cherokee and the abilities of educators to guide them.

The third (and rare) response is that of the teacher who recognizes the cultural difference between himself and the students and struggles to cope with this staggering complexity. Even though teacher and students confront each other across a linguistic barrier, both sides appreciate the nature of this handicap and try to communicate across it. While the class could still utilize expert linguistic assistance, lessons nonetheless proceed with a quickness amazing in its contrast to the conventional Cherokee classroom, and—most dramatic of all—the students talk in the class, participating freely in organized discussions.

The tragedy of these rural schools is the lack of preparation of their teachers, for they are no worse than teachers elsewhere, and would presumably like to perform their jobs competently. But they do not realize their own ignorance, and, coming from a parochial and constricted rural background, they have no understanding of what it is to be linguistically and culturally alien to the school and its teachers. The teachers require special skills, but the politically oppressed Tribal Cherokee have no one to present their educational needs. The parents can express their desires only through such media as this survey:

> We would like to see our children that go to school do something like the teacher has done when they went to school. They learned how to be teachers and then children could go in the footsteps of what they have done, trying to be teachers. So we would like to have good teachers in our school for our children where they can be good students. All I am asking is to have a good teacher in our community school, where our children go, because they sure do have a hard time in school. They have a hard time to learn anything that they should. The Cherokee Indians—it's hard to understand the English to start with. The teacher has to explain well; understand, because they are Cherokee. We send the children to school to read and write and talk English, not to just get punished.

How striking is this metaphor by which the parent relates the learning of the young pupil in the local classroom to that of the novice teacher in the college classroom. Moreover, how profound is the respect for teaching as both dealing with a body of knowledge and requiring the most sensitive interpersonal skills. Indeed, it is plain from the survey responses that Cherokee parents expect too much from the schools. They are concerned as the proverbial college-oriented parents of the suburban middle class and, like them, have instilled in their children attitudes and habits to enable them to perform well, providing that the school itself is prepared to cope with their special needs.

Image of the Good Teacher

We have remarked that the Tribal Cherokee are surprisingly knowledgeable about the schools serving their children. Nowhere is this more clearly
revealed than in their responses to the questions, "Do you think that
there is something that could be done to make the schools better now?
What is it?" (See Table 5–15.) Over half the respondents mentioned improvements that could be made to the schools, most of them concerning
better teachers and better teaching. Compared to the responses of Sioux
Indians of the Pine Ridge Reservation, this pattern of responses is startling: the parents at Pine Ridge generally took the attitude that the school
knew best, and that by virtue of their title and role the teachers must be
qualified. It might have been assumed that a depressed and enclaved
people such as the Tribal Cherokee would regard the schools as a blessing not to be questioned or criticized. Yet only a quarter of the respondents expressed the view that the schools were good as they were, and such
affirmations were generally in the context of remarks about the tribula-
tions of the older generations in attending school, and the advantages

TABLE 5–15

"DO YOU THINK THAT THERE IS SOMETHING
THAT COULD BE DONE TO MAKE THE SCHOOLS
BETTER NOW? WHAT IS IT?"

Responses	Persons	
	No.	%
	158 =	100%
Improvements of the school (total)	81	51
Better teachers and better teaching	37	23
Indian teacher	11	7
Better curriculum	10	6
Better administration	3	2
Better facilities (bus, library, etc.)	20	13
Economic for pupils		
More support for clothes, fees, supplies	20	13
Schools are satisfactory		
Good as they are	36	29
Schools lead nowhere		
No jobs	2	1
Total responses	139	88
No comments	34	21
Don't know	24	15
No response	10	6

SOURCE: K.U. Household Survey, 1966.

now proffered the young in the form of programs of clothing, bussing, and lunching.

While the several categories of suggestions for improving the schools —better teachers, better teaching, Indian teachers, and so on—are significant, so is the manner of phrasing used by the respondents. The word *love* appears with great frequency as a way of designating the desired relationship of teacher to pupils, and of how the teachers should act (but seldom did): "love all the students alike, Indian and White." Concurrently, there was a usage of "trust," "understanding," and "giving" (e.g., "teachers gave out to teach the children"). Critically, one parent states:

> Some teachers are unable to love the Cherokee Indian. I wish they could love both Cherokee and White the same—they should. Because I know some teachers, they don't like the Indians. Seems like they have to care more for the White then they do for the Indian. Whenever they are qualified to teach they have to love their kind of people. When I went to school, I knew the teacher love more the White than the Cherokee. When I ask my problem she wouldn't teach me like she ought to.

"Love" vs. "Authority" expresses the cultural dichotomy between Cherokee parental attitudes and those of neighboring Whites. For the latter, the teachers operate within a system of contractual authority. There is consensual agreement as to the tasks which should be accomplished by the school, and appropriate authority is delegated by the parents to the educators. Parents have authority over their children and the educator stands *in loco parentis*. But, as is evident in any account of traditional Cherokee society (and its history), authority is not a traditional category of Cherokee interaction, and tasks cannot be separated from the relationships of the individuals performing them. Hence, the Cherokee look first at the relationship between teacher and pupils, and unless that relationship is harmoniously balanced and respectful of the autonomy of each individual involved, they will not regard it as satisfactory. For the Cherokee, a satisfactory relationship between teacher and pupil is moral, not contractual, and the authority of the teacher can only be moral (in the broadest sense); only within such a harmonious relation can formal teaching and learning occur. This does not mean that the teacher has to be morally above reproach, but rather the moral quality of his dealing with pupils must be primary in his actions. It means even more that when the teacher acts in the correct manner, the Cherokee children are morally obligated to assist him in the learning transaction.

At first glance it might appear that the cultural distance between the two conceptions of the role of teacher is so great as to be unbridgeable, but it became apparent to our classroom observers that the Cherokee children would participate eagerly with any teacher willing to adopt the appropriate stance. These children are trained to value precision and competence, and when given the opportunity they will cooperate. Thus, in one classroom that could usually be characterized by silent acquiescence on the part of the Cherokee, the teacher began to approach them in culturally appropriate manner—with a light and relaxing bantering tone. Shortly, the students began to answer questions and to participate in classwork in a fashion that the teacher later expressed she experienced as astounding. The exchange was sustained for about 30 minutes, and then was disrupted when the teacher felt impelled to preach to the students about the right ways to behave. The students quickly retreated into their silence.

Parents (and children) say of the teacher they consider good that "he is gentle, nice," "he treats me good," or "he jokes with us." Often this means that the teacher does not regard himself as a superior authority who, by virtue of his position, can demand a particular type of conduct or work, but that, recognizing the autonomy of the student, he probes in order to ascertain areas of difficulty. Since there are also areas where the student can be humiliated publicly by his incompetencies and ignorance, the tone most often appropriate is gentle banter (although it can under certain circumstances become the "full razz"). Quite frequently, the tone underlying the words is crucial, especially to students whose English fluency is poor. The silence of the Cherokees can become a trap for the teacher, leading him to respond with an excessive verbosity which, by its indifference to the response of the pupils, aggravates their withdrawal; the teacher, in turn, employs increasingly aggressive tones. Since the Cherokee do not recognize his authority, they do not acknowledge his right to be aggressive, but judge it as a manifestation of incompetence and lack of emotional control. There is thus generated a vicious cycle in which the teacher, unable to arouse the spontaneous cooperation of the pupils, must increasingly resort to demands, commands, and other tokens of aggressiveness, while the children disassociate themselves still further from what they interpret as a tantrum. Only respect for the other, combined with affectionate regard and trust in a union that the Cherokees speak of (in English) as "love," can reverse the cycle.

Quitting School

When asked why children quit school before completing the program (Table 5–16), the largest proportion of parents referred to the child's experience with the school and, in particular, to his *hatred* for it. *Love* and *hate* are strong words, and the Cherokee employ them in order to denote what the relationship ought to be and what it really is: "I guess they just

TABLE 5–16

"WHY DO YOU THINK SOME CHILDREN
QUIT SCHOOL BEFORE THEY FINISH?"

	Persons	
Reasons	No.	%
	158 =	100.0%
Autonomy: own boss, legal age to quit, marriage, army, lazy	63	40.0
School		
Hate school	42	27.0
Can't learn, repeated failure	36	23.0
Teacher's fault, not teaching correctly	19	12.0
Familial economics		
Expense, clothes, rings, workbooks, fees pictures	51	32.0
Parents can't support, didn't assist	12	8.0
Indianness		
Because of being Indian, trouble with Whites, pupils, teacher, etc.	15	9.0
Education would have no value (because of Indianness), e.g., no job	7	4.0
Total responses	245	
No answer, don't know	7	4.0

SOURCE: K.U. Household Survey, 1966.

hate in school. If you hate something that you don't like, you can't do it; that is just the way you feel." In the calmer words of another parent, they "don't like the teacher and don't get much learning—what they should—and teachers don't teach what they ought to." The hatred is closely allied with a comment that the child has repeatedly experienced failure: "I guess they give out to learn anything in school, because the teachers didn't teacher the Cherokee Indians like they should." Sometimes the hatred moves toward condemnation of the Cherokee pupil, including the self (if a dropout): "I guess they have no use for school and can't find what they want, so they get mad and quit." Or, "they couldn't get better grades, and they didn't work hard enough—like I did. I didn't get enough credits, that's why I failed to finish. I'm tired of schooling—over and over—so, I just quit, and I am now wishing I had a high school diploma, and it was my own fault."

Another major category of reasons offered by parents as to why children left school was inability of the family to provide the requisite support. They are referring in part to financial support, but the issue involves more than the narrow sense of a few dollars, and reaches to encompass the whole matter of relative social status, especially as symbolized by clothing:

I think they didn't have enough clothes that is good enough to school to wear. They get ashamed to go to school with old clothes on. That is the way I was, and, also, the teacher don't teach enough to learn anything what they should, so they give out too easy to learn anything in school. That's why they quit in school, and we don't have a good home either, so I thought that what they look at, too. Poor Cherokee people don't have nothing to help their self.

I think this children that quit school before they finished, they think they are old enough to quit, and they thought they had enough education, and, also, they don't have good clothes to wear in school, when they are in high school. So, they get ashamed to go to school. Also, they have to buy the work books, too. So, that is what makes it so hard for this Cherokee Indian. We are not rich, or we can't afford it, like this White people does, so that's why I think they quit school.

A third category of reasons for children leaving school refers to the autonomy of the child and his maturation to the age at which he can go to work, join the armed services, marry, and so on. It is a moral norm for Cherokee that a decision be left to the actor. While governmental regulations and attendance officers have attempted, with considerable success, to enforce compulsory attendance and to involve the family in assisting that enforcement, the Cherokee elders still regard the decision to attend school as in the hands of the child. If the school desires his presence, it ought to enlist his voluntary cooperation. As we have noted earlier, a fair proportion of Cherokee elders desire that the children acquire a maximum of education, but they are thwarted by the child's dislike of school, his finding alternatives (e.g., the armed services) more attractive, and their own lack of social and economic resources that might make a continued stay at school somewhat more palatable (even if not more attractive). Moreover, we should note that here again parents refer to the inutility of education. A small percentage (7 of 158) pointed out that the child might as well quit school, since there would be no job for him anyway even if he were to complete high school. The Cherokees wish to resolve their economic situation, and they have viewed formal education as a possible instrumentality, but if completion of schooling (or at least the high school diploma) brings no economic reward, they feel they might as well retire from that system and continue their attempt to live their lives as best they can within their own communities.

Proposals and Avenues for Change

We have noted that the Cherokees seek different and more congenial teachers for their young. They also propose (Table 5–15) correlated changes in the classrooms. Several suggest that Indian teachers be recruited to work along with the Whites. Others want Cherokee added to the instructional curriculum. One respondent makes the sweeping proposal that the Cherokees have their own school system:

> I wish they could have their own school for the Cherokee Indians, because they might get a better education where they can use it, because now that some children they finish the twelfth grade and they don't have no job any place.

Revolutionary as these words seem, they are not so novel as they might appear. Until dissolution of the Cherokee Nation in 1906, the Cherokees had their own school system. For a brief period, the elementary school system was operated within the Cherokee language, although there is evidence of conflicts associated with the choice of the instructional language. In any event, the Cherokee are familiar with a variety of school systems—federal, public (local), and religious mission—while some adults may have heard from their elders about the Cherokee National system. Early in the course of our project, we were told that, when the large claims settlement was won for the Nation in 1962, one of the Tribal associations approached a member of the Executive Committee with the suggestion that the funds be used to buy land on which Cherokee could settle and establish their own schools. Their experience had been that few students from their community achieved as much as the eighth grade, but those that did, and then remained in school, usually left the community and did not return. They needed Cherokee who were educated yet remained linked to their natal communities.

Because subordinated and enclaved people such as the Cherokee are so often accused of apathy, indifference, and idleness, it is important to stress the contrary orientation characteristic of these Tribal Cherokee: they are strongly concerned about the schools and their offspring; they have good reason to be critical of the educational process as it affects their children; and they are not beyond proposing a variety of reforms to improve this difficult situation. Moreover, these reforms go beyond the carping that is distinctive of persons who defend their own incompetence and inaction by casting aspersions on those who try to assist them. Quite the contrary, there are Cherokee who would like nothing better than to assume greater control over their own destinies, including operation of their own school system.

"Outside Agitators"

Recognizing the difficult situation of the Tribal Cherokee, Professor Sol Tax and associates at the University of Chicago designed a project intended to assist the Cherokees in helping themselves. The guiding notion was that, because of their lack of fluency and comprehension of English, many Cherokee were unable to understand and cope realistically with events involving the greater society exterior to their rural communities. The assistance was to come through expanding the field of usage of the Cherokee language by making significant types of information available in Cherokee. Because so many Cherokee participate in religious services which utilize the Holy Scriptures in a Cherokee edition (prepared during the nineteenth century), literacy in the syllabary has remained relatively widespread. An active tradition of literacy and of intellectual discourse within the Cherokee language has been maintained, but, since the destruction of the printing press of the Cherokee Nation, there has been no avenue for feeding new printed materials into the cultural milieu. In consequence, the Tribal Cherokee have not been able to utilize their traditional intellectual tools to acquire a sophisticated understanding of the institutions and agencies of the greater society.

Tax and associates secured funding from the Carnegie Corporation for a project which came to include elements such as the following: (1) providing the Tribal Cherokee with a facility for printing materials in the syllabary; (2) providing instruction in use of the syllabary for those Cherokee (young or old) who were illiterate within it; (3) initiating radio broadcasts in the Cherokee language in order to enlarge the information available to the Tribal Cherokee; (4) generally improving the status of the Cherokee language in the eyes of non-Cherokee inhabitants of Oklahoma, so that its knowledge would be regarded as an asset rather than a deficiency of the speaker (e.g., trying to introduce the Cherokee language as a recognized academic subject in Oklahoma colleges); (5) facilitating the interaction of Cherokee with exterior institutions by such devices as introducing directional signs, printed in the syllabary, at strategic junctures of stores, offices, or other locales.

During the 1960's the Carnegie Cross-Cultural Educational Project of the University of Chicago profoundly stimulated the Tribal Cherokee. An indigenous organization, the Original Cherokee Community Organization (O.C.C.O.) emerged and assumed control of the printing facility in order to publish a newsletter, *The Cherokee Report*, issued with parallel columns in English and Cherokee. Leaders of rural Cherokee communities cooperated with a social worker, Armin L. Saeger, Jr., in improving the patterns of utilization of the Indian health facilities.

As the Tribal Cherokee took advantage of the Tax-Carnegie Project, problems developed. Although impoverished and politically without power—even without control over the "Cherokee Nation" which represents them to the federal government—the Tribal Cherokee had never acquisced to their position. Many wanted restoration of an independent status for a self-governing Cherokee republic, and did not conceive that the goal of their people should be assimilation and loss of indigenous institutions. The Tribal Cherokee also did not recognize the right of the State of Oklahoma to regulate hunting on what were—in their view—the national lands of the Cherokee people. Conversely, those who were positioned in the higher reaches of political and economic power in eastern Oklahoma felt threatened by the Tax-Carnegie Project. The Principal Chief, his associates, and the tribal attorneys had enjoyed the position of "speaking for" the Cherokee and of running the affairs of the "Cherokee Nation," as officially recognized by the federal government. Governmental officials (at all levels) looked askance at social movements which threatened to alter an existing balance of power. Moreover, generations of sheriffs, welfare workers, merchants, ranchers, and county officials had been accustomed to treating the Tribal Cherokee as an inferior, incompetent, and impotent breed—"Indians"—fit only for the lowest and dirtiest of work. Such persons perceived the Carnegie Project as a threat, and began to speak of its staff as "outside agitators" who had come to disturb the preexisting harmony of rural Oklahoma by stirring up simpleminded and credulous natives. Congressional investigations were threatened, and sympathetic Whites, like Armin Saeger, Jr., were confronted by their superiors with a choice between transfer to a position elsewhere or leaving governmental employ, for the offense of having tried to work directly with local leaders of rural Cherokee communities.

In a sense the educational project launched by Tax and his associates had proven a success, if a painful one. The Tribal Cherokee had begun to appraise their situation more accurately and started to enter the political arena, thus upsetting the balance of eastern Oklahoma power. The O.C.C.O. had filed a test case against the imposing of state game laws on what it contended were "Indian lands," and this judicial challenge to state agencies was widely interpreted as a threat to Oklahoma "law and order," as if the Cherokee were declaring that they need no longer obey the law. The kind of assistance now required by the Tribal Cherokee was no longer "educational" in the narrow sense, but political and judicial. Among other things, they needed an attorney to represent them against those agencies and persons who presumed on their impotence in order to seize their possessions and restrain their actions. Fortunately, at this juncture in 1967, the Field Foundation was willing to provide the funds to underwrite the services of an attorney for O.C.C.O., and to assist that organization generally in protecting the rights of the Tribal Cherokee. As of 1970, the Carnegie Cross-Cultural Educational Project was no longer operative, but O.C.C.O. and its attorney, Stuart

Trapp, were vigorously in existence, although struggling against the most formidable adversaries.

SUGGESTED READINGS

Cullum, Robert M. 1953. *The Rural Cherokee Household: Study of 479 Households within Fourteen School Districts Situated in the Old Cherokee Nation.* Muskogee: U.S. Bureau of Indian Affairs. Mimeo'd.

Debo, Angie. 1951. *The Five Civilized Tribes of Oklahoma: Report on Social and Economic Conditions.* Philadelphia: Indian Rights Association.

Dickeman, Mildred. 1969. The Integrity of the Cherokee Student, in Murray L. Wax *et al., Indian Education in Eastern Oklahoma.* Lawrence: University of Kansas.

———. 1971. *The Culture of Poverty: A Critique,* ed. Eleanor B. Leacock. New York: Simon and Schuster, Inc.

Dumont, Robert V., Jr. 1971. Learning English and How to be Silent: Studies in American Indian Classrooms, in *The Functions of Language in the Classroom,* eds. Courtney B. Cazden, Vera P. John, and Dell H. Hymes. New York: Teachers College Press.

———, and Murray L. Wax. 1969. The Cherokee School Society and the Intercultural Classroom. *Human Organization,* 18, 3 (Fall), 217–226.

Gearing, Fred O. 1962. Priests and Warriors: Social Structures for Cherokee Politics in the 18th Century. *American Anthropological Association,* Memoir #93 (*American Anthropologist,* 64, 5, Part 2).

Gulick, John. 1960. *Cherokees at the Crossroads.* Chapel Hill: Institute for Research in Social Science, University of North Carolina.

Kupferer, Harriet Jane. 1966. *The "Principal People." 1960: A Study of Cultural and Social Groups of the Eastern Cherokee.* Smithsonian Institution, Bureau of American Ethnology, Bulletin 196, pp. 215–325; Anthropological Papers, No. 78. Washington, D.C.: U.S. Government Printing Office.

Oklahoma Employment Security Commission. 1963. *Economic Base Report: Adair County.* Oklahoma City.

———. 1962. *Economic Base Report: Cherokee County.* Oklahoma City.

———. 1966. *Economic Base Report: Delaware County.* Oklahoma City.

———. 1964. *Economic Base Report: Sequoyah County.* Oklahoma City.

Oklahoma Public Welfare Commission. 1965. *Annual Report,* fiscal year ending June 30, 1965. Oklahoma City.

Original Cherokee Community Organization (O.C.C.O.). 1967 f. *The Cherokee Report.* Tahlequah, Oklahoma.

Underwood, J. Ross. 1966. An Investigation of Educational Opportunity for the Indian in Northeastern Oklahoma. Unpublished Ed.D. dissertation, University of Oklahoma.

U.S. Bureau of the Census. 1963a. *Census of Population*; Vol. 1: *Characteristics of the Population*; Part 38, *Oklahoma*. Washington, D.C.: U.S. Government Printing Office.

————. 1963b. *County and City Data Book, 1962*. Washington, D.C.: U.S. Government Printing Office.

————. 1966. *Negro Population by County*. Washington, D.C.: U.S. Government Printing Office.

U.S. Senate. 1969. Hearings before the Special Subcommittee on Indian Education of the Committee on Labor and Public Welfare, U.S. Senate, 90th Congress. Part 2 (February 19, 1968; Twin Oaks, Oklahoma). Washington, D.C.: U.S. Government Printing Office.

Wahrhaftig, Albert. 1965a. *Social and Economic Characteristics of the Cherokee Population of Eastern Oklahoma*. Chicago: Carnegie Cross-Cultural Education Project of the University of Chicago. Mimeo'd.

————. 1965b. *The Tribal Cherokee Population of Eastern Oklahoma*. Chicago: Carnegie Cross-Cultural Education Project of the University of Chicago. (Published with map in *Current Anthropology*, 9, 5 [December 1968] pp. 510–518.)

————. 1969. Renaissance and Repression: The Oklahoma Cherokee. *TRANS-action* (February), 42–48.

Wasserman, Miriam. 1970. *The School Fix, NYC, USA*. New York: Outerbridge and Dienstfrey.

Wax, Murray L. 1971. Poverty and Interdependency, in *The Culture of Poverty: A Critique*, ed. Eleanor B. Leacock. New York: Simon and Schuster, Inc.

————, Rosalie H. Wax, and Robert V. Dumont, Jr. 1964. *Formal Education in an American Indian Community*. Monograph #1 (Supplement, *Social Problems*, XI, 4), the Society for the Study of Social Problems.

Wax, Murray L. *et al.* 1969. *Indian Education in Eastern Oklahoma*. Final Report, U.S. Office of Education Contract No. OE-6-10-260, Bureau No. 5-0565-2-12-1. Lawrence: University of Kansas. Mimeo'd.

Wolcott, Harry F. 1967. *A Kwakiutl Village and School*. New York: Holt, Rinehart and Winston, Inc.

INDIANS AND
THE GREATER SOCIETY

Part Three

We have already seen how Indian tribes altered themselves in order to meet the challenges posed by the White invasion. The Yaqui elaborated a social and religious reorganization begun by the Jesuits; the Apache became equestrian raiders; the Iroquois confederacy became more tightly organized and more encompassing; the Cherokee shaped themselves as a republic. But so far we have not touched upon developments and transformations which were not specific to a particular tribe, but which had a larger or intertribal frame of reference. Some can be classified as religious movements, some as a spread of a common pan-Indian "popular" culture (displacing the distinct cultures of the separate tribes), some as the emergence of political agencies for pan-Indian action, and some as pathologies of the cultural frontier where Whites and Indians interact. A religious movement such as the Good Message of Handsome Lake had a strong intertribal potential but became fixated as a cult of just the Six Nations. Another movement, the Ghost Dance, appears to have been more pan-Indian than it was because it functioned more to renew the native traditions of participating tribes than to unify diverse tribes into a new religious unity.

Pan-Indian Responses to Invasion and Disruption

In the present century, pan-Indianism is more of a social reality. Despite fierce opposition, the Native American Church has won converts among all the major tribes and is at home in the city as well as in the reservation. In like manner, the powwow attracts participants from every tribe and every locale and, even though its inner impact is small, becomes a visible token of a common Indianness. Finally, there are organizations (the National Congress of American Indians, the Coalition of American Indian Citizens, the National Indian Youth Council) which strive to marshal Indians for political purposes. Pan-Indianism is thus a polymorphous process, rather than a reality. In the previous century and today, the process of pan-Indianism has been abetted by educational and custodial institutions which have confined together Indians of varied linguistic and cultural backgrounds and subjected them to a common discipline. Institutions which were designed to deracinate instead fostered pan-Indianism.

THE GOOD MESSAGE
OF HANDSOME LAKE

On June 15, 1799, an Indian named Handsome Lake went into a trance. His people, the Seneca, had sided with the British during the American Revolution, and their lands had consequently been reduced through confiscation, sale, and swindle. Food was scarce, and trade was not a reliable source of help, since whiskey was a prominent constituent of the goods received in exchange for Indian furs, often resulting in parties which lasted several weeks and might lead to deaths from exposure or brawling. Handsome Lake was brother to the famous Seneca chief, Cornplanter, but on the date in question he was himself suffering from the effects of an extended bout with trade whiskey (received at Pittsburgh in exchange for furs).

In the course of this and subsequent trances, Handsome Lake was visited by several spiritual beings whose admonitions and exhortations were to become the basis of his "Good Message." When he reported these events to his brother and others in the community, they questioned a White Quaker teacher as to the significance. The Quaker admitted that some of the elements of the vision were similar to those of his own belief, but naturally he was cautious about accepting the validity of the experience. In retrospect, the Good Message does seem to be a blend of what had been traditionally preached by the wise men among Seneca, together with novel messages similar to those preached by the Quakers.

The spiritual visitors advised Handsome Lake that he and his brethren should give up the use of alcohol, and "quit all kinds of frolics and dancing, except for their Worship Dance." In regard to Whites and the cultural innovations which they were bringing, the message was peaceable accommodation:

> It is all right to learn to farm in the white man's way, but only that you may grow more to give away to the needy—not that you may have more to sell for profit; reading and writing are not good for Indians, but it is well that some of your children learn them so that they may deal with the whites for you [Deardorff, 1951, p. 103].

As the Good Message was elaborated, it was applied to many relationships: children should not be disobedient, nor should they be punished unjustly; marital partners should be faithful to each other; children should respect and care for their parents; antagonisms with in-laws should be avoided; men were not to boast; women, when visiting, should help their hosts with the work; visitors arriving during mealtime should be offered food, and they should not refuse; adherents of the religion should look within themselves for spiritual guidance; and so on (cf. Wilson, 1960, pp. 80 ff.).

These moral exhortations were accompanied by the cultic beliefs of an organized religion. There was a Heaven ("The New World") and a Hell. Whites were not allowed to enter Heaven, since their sins included the crucifixion of Christ, whereas Indians had not been involved. Nonetheless, no one who repented would be damned, even if that repentance came only at the end of a wicked life. Those who adhered to this new religion came together as congregations in a "Longhouse," and the religion is often known accordingly.

Following his visionary experience, Handsome Lake devoted much of the remaining 16 years of his life to preaching among the Iroquois peoples. He acquired a following of apostles, and the Good Message was received everywhere with enthusiasm. While visiting in Washington, he received a letter from President Jefferson enjoining all Indians to listen to the Good Message; Indians still regard this as governmental endorsement of the religion. After his death, the religion fluctuated in popularity, but never died out completely. Intensive evangelical efforts by White Christian missionaries during the nineteenth century caused significant attrition, and the religious organization was affected by factionalism, while reinforced by a succession of minor prophets.

Over a century and a half later, the religion of Handsome Lake was still important on the Six Nations Iroquois Reserve in Canada. Shimony (1961, p. 35) notes that its four congregations form the most actively functioning social units on the Reserve, and their Longhouse affiliation serves to integrate most of the congregants' social activities. The congregations now represent the most conservative or tradition-oriented perspective of all Iroquois groupings, as evidenced by such facts as their use of no English in their meetings. Political factionalism is connected with religious participation, and the Longhouse congregations insist that the only legitimate community leaders are those who have been invested at their special ceremonials. The elected Christian leaders have resisted such investiture, and in consequence no tribal government enjoys the role of legitimacy among all factions.

Emerging on the frontier of Indian–White interaction, the Longhouse religion combined elements from both parties. Some of its symbols and norms are related to the presence and missionizing of the Whites, but its basic emphasis upon proper and harmonious personal relationships was wholly consonant with traditional Indian values. Any criticism by White observers would have been disarmed, because the Longhouse religion had rid itself of that traditional paraphernalia and imagery which missionaries customarily denounced as heathen, superstitious, or even satanic. Equally important was the moral and pacific nature of the Message. The congregational nature of the religion, perhaps adapted from Christian practices, helped Indians to integrate themselves socially and ritually under the new conditions of a life in which traditional ceremonies had become meaningless or incongruous.

Now, in contrast, we turn to a congeries of religious movements developing later on a frontier further westward. Paradoxically, these movements were more intertribal in their spread, although more specifically tribal in their local adaptations, some of which were more conducive to armed struggle. Some were also more clearly nativistic in the sense of providing a ceremonial occasion for reviving the practice of traditional rites. These were broader movements than the Longhouse religion, appealing in different ways to peoples whose lives had deteriorated.

THE GHOST DANCE MOVEMENTS

During the third quarter of the nineteenth century, a set of religious movements developed among the tribes of the West. Their common feature was a prophet thought to have visited the abode of the (Indian) dead and to have returned with the message that they and the living were going to be reunited, and that the Whites were going to disappear. Deriving from these messages were cultic ceremonials (mainly circular dances) which helped to engender trance states or "dreaming" during which the participants might themselves visit and converse with the dead.

In the 1870's the "Smoholla Religion" was active in the Oregon region, and at the same time the initial phase of the Ghost Dance appeared among the Northern Paiute. Following a vision in 1870, Tavibo prophesied that those who adhered to the cult and participated in its distinctive circular dance would witness a miraculous return of their dead relatives, become immune to sickness or death, and enjoy a state of prosperity. From its origin among the Paiute, this good news spread north and west, where it had a major appeal to those tribes whose lives had been most severely disrupted by recent invasions of Whites. The Ghost Dance preacher among the Tule Lake Modoc held that the Whites would be consumed with fire and the Indian dead would return. Those Indians who participated in the new cult would enjoy the coming prosperity, while the skeptics would be turned into rocks. The exact relationship between the cult and the further military campaigns of that region cannot now be determined, but it is known that the Whites were greatly alarmed when news of the movement reached their attention ("the natives are restless"). The so-called Modoc and Nez Percé Wars occurred in

1872 and 1877, respectively, but it is difficult to say whether the Ghost Dance (or allied movements) provided the stimulus for Indian militancy or the excuse for campaigns to suppress and slaughter Indians whose lands were being taken.

A generation later, the Ghost Dance received fresh inspiration from the vision of another Paiute, Wovoka (Jack Wilson). When he was about 30 years old, there was a solar eclipse visible to inhabitants of his area; Wovoka had fallen ill, and during the eclipse he had a revelation. His partisans believed that on that occasion he, like the sun, had died and been revived after a brief period. The elements of the vision were similar to those of the earlier prophet: a millenarian prophecy of the return of the Indian dead; eradication of sickness and death; provision of abundance and prosperity for the faithful. The millenial date was set for sometime during the Spring of 1891. The orientation was peaceable— "You must not fight!"; no overt hostility was expressed toward the Whites, Wovoka reportedly believing that it would be best for Indians if they became "civilized."

While the new prophecy had little impact among the Western tribes who had participated in the earlier phase of the Ghost Dance, it struck fire among the tribes of the Great Plains. These tribes had gone in one century from the dramatic prosperity and cultural efflorescence of their novel existence as horsenomads to a condition of humiliation, malnutrition, and decimation. Their young men were raised to be bold and reckless warriors. They disdained the ethos of pacificity and diligent drudgery preached by such missionaries as the Quakers, and they chafed under the regimentation and boredom of reservation life. In a brief period their peoples had changed from self-determining bands to mere groups of families subject to the will of alien masters. Realistically, they had nothing to look forward to except slow starvation on government rations.

The Plains peoples were fired with excitement by the news of Wovoka's prophecy. The Oglala Sioux (as did many others) sent envoys to Nevada to learn more from the prophet himself. In the process of communication and translation, new elements were added to the message. The return of the envoys was recalled later by Black Elk, who was himself to become a holy man among the Sioux: Wovoka was the son of a great spirit; he had been killed once by Whites but had returned to the Indians; he was indeed Jesus Christ. He prophesied (according to Black Elk):

> ...that there was another world coming, just like a cloud. It would come in a whirlwind out of the west and would crush out everything on this world, which was old and dying. In that other world there was plenty of meat, just like old times; and in that world all the dead Indians were

alive, and all the bison that had been killed were roaming around again. ... If they did this [the circular dance, preached by Wovoka], they could get on this other world when it came, and the *Wasichus* [Whites] would not be able to get on, and so they would disappear [Neihardt 1961, pp. 236–238].

Some of the envoys were temporarily imprisoned, but despite the efforts of the Indian Agent, most Sioux were participating in the new ritual by the late summer of 1890.

Some participants experienced visions during the circle dance and fell to the earth. In such a vision, Black Elk first "felt queer" in his legs, and then had the sensation that his arms were outstretched and he was leaving the ground and flying through the air. He flew over a beautiful land where everyone had plenty, and he received the design patterns for a holy shirt. Believing that these designs would protect against harm—even against the bullets of the U.S. Cavalry—adherents of the cult made and wore these Ghost Dance shirts.

The movement climaxed among the Oglala Sioux with the massacre at Wounded Knee (located in what is now the Pine Ridge Reservation, South Dakota). Prior to escorting a Sioux band to a camp on the reservation, U.S. cavalrymen had been confiscating the Indians' guns. While this action appeared to make for peace, it was deeply disturbing to a warrior people, and left them without means to engage in hunting. The soldiers were green, and the Sioux may have been defiant. The Sioux may also have felt protected by the new powers associated with the Ghost Dance, and the soldiers were nervous. A minor incident triggered panic among the soldiers, and when their barrage had lifted, nearly 300 Sioux—of both sexes and all ages—lay dying; cavalry losses were 31. Mooney (1896, p. 828) emphasizes that the real cause of "The Sioux Outbreak" was the economic hardship suffered by these people, and that the Ghost Dance activity merely provided an occasion for rousing panic among the Whites. If Mooney is correct, the real threat of the disarmament was starvation. In any event, the incident at Wounded Knee altered and weakened the Ghost Dance among the Oglala; where it survived, it was as a secret cult among the persecuted.

The Ghost Dance cult triggered no such violent confrontation among other Plains Tribes. Failure of the millenial era to arrive must have occasioned bitter disappointment, but it did not cause the cult to disappear (any more than failures of the millenarian prophecies of Christian sects have caused them to disappear). Among tribes such as the Pawnee the cult had at first been the vehicle whereby traditional ceremonials could be revived, despite the deaths of those priests who had been solely authorized to perform them. (Visits to the abode of the dead via Ghost Dance trances became the ritual means for authorizing new persons to stage ceremonials which had formerly been exclusive property.) Now the Ghost Dance cult assumed a new form among the Pawnee, as it was used to give sacramental value to a traditional gambling game. Play in the game came to have a ritual and prophetic value. The Ghost Dance hand game flourished among the Pawnee at least until the 1930's, perhaps longer (Lesser, 1933).

The millenarian qualities of the Ghost Dance retained a strong appeal for other tribes. Traditionalist Indians, recalling the days of their youth, continued to hope for the great transformation in which the Whites would be swept away, the dead animals and Indians return, and the Indians again freely enjoy the land that had once been theirs. It would be difficult to discover where and to what extent these beliefs are still held and expressed in rituals such as the Ghost Dance. But the observer can no more disregard them than he might disregard Zionism among the Jews before World War I or the demands among American Negroes that they be regarded as Afro-Americans and allowed to form their own distinct nation.

In contrast to the dramatic rise and decline of the Ghost Dance and its millenarian intensity has been the steady growth of a more quietistic cult based on the sacramental use of peyote. While it can be referred to as "the peyote cult" or "the peyote religion," that nomenclature would be as misleading as an Imperial Roman speaking of the Christianity of his time as "the bread and wine cult" because of the central role of the Eucharistic sacrament. To comprehend it in terms of English verbal patterns, it is more useful to speak of it, as do its participants, as the Native American Church, and to deal first, not with the pharmacological nature of peyote, but with the ritual service (or communion) and the ethos.

THE NATIVE AMERICAN CHURCH

The ritual service is a formal communion that lasts an entire night. In the Plains format the participants in the service should be sheltered within a tipi and seated in a ritual circle about a fire, but in practice there may be symbolism instead of actuality. As the service proceeds, a tray of peyote in the form of dried "buttons" is passed about the circle, and each participant is free to take as many as he chooses. A special sacramental drum and gourd rattle are used, and in ritual succession each participant chants his own sacred song. The ritual and singing may be in the native tribal language or in English, but the rhythms are quite distinctive to the cult. Each individual is free to compose his own words and melody. Christian imagery is freely employed; Bibles are often part of the ritual paraphernalia, and figures of the cross and of Jesus are carved or painted on ceremonial objects. Participants sometimes say that Christianity is for Whites and Peyote for Indians. They do not mean simply the drug or its psychedelic qualities, but a beneficent and spiritually powerful being who can assist them to achieve health, prosperity, and harmonious relationships with their fellows. Peyote is never used casually, but always regarded as a sacred substance; in case of illness it may be taken as an herbal tea, but it is never eaten or drunk in the fashion that a person might light a cigarette or sip a beer.

The religious ethos associated with participation in the Native American Church (N.A.C.) includes brotherly love, care of the family, self-reliance, and avoidance of alcohol. Anti-White sentiments are almost completely absent from the doctrine, although Indian members will say that it was the Whites, not the Indians, who killed Jesus. Typically, the creed emphasizes that the cult of peyote is an alternative for Indians—it is their sacramental way. Whites who express an interest in the cult are frequently invited to attend the ritual service in order "to see for themselves" the prevailing atmosphere of meditation and comradely warmth; as visitors, they may choose for themselves either to observe or participate.

The N.A.C. is less tribal and yet both more individualistic and more congregational than traditional Indian cults. Through its service, the individual Indian seeks his own solutions to his own problems (as compared to the collective salvation envisioned in the Ghost Dance). At the same time, there is considerable intertribal visiting among the membership. Individuals and kin groups travel great distances to visit coreligionists on other reservations and gather with them for the service. Members of southern Plains tribes will take with them considerable quantities of peyote to be given to their coreligionists in the northern Plains. Where Indians gather together in a city, there may develop pan-Indian (intertribal) congregations which encompass people of radically different ethnic backgrounds.

Outside opinion about the cult varies considerably. Knowledgeable anthropologists who have witnessed many ritual services—or even participated—assert that the effects of the drug are temporary and that the congregants tend over time to become the most stable and reliable members of the Indian community. Missionaries, administrators, and educators have usually remained hostile. One minor phenomenon should be mentioned: since the participants in a service have been awake all night, they are not likely to be in the most lively or spirited condition the next day. It is a moot point whether an institution, such as school or local government, should accommodate its time schedule to that of the N.A.C. (as it has to the seven-day week of Judaeo-Christianity and to the secularized holidays of Euroamerican Christianity), or whether the N.A.C. must structure its sessions to meet the conventional calendar and scheduling of White bureaucracies. Another phenomenon is the use of peyote as a therapeutic, the difficulty being that persons so doctored may display peyote symptoms that conceal a serious illness.

As a matter of basic religious principle, Protestantism has been hostile to intoxicants and hallucinogens, and at various periods has launched holy crusades against alcohol, tobacco, coffee, and opiates, marijuana, and other drugs. As Christian missionaries and reformers became aware of the religious cult centering about peyote, they responded with energetic hostility. All manner of deleterious effects were attributed to the substance, and it was rumored that cult meetings were the occasion for sexual license. The legislatures of several states and the councils of several tribes have passed laws barring the use or transportation of peyote. Responding to these onslaughts, members of the movement incorporated themselves in 1918 as "a religious and benevolent association" known as the Native American Church. The first corporate charter was valid only in the state of Oklahoma, but by the mid-1930's the association was national in scope. It quickly gained the support of most anthropologists involved in Indian affairs: Sidney Slotkin served as its national secretary, and others, such as Omer Stewart, testified as expert witnesses in court hearings designed to test the constitutional validity of state laws interfering with the use of peyote. The Church has remained congregationally decentralized. Rituals vary somewhat among the tribes, there is little formal creed, and no elaborate buildings or institutions are associated with it. Accordingly, it remains highly consonant with a population many of whose members are impoverished and nomadic.

In judging the N.A.C., most Protestants tend to place too much emphasis upon the use of peyote. Many peoples of the world have given affirmative religious sanction to visions and have sought to secure them through drugs, ascetic practices, torture, suggestion, and group hysteria. Plains peoples practiced the Vision Quest, in which the seeker would isolate himself and abstain from food and drink for four days, and perhaps even mutilate himself, in order to induce a vision. Contemporary denominational Protestantism is unusual among world religions in its derogation of visionary experiences and hostility towards drugs or other means for inducing them. (The evangelical sects encourage trance experience in the context of their religious services, but tend to be even more hostile to drugs, intoxicants, and the like.)

When dried, the peyote plant furnishes a natural organic substance which can help to engender psychedelic effects of a mild nature. It is a cactus (*lophophora Williamsii*) native to the deserts of Mexico and the

U.S., and it contains low concentrations of nine psychotropic alkaloids; these are water soluble and thus eliminated relatively quickly from the body. (Labarre [1960, p. 45] cautions that the peyote cactus should not be confused with the mescal bean [*Sophora secundiflora*] or with the Aztec narcotic mushroom [*teonanacatl*, which is a Basidiomycete] or with Jimsonweed [*Datura*].) To achieve significant effects from peyote, the consumer must force himself to ingest a large quantity in a relatively short time. It is notoriously unpleasant to take, and on many persons acts as an emetic. Even persons who have used it for years find it difficult to ingest, so there are severe natural impediments to using it just for kicks.

As with several other psychedelic substances, the effects of the alkaloids depend upon the mental set of the consumer, and in any case, peyote serves more to intensify a mood than to stimulate free visions. Many communicants of the N.A.C. have faithfully taken peyote for years and never experienced a vision. Receiving a vision is regarded as a special blessing, enjoyed only by a select few.

Reconstructing the history of the cults preceding the rise of the N.A.C. is not easy. Tribes neighboring to the region where the cactus grows have evidently employed it ritually for centuries. The conquests of the Americas, and improvements in communication—via the spread of Spanish and English as lingua franca—as well as improvement in transportation, facilitated the spread of the cults. During the nineteenth century, tribes which previously had not employed peyote—or at least not as a regular ritual—became participants in an intertribal cultic practice, and by the turn of the century it had spread throughout the Plains. At the present time, the N.A.C. has become a significant form of association of many contemporary Indians. Its ritual and ethos remain compatible with a wide range of Indian problems and needs, and it appeals to Indians from a variety of tribes and in multiple social and economic contexts, both on the reservation and elsewhere. It is regarded as a distinctively Indian religion in which its member can take pride, and it allows Indians to incorporate and integrate diverse elements of their heritage.

PAN-INDIAN POLITICAL
NATIONALISM

North American Indians have traditionally regarded themselves not as a single people but as members of numerous, separate bands of kith and kin. Contact with Europeans encouraged the growth of larger and more centralized entities, such as tribes or even nations. However, even though Whites grouped the American natives together, labeled them as Indians, and created agencies—such as the Indian Service—to deal with them, it required a multitude of social changes and novel experiences for the lives of Indians to be so altered that they came to feel that, at least to some extent, they were but a single people with common needs and goals. This development, which is still in process, is given the label of pan-Indianism, and in this section we will deal with the rise of political associations expressing pan-Indian nationalism.

Whenever Indians in the past dealt with agencies of the encompassing society, it was as bands or groups from the same tribe. During the Indian Wars of the nineteenth century, the Army would recruit a band of warriors from one tribe to use as scouts and light cavalry against a tribe of "hostiles." Even in the boarding schools of the Indian Service, where Indians of several tribes mingled together, the conditions encouraged (and still encourage) them to band together in cliques and factions of their native tribe. Moreover, the humiliations and deprivations suffered by tribes on the frontier made several generations of Indians too fearful to indulge in such major innovations as building political associations with other tribes. Even today, the older generation on many Indian reservations, recalling the hardships suffered by themselves, their parents, and grandparents, tend to be extremely conservative about any innovations in their relationships with federal authority. While the outsider may visualize opportunities for constructive change, the older generation realizes that change can be for the worse, and mistrusts those who wish to alter the fabric of a style of living which it has come to find tolerable. Existing on such a slender margin of resources, it has little interest in the creative innovation which might, by failing, leave the situation worse.

The experiences of World War II made a great difference. Some 25,000 Indians served in the Armed Services, where they had the opportunities to serve in novel capacities, undergo new types of training, and enlarge their realm of experience. A new generation was created, and possibly the most influential factor in their experiences was the contact with other distinctive peoples who were also of lower class and status. The Indian serviceman came to realize that the disadvantages suffered by his people were not so much the result of the disabilities of Indians as of their failure "to work the system." Many of those who returned to their home communities did so with fresh perspectives on the larger society and a new consciousness of how to relate to it.

In 1944 a group of acculturated Indians organized the National Congress of American Indians (N.C.A.I.). Since the intertribal confederacies of the frontier (the Six Nations, the League of Tecumseh, etc.), this was the first designed for Indians to advance their political interests in the exterior world. While there had been such organizations as the

Indian Rights Association or the Association on American Indian Affairs, these had been benevolent associations of liberal and religious minded White reformers designed to be *for* Indians, but not *of* and *by* them (even though Indians are now included on their boards of control). The N.C.A.I. solicited memberships from various tribes as well as from Indian individuals, and it permitted Whites to join only as nonvoting members who paid a higher rate of dues.

Existing mainly as an intertribal association, the N.C.A.I. suffered many of the handicaps of a league of sovereign nations. Not all tribes perceived an advantage in joining, in maintaining an enduring membership, or in paying their dues. Since dues had to be set at a low figure in order to encourage membership from so many impoverished tribal groupings, the central office was poorly funded, and for many years the only permanent employee was the Executive Secretary.

In due course, other national, political, pan-Indian associations began to emerge. The National Indian Youth Council (N.I.Y.C.) was formed in 1961 by young college-educated Indians of radical persuasion who had deep roots in impoverished, traditional, Indian communities. They levied strong criticisms against the N.C.A.I. and the established group of tribal governments which it represented. In their critical judgment, most of the tribal governments (and therefore the N.C.A.I. as a whole) were not representative of the "real Indians"—i.e., the impoverished, more traditional peoples—but instead stood for the interests of wealthy and acculturated peoples whose claim to Indianness was a blood quantum rather than any social relationship. Even more important, they perceived within the N.C.A.I. a powerful bloc consisting of representatives from "The Five Civilized Tribes" (Cherokee, Creek, Choctaw, Chickasaw, Seminole) of eastern Oklahoma. During the nineteenth century, these tribes had been organized as autonomous, democratic republics, but those structures had been dissolved by act of Congress early in the present century. The chief executive officer of four of these tribes was an appointee of the President of the U.S., serving for an indefinite term and without any organized procedure which would force him to account to the Indian people for his political acts or his employment of their funds. Since the chiefs of The Civilized Tribes were shrewd and able men, well connected with the state administration of Oklahoma and agencies of the federal government, and since some were wealthy enterprisers, they had come—in the judgment of Indian radicals—to exert a disproportionate influence within the N.C.A.I., tending to commit it to a conservative rightwing line on any major political issue. Most significantly, the N.C.A.I. was committed to denunciation of the tactics of civil rights workers and the struggles of Negroes to improve their lot radically as a minority. Accordingly, from the point of view of the leadership of the N.I.Y.C., the N.C.A.I. had estranged the Indian peoples from their natural allies among the impoverished and suppressed of other minorities; the N.C.A.I. also deterred Indians from the militant tactics by which they might have made their abused condition known to the general public.

Whatever the validity of these criticisms, the N.C.A.I. has come to assume as its primary duty serving as a lobby in Washington for the organized Indian tribes. Thematically, its role was symbolized by its persistent opposition to two major acts of Congress passed in 1953: Public Law 280 and House of Representatives Concurrent Resolution 108. Public Law 280 authorized individual states unilaterally to assume jurisdiction over crimes committed on Indian reservations, and thus to take over a function formerly controlled by the federal government jointly with the tribal governments. Concurrent Resolution 108, popularly known as "the Termination Policy," called for withdrawal of federal governmental supervision of the several tribes "at the earliest possible time." Both congressional acts were regarded by Indian organizations and their liberal associates (e.g., the Indian Rights Association) as threatening to erode the last vestiges of treaty rights, and so diminish the Indian right of self-determination. Fear of "termination" has been a major guideline of N.C.A.I. policies and motivated their condemnation of the 1967 proposal to transfer schools operated by the B.I.A. from the Department of the Interior to the U.S. Office of Education; it is testimony to their influence that their veto was determinative in this issue, for the move had already received major approval within the administration.

Fundamentally, the N.C.A.I. has sought to improve the position of Indians within the present structure of federal relationships, and has been wary of any alterations which seem to imply "termination" of federal responsibilities. On the other hand, organizations such as the N.I.Y.C., the Coalition of American Indian Citizens, or United Native Americans have condemned the entire fabric of the present structure. They advocate such changes as abolishing the present B.I.A. and replacing it with agencies which would offer counsel and advice to Indians, as the Department of Agriculture does the farmers. In their judgment, the major share of funds for Indian purposes should be channeled directly to Indian communities—not through federal bureaucracies—and used for community development according to local designs and leadership. They frequently take as their models the new nations which were formerly colonial but have become self-governing. Tactically, these more radical organizations have not hesitated to utilize the techniques of picketing and confrontation employed by Black and Chicano militants. The

N.I.Y.C. sponsored the "fish-ins" of the 1960's in order to combat the attempts of state game and fish commissions to impose customary state rules on Indian tribes, in violation of rights guaranteed by treaty.

The N.C.A.I. has published a quarterly news magazine, *The Sentinel*, while N.I.Y.C. has erratically published *ABC: Americans Before Columbus*. In addition to these two publications, there have been a small number of other pan-Indian periodicals issuing out of local concentrations of Indians in such urban centers as the Bay Cities or Los Angeles.

The Executive Secretaries of the N.C.A.I. have included Robert Burnette (Rosebud Sioux), Vine Deloria, Jr. (Standing Rock Sioux), John Belindo (Kiowa Navajo), and Bruce Wilkie (Makah). Recent Presidents have included Earl Old Person (Blackfeet), Wendell Chino (Mescalero Apache), and Walter Wetzel (Blackfeet). The founding group of the N.I.Y.C. included Mel Thom (Paiute), Clyde Warrior (Ponca), Robert V. Dumont, Jr. (Assiniboine), Bruce Wilkie (Makah), Fran Poafpybitty (Comanche), and Herbert Blatchford (Navajo).

Despite the emergence of these national pan-Indian political organizations, the political and social interests of most Indians are still tribal or local. The Quechan of the Southwest consider retrieval of their ownership of Colorado River bottomland as primary, and cannot understand why tribes like the neighboring Navajo are "getting all the gravy" of federal assistance. At the same time, they themselves proudly declare their superiority over their erstwhile enemies to the south, the Cocopa. The Quechan are a small tribe and, save for their claims to the bottomland, an impoverished one without political strength. Yet their attitudes are not untypical, and they represent the difficult tasks confronting nationalistic Indian associations. For most Indians, problems remain tribal and local, the tangle of tribal, state, and federal laws, and of treaty rights, as well as decisions in state courts, mean that these problems must indeed be taken up at the local level. Because of the large role which the federal government has played, and the impact of congressional law, Indians need organizations to lobby and represent them in Washington, but these cannot solve the local problems of tribal communities.

PAN-INDIAN POPULAR CULTURE

All over the U.S. and Canada, but especially in areas west of the Mississippi, Indian powwows have become familiar summer spectacles. At one extreme, they are an essential feature of formal tourist attractions organized by Chambers of Commerce which have come to include such elements as parades, rodeos, pageants of frontier history, "Indian villages," and contests for frontier and Indian skills. At the other extreme, they are events occurring annually in small reservation communities which may also involve small rodeos and fairs, but essentially are organized by local communities for their own pleasure and sociability. What is culturally pan-Indian about the participation of Indians in either kind of powwow are the common styles of dancing, singing, and costuming, and the rapid communication from one group to another of innovations in these matters. This national spread among Indians of a common set of cultural traits and concomitant institutions for sociability and expression represents a different order of phenomena from the rise of pan-Indian political nationalism (described in the preceding section).

Historically, the powwow styles of dancing, singing, and costuming evolved out of the Plains cultures, especially that of the Sioux. Until their adoption, each of the various Indian cultures had its own styles, and the knowledgeable trader, frontiersman, or ethnographer could infer the region an Indian was from, or the tribe within that region, from his style of dress, dance, or song. Furthermore, while tribes usually had some types of dancing, singing, and adornment that were purely secular or social, most were ritual and held an assigned place within ceremonials for healing, hunting, warfare, or general divine blessing. Today, the traditional context of these ceremonials has vanished, and, insofar as dances are performed for sociability and entertainment, Indians have been more free to borrow and innovate. Indians as performing artists and Whites as occasional spectators have both found that the dances and costumes which developed among the Plains cultures are more exciting and offer greater opportunity for the performer to display his artistry.

The costuming, dancing, and singing are a trio of interlocking art forms. They can be performed by persons of any age and either sex, although in most cases women's dancing differs from men's in being less flamboyant and offering less opportunity for intricate variation. Of the three arts, singing is the most subtle, sophisticated, and, being far from Western patterns, the most difficult for an outsider to comprehend and appreciate. In most local powwows or ceremonials, the singing is still done in a native Indian language, making the lyrics incomprehensible to an outsider. This barrier is doubly unfortunate, since Indian singers are judged (among other criteria) on their virtuosity in composition, and dancers in a tribal powwow are judged on their interpretation of a lyric. The high-pitched singing of the Sioux may sound like rhythmic but discordant shrieking to the naive outsider, and it takes either a musical ear or some familiarity before the listener can appreciate the subtleties of a pitch modulation which uses even quarter-tones. It is quite clear to the Indians that the costuming, dancing, and singing are arts subject to normative judgment. In many powwows there are contests for best costume, best dancer, and best band of singers. While the prizes are seldom large (and the entry fees may be significant), Indians will travel considerable distances to participate, and some, as we shall note, devote such time and energy to these competitions that they can be classed as professionals.

While this trio of forms can be considered as performing arts, they can also be indulged in for fun. Indians enjoy the singing and dancing, and once a powwow is started the activities may last for hours or days, until the participants have thoroughly satisfied themselves. The activities, particularly the costuming and dancing, are appealing to others as well as Indians. Until the rise of "rock music" and its style of dancing (or the earlier jitterbugging), there was little sociable dancing within the U.S. which offered men the opportunity for colorful display of their individual virtuosity. It is not surprising to learn that some cities have teams of "Indian dancers" none of whose members are Indians, or that attached to some companies of "professional" Indian performers are persons of non-Indian background who have developed a high competence in these Indian arts.

According to Beatrice Medicine (personal communication), several sets of powwow cycles, and corresponding routes traveled by professional participants, can be mapped in the Great Plains. Some bands of kith and kin (dancers or singers) will travel for months over many miles, participating both in the large tourist attractions (e.g., "Frontier Days," Cheyenne) and some of the small community powwows. The large attractions offer the opportunity for special prizes, or the band may be rewarded or reimbursed for special types of novelty performances (e.g., the hoop dance, or dances with flaming wands). In the smaller fairs there is less formalized procedure of the "giveaway," and the visitors are frequently the objects of gifts of food, money, automobile tires, or other valuables. We may guess that few of these professionals make much money during their travels, but if a performer enjoys his art and the traveling, and is competent enough to win some honors and prizes, then surely there are many satisfactions. The major barriers to these performing artists earning real income are twofold. First, the spectator Whites who might be able to afford reasonable payment are usually unable to judge excellence in performing, and are thus reluctant to expend a sum reasonable to compensate the outstanding performer. Second, the Indians enjoy performing so much that most are in a poor psychological position to bargain for a reasonable price for their participation in a tourist attraction. We have observed tourist attractions with only a modest set of prizes where a promoter has been able to recruit large teams of excellent singers and dancers who willingly performed lengthy shows for several days.

From New England to Southern California, American Indian

groups have consciously adopted powwow dances, songs, and costuming, as well as other symbolic traits (e.g., tipis) characteristic of Plains life during the nineteenth century. Some have chosen to rationalize their conduct on the grounds that if they do not comport themselves as Whites think Indians do, their claims to Indianness will not be accepted. When queried about the Plains headdresses, red shirts, beaded belts, and white trousers that his tribe were wearing in a parade, one member of a Southern California tribe remarked to Robert L. Bee (personal communication): "Sure, we all know *our* people didn't wear headdresses like that in the old days; but, unless the band wore them now, how would the people know we're Indians?" Doubtless this is true, but I cannot escape the feeling that Indians are doing these things because they enjoy them. Of course, not all Indians view the powwow orientation as desirable: some condemn powwows as "drunken brawls" which do not represent "the real Indian way"; others (e.g., the N.C.A.I.) object because the larger powwows are not controlled by Indians, but are organized by Whites who use Indian spectacles to make money from the resultant crowds of tourists. The N.C.A.I. also argues (*The Sentinel*, Vol. II, No. 5, 1966) that the brief homage paid to "Indian Culture" during these tourist spectacles is at variance with the shabby treatment accorded to the same Indians by the same Whites at other moments.

Whether Indians participate in powwows because they enjoy the arts and the sociability, or because they thereby define themselves to outsiders as being "Indians," the fact remains that the spread of this popular culture represents the emergence among Indians of a common set of traits, institutions, and symbols. Just as Yiddish jokes and phrases are employed by Jews whose ancestors did not speak that language, so the pan-Indian popular culture serves as a basis for the informal unity of Indians generally. Wherever Indians meet, whether in student clubs on a campus or intertribal centers within a city, powwow activities are generated, and teams of singers and dancers are organized. Thus these pan-Indian activities have become symbols of the emergence within the U.S. of a new ethnic group or a new nationality.

PATHOLOGIES:
ALCOHOL AND CRIME

The vulnerability of Indians to distilled liquors rapidly became apparent to frontiersmen, traders, and government emissaries. Those who wished to secure furs or to obtain possession of Indian lands often found that they could make more favorable deals more rapidly—if more hazardously—by plentiful lubrication with "firewater." Yet this vulnerability has remained something of a puzzle, perhaps because human use of alcohol is itself something of a puzzle.

Many peoples, today or in the past, have considered usage of alcohol to be a social problem. When temperance workers in the U.S. managed adoption of the eighteenth amendment to the Constitution and passage of the Volstead Act, they displayed eloquent examples of the disasters that had accompanied use of alcohol. Today, among the general population of the U.S.—as among the population of many nations—alcoholism constitutes a significant problem, and no system of therapy has been judged reliably successful for all types of drinkers.

In order to facilitate further discussion, let us distinguish among four styles of consumption of alcoholic beverages: (1) chronic alcoholism; (2) ritual drinking; (3) social drinking; (4) binge drinking. Alcoholism, properly speaking, is an *addiction* to alcohol, based on physiological habituation to a high level of alcohol within the bloodstream; when that level falls, the body is disequilibrated and the person suffers "withdrawal distress" (hangover), which he relieves by drinking (raising the level of alcohol in the bloodstream to what has become his norm). In order to stay comfortable, a chronic alcoholic finds that he must consume sizable quantities of alcohol at regular intervals. Unless he exercises caution, the effect of this consumption is deterioration of basic organ systems of his body (notably the liver) and marked reduction of his life span. While there are a few Indian alcoholics, the problem of Indian drinking is something quite different.

The religious rituals of many peoples require the participants to consume specified quantities of liquor. For example, adult participants in the Jewish Passover service are obliged to drink four glasses of wine; the communion service of some Christian denominations requires some or all of the participants to drink a small quantity of wine. As part of their ceremonials for rain, the Papago Indians of the Southwest attempted to achieve a state of drunkenness through consumption of fermented liquor from cactus fruit. The Indians of highland South America have incorporated periods of ritual drunkenness into their observance of certain Catholic ceremonials. These kinds of ritual drinking are clearly far different from chronic alcoholism, and since they are required as religious norms of the group, can scarcely be considered "social problems."

While sociable and binge drinking intergrade, the basic distinction is in the normative attitude of the company drinking together. In sociable drinking, the norm is "to hold one's liquor like a gentleman," while the norm in binge drinking is to get drunk. In the first case, the drinking companions are supposed to be convivial but to retain self-discipline in a number of basic categories (e.g., refraining from fighting, sexual assaults, and activities that are dangers to life or valuable property). In the second instance, the psychic condition of feeling drunk is valued. To some extent, the differences here may simply be of youth and social class, for the young men among many peoples spend much of their leisure hours in autonomous gangs that seek "kicks" or "action," and drinking in such "action-oriented" groups is often associated with public disorder, violence, or even death. The age range in sociable drinking is wider, often including the middle-aged or elderly, and the drinking situation is more routinized and regulated. If any individual begins to behave too boisterously, he is subjected to group sanction and ultimately to dismissal from the group.

Simply put, there is a high incidence among Indians of binge drinking. The context of this drinking is the peer association of young men, frequently resulting in an encounter with the police that leads to jailing, or in drunken driving at high speeds, which can lead to disaster for the occupants of the vehicle.

Given these sociocultural differences in the usage of alcohol, most attempts to "explain" drinking on the basis of individual psychology (e.g., people drink to escape from their problems) seem naive. In a fundamental sense, there is no more need to explain the use of alcohol than there is to explain the prevalence of sexual relationships, for the simple fact is that both are gratifying and pleasurable. What needs to be explained or understood are the ways people have evolved for curbing, disciplining, or ritualizing the consumption of alcohol (or the enjoyment of sexual relationships). Omer Stewart has argued that Western peoples have had a longer period of familiarity with both fermented beverages and distilled liquors, and therefore have had centuries, even millenia, in which to elaborate codes and rituals for handling them. Even so, these peoples remain dissatisfied with the consequences, and think of drinking as a social problem. The Indians of the Americas have had a briefer time to work out cultural responses to this novel and deadly challenge. Indians have the same problem in handling alcohol that is experienced by many other folk peoples, because they place positively high value on trance and vision states. Whereas a people with strong norms favoring disciplined rational conduct would be discomfited by the experiences of inebriation, these folk peoples give it a positive social reward.

However we endeavor to understand the differences between Indian and non-Indian relationships to alcoholic beverages, the fact is that much of the troubles Indians encounter with law enforcement agencies are grounded here. The rate of Indian arrests in 1960 for crimes related to alcohol was twelve times the national average and five times that of Negroes. Of all Indian arrests in that year, almost three-quarters were for drunkenness. Moreover, the problem is exaggerated in urban areas, for the rate of Indian arrests in the city is 24 times that in rural areas, and when only arrests for crimes related to consumption of alcohol are considered, the rate of arrests in cities jumps to 38 times that of rural areas (Stewart, 1964, p. 62).

Whether or not drinking is the major contributing factor, the statistics also show a disconcertingly high proportion of Indians in penal confinement. In South Dakota, where Indians form about 5 per cent of the total state population, they constitute over one-third of the prison population. About a quarter of the boys and half of the girls within the South Dakota State Training School (juvenile detention) are Indians (Stewart, 1964, p. 62). Figures such as these do not bear their meanings on their face: they may indicate differences in conduct, or they may—and this is more likely—indicate differences in social status and wealth which affect the ways in which agencies of criminal justice deal with deviant behavior. For example, in some small towns neighboring to the Pine Ridge Reservation, a high proportion of White drunks are sent home, but Indian drunks are incarcerated and sentenced to labor on public projects. The police might defend themselves on the grounds that, since the Indians come from the Reservation, which is dry, to drink in town, they have no "homes" to which they may be sent when drunk. It would, in addition, be a costly service to house them in jail. In areas where police forces utilize "arrest quotas" as devices to keep their men actively patrolling, there is a natural tendency for some patrolmen to meet their daily quota by victimizing a population that is politically powerless and socially conspicuous in a fashion judged negatively by community leaders.

CONCLUSIONS

This chapter has grouped together a number of ways in which Indians, as an ethnic group or national minority—rather than particular tribes—have responded to the invasion of the White Europeans. We began and ended with an emphasis on the use of alcohol, starting with Handsome Lake, whose creed had some of its psychic roots in his own and his fellows' struggles with drink, closing several centuries later with statistics showing the legal penalties Indians suffer through their drinking practices. Between these two points we have noted a number of social, political, and cultural movements, each of which has served to draw Indians together, so that slowly but significantly there is emerging a set of cultural practices, social institutions, and political agencies that are constitutive of Indians as a national minority within the total life of the U.S.

We should not oversimplify this development. Pan-Indian popular culture and pan-Indian political movements were for a time associated with each other, but in recent months have tended to diverge. Especially in the urban context, an increasing fission has grown between Indians oriented toward aggressive political action and those who wish to engage in singing and dancing. Nonetheless, the activists claim to represent the cultural Indians and regard themselves as the spokesmen of those who, being traditionalist in mentality and lower class in social position, are reluctant to speak for themselves in public confrontations. Thus the activists require a close linkage to those who engage in pan-Indian cultural performances, while the latter compose an unreliable political constituency.

SUGGESTED READINGS

Deardorff, Merle H. 1951. *The Religion of Handsome Lake: Its Origin and Development.* Washington, D.C.: U.S. Bureau of American Ethnology, Bulletin 149, pp. 79–107.

LaBarre, Weston. 1960. Twenty Years of Peyote Studies. *Current Anthropology,* 1, 1 (January), 45–60.

Lesser, Alexander. 1933. *The Pawnee Ghost Dance Hand Game.* New York: Columbia University Contributions to Anthropology, #16.

Lurie, Nancy O. 1969. *A Suggested Hypothesis for the Study of Indian Drinking.* Paper delivered at the annual meeting of the Central States Anthropological Society, Milwaukee, May.

Mooney, James. 1896. *The Ghost Dance Religion.* Washington, D.C.: U.S. Bureau of American Ethnology, Annual Report 14, Part 2.

Nash, Philleo. 1955. The Place of Religious Revivalism in the Formation of the Intercultural Community on Klamath Reservation, in *Social Anthropology of North American Tribes* (2nd ed.), ed. Fred Eggan. Chicago: University of Chicago Press.

Neihardt, John G. 1932. *Black Elk Speaks: Being the Life Story of a Holy Man of the Oglala Sioux.* Lincoln: University of Nebraska Press, Bison Books #119, 1961.

Parker, Arthur C. 1913. *The Code of Handsome Lake, The Seneca Prophet.* Albany: Education Department Bulletin No. 530; November 1, 1912, New York State Museum Bulletin #163, University of the State of New York.

Shimony, Annemarie A. 1961. *Conservatism among the Iroquois at the Six Nations Reserve.* New Haven: Yale University Publications in Anthropology #65.

Slotkin, James S. 1956. *The Peyote Religion: A Study in Indian-White Relations.* New York: The Free Press.

Stewart, Omer C. 1964. Questions Regarding American Indian Criminality. *Human Organization*, 23, 1, 61–66.

Thomas, Robert K. 1965. Pan-Indianism. *Midcontinent American Studies Journal*, 6, 2 (Fall), 75–83. Reprinted in *The American Indian Today*, ed. Stuart Levine and Nancy O. Lurie. Deland, Fla.: Everett/Edwards, 1968.

Wilson, Edmund. 1960. *Apologies to the Iroquois* (with Mitchell, *The Mohawks in High Steel*). New York: Random House, Inc., Vintage Books V-313, 1966.

NUMBERS, PLACES,
AND SOCIAL CLASSES

In order to speak precisely of Indians in cities, we should be able to specify exactly how many persons of what sort and in which places. But we encounter the familiar problem of trying to discover who is an Indian, or who is what kind of Indian. There are a few distinct urban tribal enclaves, as the Mohawk in the North Gowanus area of Brooklyn, N.Y., or the Sioux camps bordering Rapid City, S.D.. However, in most situations we run the risk of undercounting and ignoring those at the extreme points of the socioeconomic continuum. Those at the upper end of the scale may seek to avoid being identified as Indians except under special circumstances, while those at the lower end may either be so transient as to evade a survey or be so unprepossessing as to be ignored by survey workers or census enumerators.

Indians

in

the

Cities

At the upper end of the socioeconomic scale are persons, some of whose ancestors were Indians, but whose contemporary lives involve neither social ties with Indian communities nor membership in Indian associations. Their claim to Indian identity may emerge only in cases of distribution of a tribal estate. In short, they identify as Indian in an heirship sense, when there is benefit to be gained, but otherwise they prefer to dissociate themselves from both the tribal Indian, whom they consider backward, and from the lower class Indian, whom they consider inferior. This kind of conduct is not peculiar to middle or upper class Indians, but can also be found among "The Black Bourgeoisie," just as it was for a time characteristic of relationships between German Jews and Eastern European Jews in the United States. A significant difference between the Jewish and Indian cases is that the German Jews could not evade being identified with and held responsible for their lower class coreligionists, so, in addition to ethnic sentiment, they felt social pressures to assist and uplift them. The tribal nature of Indian life, and the pattern of diffused responsibility for the Indian condition, have led to a situation in which, for example, a middle class

Cherokee living in Los Angeles might well feel no relationship to or responsibility for a lower class Apache he encountered there. Accordingly, it is easy to underenumerate individuals of Indian background who have successfully achieved a middle class urban style of life in the generalized American format.

At the lower end of the socioeconomic scale are Indians plagued by poverty, disease, personal disorganization, and encounters with police and courts. They are usually residentially unstable, and therefore hard to locate and enumerate. Often they are strangers to the urban environment and unused to its institutions, but even when familiar with the city they may experience discrimination and derogation which lead them to withdraw from the use of service institutions. Their concentrations tend to be most extreme in cities near reservations or other aggregations of rural Indians: e.g., Gallup, N.M.; Rapid City, S.D.; Ponca City, Okla.; Scottsbluff, Nebr. The numbers and social patterns of the Indians in such areas tend to be unknown, for few persons are interested in establishing the facts. The federal census has relied heavily on lower middle class housewives, and they have proven to be less than thorough in their enumeration of lower class folk. To add to the confusion, these Indians tend to pack their modest baggage and flee, either to avoid the law and the bill collector, or to seek fresh opportunity elsewhere.

The easiest to enumerate and survey among Indians in the city are those in the stable working class, as they tend to maintain active participation in Indian institutions, including institutions with a substantial Indian membership or with an Indian service orientation, e.g., churches, mission societies, powwow associations, and Indian welfare centers. They are likely to be members of congregations which have a markedly Indian composition, and may even be participants in an urban section of the Native American Church. If there is a social center or association catering to Indian singing and dancing, they will probably be participants there. Finally, they are likely to have preserved strong attachments to family and kin in a reservation or rural context, and to journey there frequently. Obviously, such persons are easy to identify as Indians.

Turning to the U.S. Census, we remind the reader that a change in technique of identifying Indians may have led to an apparent increase in their numbers in 1960. In the 1950 census the population of Indians is given as about 350,000, whereas in the 1960 census it is 525,000. Some of this change may reflect the high rate of natural increase of Indian peoples, and some may simply reflect a superior technique of identifying them. With this caution in mind, we note that the 1950 census showed 56,000 Indians in urban localities, whereas in 1960 the number had risen to 146,000. The percentage increase in urban population is quadruple that of Negroes.

Cities like Los Angeles attract Indians from all over the U.S. Surveying that area in 1968, John Price found Indians from over 100 tribes, with predominant blocs from the Navajo, Sioux, and Civilized Tribes (Cherokee, Creek, Choctaw, Chickasaw, Seminole). Plains peoples predominated, but there were also representatives of such eastern seaboard peoples as Nanticokes. In all, Price estimates a population of about 25,-000 Indians for Los Angeles.

In contrast, the Twin Cities (Minneapolis and St. Paul) of Minnesota have recruited a much more homogeneous Indian population, of whom two-thirds were Chippewa, and an additional 10 per cent were either Sioux, Winnebago, or Menominee. This urban area attracts Indians from a smaller geographic region, mostly Minnesota, Wisconsin, and the Dakotas. Estimates are that its Indian population numbers six to eight thousand.

Quite a number of studies, as by the Boeks in Winnepeg (1959) or Hodge in Albuquerque (1969), do not even attempt an estimate of numbers of Indians, but instead report helpful data about particular samples encountered by interviewers or about contacts between Indians and caretaker agencies (e.g., schools, police, health clinics, welfare agencies).

FROM CAMP TO TOWN
IN ALASKA

Rarely do people move in one leap from a small rural camp to an urban metropolis. Usually the movement is by slow stages from rural camp to village to town to city to metropolis. The entire process may take several generations, as emotional and social ties to the earlier home are cut and the decision is eventually reached that greater opportunity is afforded by the more urbanized environment. Those who migrate tend both to be sentimental and cautious; many hope that they will make enough money to return to their homes in the more rural location and live in comfort and dignity rather than their previous condition of hardship. At the same time, their ties to the rural community are a kind of insurance, for should they fail in the strange world of the city, they can always return home and continue their lives.

The migrations of Alaskan Eskimo illustrate some of the earlier stages in the contemporary urbanizing process. Traditionally, the Eskimo practiced a hunting and gathering economy under conditions of great severity. Although they had evolved a highly complex series of skills and tools—such as the ice-house or igloo, the kayak, and fur clothing—they could manage to exist only as small bands who traveled far distances to exploit the biological resources of a vast territory. Since World War II— and the rise of military tension between the U.S. and the U.S.S.R.—these northernmost territories have been affected by all manner of projects for military defense, research, exploration, and development. The Distant Early Warning (DEW) line has involved a massive set of constructions under difficult arctic conditions, and for this labor the Eskimo have proven valuable employees. They in turn have perceived that life in towns is more comfortable, congenial, and secure than their previous nomadic existence. Unhappily, the job market continues to be of the boom or bust variety. A massive military project will get underway, offering abundant employment at good wages; after it is completed or phased out, there may follow a long period of dormancy until another agency with another project enters the area. Meantime, the Eskimo are trying to cope with problems generated by erratic monetary income and life in contact with institutions of a larger society.

In a study of Barrow—the northernmost permanent U.S. settlement —Arther E. Hippler (1969) sketches some of the dynamics of "urban" immigration and adaptation. Even though Barrow is a small town (population of 1,811 in 1967), he argues that the problems of a tribal folk undergoing urbanization are easier to perceive there. Eskimo began to move to Barrow in response to employment offered by the military, and remained there after the employment had disappeared. Then the U.S. Public Health Service (P.H.S.) decided to establish a medical facility in order to reduce high rates of infant mortality and infectious diseases among northern Eskimo. Perceiving in Barrow a high concentration of Eskimo at a strategic point, they decided to locate the facility there; the B.I.A., perceiving the high concentration of Eskimo youngsters, decided to establish a new school in Barrow. Coming together at the same time (1964), the two projects created a boom employment situation, and in consequence the neighboring rural regions were emptied of Eskimo; the process has been so extreme that some traditional Eskimo campsites are almost totally deserted.

When the boom employment failed again, the Eskimo remained, attracted by the school, the medical facility, other amenities of town, and the hope for further employment. Since the Eskimo have always been nomadic and enterprising, it is not surprising that they should come to Barrow to visit and observe; the significance is that, once there, they remain. One adaptation that has emerged is a family cluster in which one or two men work full time for cash, and another one or two devote themselves full time to hunting. The combination supports food, shelter, and

the pleasures of town living. The current style of hunting involves substantial cash investment, for dogteams have been displaced by snow ma-
chines which require parts and fuel.

Thus the Eskimo have become dependent upon cash income and
accustomed to the amenities of town life, but the process has exacted a
severe psychic toll. The history of contacts with the Whites has given the
Eskimo the notion that their ways of life are inferior; the town life confirms it. One sign of this is the pattern of intermarriage. Of the 35 marriages traced by Hippler in 1966 and 1967, no less than nine were Eskimo-
White, and all were of Eskimo women to White men. The same pattern
is widespread throughout Alaska and has generated strong anti-White
feelings among Eskimo men. Meanwhile, the out-migration of women is
abetted by agencies such as the B.I.A., whose orientation encourages Eskimo girls to think they are advancing themselves by marrying Whites
and leaving the area. Moreover, the high school which serves Barrow's
children is located in the southern part of the state; the brightest and
prettiest of the Eskimo girls are encouraged to enroll there and do not
return once they have departed.

The local magistrate and the town Elders, who are Eskimo, have so
internalized a puritanical White standard of morality that they actively
persecute youngsters of their community for engaging in conduct which
Eskimo traditionally have considered proper and natural. In recent years
the magistrate (an Eskimo woman) has had removed from the town no
less than 14 adolescent girls because they were indulging in "sexual
promiscuity": nine went to correctional institutions and five to foster
homes. Given these patterns of female out-migration, whether volun-
tarily to school or forcibly to correctional agencies, the sexual composition of the population is becoming badly skewed. More important, a dis-
astrously negative self-image has arisen among the Eskimo. For example,
the Eskimo authorities conceive that they have a drinking problem, yet
Hippler produces evidence to show that the Whites in Barrow drink 15
times as much per capita as do the Eskimo. Even if some of his data are
misleading, and some of the liquor purchased by Whites finds its way
into Eskimo bellies, it is clear that what constitutes "a drinking problem"
is mostly a matter of social perception. The Eskimo indulge in binge
drinking in public and in gangs, and the consequent behavior is much
more visible than the cocktail drinking of the Whites. The problems of
the Eskimo seem to be neither sexual activities nor drinking parties, but
the destructive self-hatred and self-derogation developing in these situations of intensive contact.

All too many of the teachers in the local school act to confirm the
self-derogation of the Eskimo children. As is typical of B.I.A. operated

schools, the building seems to be "surrounded by an invisible moat" (Hippler, 1969, p. 14). The educational personnel constitute a separate enclave, and most have never spent an evening with any of the Eskimo. Some teachers seemed to reach a satisfactory accommodation with their students and the community at large while keeping in balance with B.I.A. policy, but a significant core were disgruntled both with the B.I.A. and the Eskimo community, and defined their task as primarily one of instilling discipline into native children. Like many White persons, these teachers conceive of Eskimo children as "permissively raised," and believe there is a real need for physical punishment within the schools. These teachers do not perceive that the Eskimo have styles of disciplining children completely different from those that are traditional in White cultures. The problem for the pupils is the nature of the school as an agency controlled from without and serving as a missionary institution of the greater society. Not merely by its curriculum but by its very organization and system of status, the school provides an orientation in which the Eskimo are defined as a backward and inferior folk who must be transformed in order to fit with the greater modern society.

When the P.H.S. registered dramatic gains in its work, the consequence was a population explosion and more pressure upon the economy. In line with new federal policies, the P.H.S. began to preach the gospel of birth control, and in 1967 fitted 180 women of childbearing age in Barrow with intrauterine contraceptive devices (IUCD's), while providing general assistance in contraception to the women. The Eskimo men were not always consulted, and in this situation of erratic employment and psychic inferiority have responded with hostility, labeling the program as "genocidal." In consequence, relationships between the P.H.S. and the Eskimo community have deteriorated badly.

The situation in many other towns of Alaska is even more troublesome than that in Barrow. The Eskimo in Barrow maintain considerable control over their own community, but in towns like Kotzebue, the Whites control every agency of significance. Whites engage in steady criticism of Eskimo customs, and the latter have internalized this negative self-image and manifest a pathological derogation of their own traditions. In consequence, the symptoms of disorganization and conflict are far more severe, and recent years have witnessed the emergence of violent gangs among Eskimo youth.

Thus Alaska presents a picture of rapid and even pathological cultural change and assimilation among the Eskimo. The young women demonstrate a strong tendency toward hypergamy, i.e., marriage out of their group into the (theoretically) higher ranking society of the Whites. Among the Eskimo as a whole, there is a strong tendency to discard traditional crafts and the traditional style of life, and to enter the town version of urban life at the level of the lowest class. Intense rejection of their own traditions is accompanied by self-contempt, a variety of social pathologies, and abusive conflicts with the welfare agencies.

AN URBAN ENCLAVE

Immigrants who settled in America's cities during the great waves of migration between the Civil War and World War I did not do so as separate individuals randomly scattered throughout the urban area. They formed enclaves—miniature villages or cities—which became known as Little Italy, Polish Town, the (Jewish) Ghetto, Chinatown, and so on. Within this area of dense residential settlement, they elaborated distinctive institutions, catering to their special needs and tastes: churches with services conducted in the mother tongue, funeral homes, restaurants and grocery stores, lodges and sodalities and burial associations, and so on. Among the Italian-Americans of Boston, even as late as the 1930's—more than a generation after immigration—William Foote Whyte (1943) encountered a densely organized, distinctively Italian-American community. Twenty years later, Herbert J. Gans (1962) found Italian-Americans in a different area of Boston still well integrated with each other in an ethnically distinctive fashion. Less Italian in their customs (and no longer speaking the Italian language), these people were nonetheless solidary and preserved an intense and integrated social life together in the midst of the metropolis. On the other hand, they were unsuccessful in organizing themselves to preserve their neighborhood from the onslaught of "urban renewal and redevelopment." To social workers and reformers, their neighborhood appeared rundown and their society disorganized. This social critique was used by realtors and other municipal interest groups as a rationale for schemes which required destruction of the West End, and the Italian-Americans had not developed the political instrumentalities for defending their enclave against such a combined assault.

Indian migrants to the city exhibit the same patterns as European migrants of a half-century ago. Given the opportunity, they cluster together residentially and elaborate distinctive institutions which are neither traditional nor urban middle class, but which enable them as a community to fabricate a meaningful existence in this new environment. Comprehension of these patterns and institutions requires prolonged immersion within the urban community; Whyte spent three years in Cornerville, Gans about eight months in the West End. But most studies of urban Indians are performed far more hastily and with the goal of simply reporting numbers, economic conditions, and personal problems.

In a sense, most researchers act as agents of "caretaker agencies"—schools, clinics, welfare agencies—interested in measuring the quantity and quality of need for their services, and whose staff—like the settlement house workers, educators, and librarians of Cornerville and the West End—misperceive the nature of the social life of the ethnic community. Only occasionally do we encounter reports of Indian urban communities which are functioning so successfully that the investigators have had to approach them as social unities rather than as aggregates of discrete individuals. It is intriguing that the functioning communities are not so different in culture and ethos from the depressed and impoverished ones; they have just been more fortunate in their economic encounters.

In 1714 John Lawson remarked of the Tuscarora that "They will walk over deep Brooks, and Creeks, on the smallest Poles, and that without any Fear or Concern" (cited in Wallace, 1951, p. 64). The Tuscarora are a branch of the Iroquois, and it was at the tribal reserve of another branch, the Caughnawagas, that this fearless conduct impressed itself on those managing construction of a bridge across the St. Lawrence River. Thus in 1886 the Caughnawaga (pronounced Ka-na-wá-ke) men entered upon high steel work as a vocation and a style of life. The men enlisted each other and, as time passed, inducted their youth into the craft. Other Iroquoian peoples subsequently entered the field, particularly the St. Regis Mohawk and various bands of Seneca in New York State, but this account will focus on the Caughnawagas (also traditionally known as "Christian Mohawks").

Work on the high iron fitted well with the warrior ethos of the Iroquois. Much of the work is performed by small gangs who must know each other's ways and mesh their efforts in a fabric of trust and egalitarian cooperation. The fact that the work is dangerous has made it seem even more desirable. After a catastrophe in 1907—when the collapse of a bridge under construction resulted in the death of 35 Caughnawaga men —the work became, if anything, more attractive to men of the reservation. The sole effect was to lead the women to insist that so large a body of their menfolk no longer work on the same structure, lest the whole community be widowed in another catastrophe.

The Iroquois are a matrilineal people—groups of blood-related women are the core of the institutional structure of the society. Married daughters settle near their mothers, and the family units remain integrated. While the men roam in warrior style, the women maintain a separate world in which the children are raised and integration of community is preserved. Men look to the women as providing a stable locus where food, shelter, maternal affection, and domestic pleasures are available, and where their children will be conceived and reared. The women secure what they can of the men's earnings, being watchful lest all be consumed in drink and dissipation. The picture may appear pathological to observers accustomed to the patterns of middle class America, but the Iroquois have been functioning effectively for centuries, and the adaptation to high steel is merely a recent variation suiting an industrial environment.

Perhaps most congenial to these men is the opportunity for joint adventure and travel. Leaving their wives and children, they go from one construction site to another, all over North America (and perhaps today all over the world). Their stay at any particular location depends not merely on the wages or conditions, but on their interest in the job. Mitchell (1949) reports how a band left good work in Manhattan in order to journey across the country and labor on the Golden Gate Bridge; Blumenfeld (1965, p. 20) states that "to excel on the high scaffold is to prove oneself both as a man and as an Indian." Men use the occasion of a funeral wake to recite the exploits on and off the high steel not only of the deceased, but of those who have been dead for many years, and the pattern is reminiscent of Indian men praising the warrior deeds of their ancestors. While the men value work of this kind, they have little use for farming, so that while every member of the tribe has a plot on the reserve in Quebec—about two miles south of Montreal—few bother to cultivate the lands, and most rent their shares to outsiders (usually French-Canadians).

Even though the men enjoy roaming and the women prefer the company of their mothers and sisters, urban colonies have developed in Brooklyn and in other cities of steady employment, such as Buffalo and Detroit. The Brooklyn colony arose in the 1920's and is situated in a small area known as North Gowanus. Responding to the Indian presence are bars that cater exclusively to their custom and a Presbyterian Church whose minister offers services in the Mohawk language.

The size of the Brooklyn colony has varied with economic conditions. During the Great Depression, the tribal reserve provided a refuge where Indians could receive governmental and missionary assistance. With the boom in construction since the start of World War II, the Brooklyn colony has swelled in size and now numbers about 800. But North Gowanus is not home, and almost all Indians look to retiring to the tribal reserve in Quebec. Indeed, many children are sent back there to be educated, since most Caughnawagas are Catholic and the parochial school on the reserve is free, whereas that in Brooklyn charges tuition. The reserve is especially attractive in summertime, not only because of its leisure activities (swimming, boating, fishing), but because money can be made from the tourists. The fact that the reserve is less than a day's drive away from Brooklyn means that families as well situated as the Caughnawagas, and as accustomed to travel, can make the journey frequently. Blumenfeld notes that any Mohawk who wants a ride to the reserve can go to the local tavern on Friday night and be assured of a seat in a car driven by his kindred.

As a tribal offshoot from the Iroquois, the Caughnawagas came into existence under Jesuit influence. A substantial minority has since become Protestant, and some have become Longhouse people according to the revelation of Handsome Lake. The Caughnawagas have maintained Mohawk as their primary domestic language, and most speak English and some French as well. The Longhouse services in Mohawk have an appeal even to Christians, and traditional spiritual beliefs are still influential. Caughnawagas will return to the reserve in order to consult native therapists or to secure special medicines, for belief in the traditional Mohawk deities and even in witches remains strong even among those who are presumptively Christian.

The story of the Caughnawagas contains many lessons for those concerned with planning policy for Indian affairs, and especially for assisting Indians to secure off-reservation employment. Relocation is so often considered in terms of the individual or the nuclear family, when —as in the case of European immigrants to U.S. cities—it is the presence of the community and the opportunity to work together with men of one's kith and kin which is important. A strange city is a poor environment for a solitary tribal man.

THE SIOUX IN RAPID CITY

The Sioux communities of Rapid City have been under study by Robert A. White, S.J., for some years. Having taught in the mission boarding school at the Pine Ridge Reservation of the Oglala Sioux, White was familiar with Sioux reservation life before he embarked on his more urban efforts. His professional field is anthropology, and his reports on the Sioux rely both on his own observations and on surveys conducted by assistants and associates.

Rapid City is strategically located on natural routes of travel near the Black Hills of western South Dakota. Beginning as a center for mining, lumbering, ranching, and tourism, in the 1950's it became the site of an air base of the Strategic Air Command, and by 1964 its population was near 50,000. The military expansion created job and economic opportunities of various sorts, while the location—within a day's drive of several major reservations—made it convenient for the Sioux to try their luck there, and easy for them to return to natal communities for pleasure or in case of difficulties. By the mid-1950's the population of Sioux in the city had risen to nearly 5,000, living in housing that ranged from tents and tarpaper shacks to ranch style homes in the new subdivisions.

The Sioux in Rapid City may be differentiated into at least three types. At one pole are those who, following Gans (1962), we may term the "middle class mobiles." Some have been in Rapid City for a decade or more; others have moved more recently from reservation areas, but in this case they derive from these we have described as "the Mixedblood elite." They had already dissociated themselves from the Fullblood bands within the reservation, and had oriented themselves about the welfare of the nuclear family. In the reservation situation they were minor employees of the B.I.A. or other state agencies, or had worked in commercial farming or ranching enterprises. In the urban locale they think of "getting ahead," orienting themselves toward the education of their children, and talking of "improving themselves." They are at pains to express their antipathy toward reservation culture and the living habits of the Fullbloods. Despite these maneuvers, the middle class mobiles are not moving into non-Indian society, at least not in any rapid fashion.

Worthy of mention are those who might be labeled "upper middle class White Indians." On the appropriate social occasion, such as a dinner or cocktail party, knowing that their auditor is "interested in Indians," they will mention an Indian forebear, invariably female, several generations back (e.g., "My great-grandmother was a niece of Chief Crazy Horse"). These individuals are descendants of Mixedblood families which made good in ranching, mining, or trading. Their only ties to the lives of Sioux communities may be as members of the boards of benevolent associations. They live in a world far different and more secure than the middle class mobiles.

Those who are called "Indians" in an invidious sense, and who constitute "the Indian Problem," are referred to by Robert White as "Camp Indians." They come to the city from impoverished, usually rural, reservation conditions. Relatively unskilled and undereducated, they may speak little English, and what they do speak is a dialect of low status ("substandard"). They have come to the city out of economic necessity, hoping to secure a job of some sort. Lacking any resources of capital or skills, they cannot frame long-range plans, and build their lives from day to day, dealing with each crisis as it comes. Not oriented toward the middle class, they are not perceptive of the status value attached to housing, and import reservation standards as they try to survive under conditions of difficulty or desperation. In the early 1950's the low areas along Rapid Creek, and other underdeveloped areas close to places of employment, became the sites of tents or shacks which constituted Sioux encampments.

These were distasteful to the good folk of Rapid City because of the packs of dogs, litter, crowding, and social habits, such as occasional drunken brawls. Classifying these residential areas as "substandard housing," the city forced their inhabitants out, and the camps were relocated beyond the city limits, away from the judgments of building inspectors.

Life for many Camp Indians is perpetually insecure. Employment may be erratic and financial resources minimal; agencies of the larger society are perceived as indifferent or hostile. The men have been accustomed to finding security among their peers, as the women among theirs, but in the urban context they are no longer associating with a stable and well integrated society of kith and kin. Associations in the urban camps are more brittle, and the young folk of either sex tend to participate in a culture of excitement (cf. the description of "lower-class action-seekers" in Gans, 1962, pp. 24–32). The life of this culture is characterized by excessive drinking, physical violence, frequent travel, sexual exploits, and violations of the law. While some cultural threads connect this style of life to the warrior history of the Sioux, much stronger influences come from the lower class action-seekers of the general urban environment, be they Indian, Mexican, Negro, or ranchhand White. Thus the Camp Sioux of Rapid City pick up styles of conversation, dress, singing, and overall conduct from other members of the urban proletariat.

The action-seeking mode of life is not peculiar to Indians, nor is it peculiar to the lower classes. Its appeal is to the young, especially males, of all ethnicities. The surest reformatives have always been age and the opportunity for a respected, secure, and satisfactory life. As Gans reports of his action-seeking Italian-Americans, most settle down into a routine working class existence. The same transition is plainly visible in Fullblood communities on the reservation, where the wild and exciting existence of the young gives way to a more settled mode of life, as energy declines, emotional attachments mature, children multiply and develop, and some form of livelihood becomes available.

On the other hand, the conditions of life of an oppressed, urban ethnic minority tend to foster an action-seeking style. Well-paying, stable, and respected employment remains scarce, and least available to the young men. Welfare agencies regard them as the least desirable clients. Police harassment often breaks the cycle of employment, and a police record makes a man even less appealing as a potential employee. In their efforts to disrupt the peer society and emphasize the marital union, case workers often blunder and leave the individual without any stable social linkages.

It is striking to contrast the description of Camp Sioux with that of the high steel Caughnawagas. In both cases, a warrior culture prevails among the men, but in one instance it is harnessed to the performance of important, well-paying, and respected work, while in the other, it is an unwanted community resource which stimulates varieties of assault from agencies of the greater society.

Between the middle class mobiles and the Camp Sioux are a stratum desperately seeking to establish a secure and routine existence in Rapid City. Some remain in the camps and try to be good Sioux, living up to norms of generosity and hospitality, but with little use for chronic drunkenness and brawling. Others have moved out of the camps and rented modest homes; they have achieved some degree of security, but without the opportunity or interest for the future oriented planning of the middle class mobiles.

MINNEAPOLIS

Just as the other Indian and migrant peoples we have mentioned, Indians come to Minneapolis seeking jobs, but many of them are unprepared to secure and maintain employment within a competitive urban society. Coming out of an environment of rural poverty, they possess few clothes and little money. They move in with friends or relatives who—by the standards of middle class society—are already overcrowded. Faced with the usual apparatus of employment and personnel offices, including complex application schedules, interviews, referrals, and intimate questioning, they are disconcerted, and tend (as rural Indians generally do) to withdraw. Their dialect, grooming, dress, and response to bureaucratic situations make them seem less than desirable for good employment. Finding it hard to relate to conventional bureaucracies filled with strange people and difficult situations, they look for Indian agencies, but being Indian does not qualify them for special services. The B.I.A. services derive legally from its responsibilities as trustee of Indian lands; services are not provided for Indians generally, or for Indians who happen to have arrived in the city.

Responding to the social problems presented by these Indians, a research team at the University of Minnesota has attempted to gather basic facts and figures (Woods and Harkins, 1968a,b). Under the direction of Arthur Harkins, and using a variety of student and volunteer labor, it has interviewed Indians and analyzed the files of agencies which have a troublesome Indian clientele. One feature of the research is especially noteworthy: in addition to surveying Indians themselves, the researchers have surveyed agency personnel, and tried to convey some of what Indians face when coming into contact with them.

A school count (November 1967) showed 1,357 Indian children, highly concentrated in three schools. The dropout rate is high, and many are enrolled late in the fall term, some losing as much as eight weeks of school. It is likely that the lateness is a reflection of the summer rural location of a family engaged in ricing (harvesting wild rice) or hunting. As in most schools throughout the U.S., the Indian child confronts history and civics textbooks written exclusively from the point of view of the White invaders of his ancestral lands.

In disproportion to their small ratio in the total metropolitan population, Indians are heavily represented among those handled by the police and courts. Most crimes of which they are accused are misdemeanors—drunkenness, disorderly conduct, vagrancy, simple assault, traffic offenses—but the records show that of those persons sent to the Minneapolis Workhouse in 1966, 22 per cent of all women and 11 per cent of all men were Indian. Generally speaking, Indians seem ignorant of the law and of their rights and duties in relation to it. Moreover, they are also ignorant of the mechanisms of probation, and when offered it they frequently violate its terms. Their arrests probably come as much from poverty and homelessness as from conduct, for a man who is encountered drunk, penniless, and without identification on skid row is more likely to be arrested than a similar individual with a wallet full of money in a fashionable neighborhood. None of the agencies of criminal justice had any Indian employees.

Again in disproportion to their small ratio in the population, Indians are heavily represented among the recipients of public assistance, numbering 10 per cent of those receiving public relief in Minneapolis. Of all counties in Minnesota, Hennepin has the most Indian families receiving A.F.D.C., amounting to one-third of the Indian A.F.D.C. group for the state.

Erratically, there has been an American Indian Employment and Guidance Center. Operating with sporadic funding, it opened in 1962 and closed in 1968. An analysis was conducted of the records of 743 persons who had sought assistance during the summer of 1967. The data reveal a population which is young, single, male, and largely Chippewa, has strong ties to the reservation, and is highly mobile between the reservation and the city, and within the city itself. These persons are poorly educated, lacking skills, and without union affiliation. Their income is marginal, and they have neither debts, car, nor welfare monies; over half of them either did not know or could not report the cost of their rent or utilities. While some had graduated from high school, differences between their status and that of the dropouts was minor.

When interviews were conducted in residential areas known to have heavy concentrations of Indians, a different sort of image appeared. The persons encountered were middle-aged, reasonably stable, married, and with children. Mainly Chippewa, they had been born on a reservation and lived there for years; although they return to the reservation occasionally, they have become stable residents of the city. While they are employed at blue collar, nonunion labor, they manifest some striving for upward occupational mobility. This population appears to have made a successful adjustment to the city and to be markedly similar to their White neighbors.

The findings of Harkins and his associates for Minneapolis and of White for Rapid City present a neat counterpoint. It is likely that if White were to work in the Twin Cities he would encounter some of the same types of communities and adaptations he found in the west. On the other hand, the sheer size and density of Minneapolis make it impossible for Indians to construct their "camps" within or near its center. Accordingly, phenomena which White found for the Rapid City camps could occur in Minneapolis only in the more heterogeneous slum neighborhoods of the inner city. Harkins argues that some of the difficulties experienced by new migrants to the city could be obviated or reduced by special intake agencies and centers for Indian sociability and assistance; it is likely that Robert White would agree.

CONCLUSIONS

Given the difficulties and instabilities of life in a modern urban industrial society, no mode of adaptation can resolve all problems. Some adaptations, such as the Eskimo in the Alaskan town or the Camp Sioux of Rapid City, appear to be pathological, not merely because of the critical judgments of outsiders, but because the Indians themselves have internalized severely self-critical judgments. They think of their peoples and traditional ways as inferior or even evil, and in trying to come to terms with these judgments indulge to excess in drinking, violence, and erratic conduct. As reformers have argued, one way out is cultural assimilation on the model of the Anglo-Saxon middle class. Some Indians, being of Mixedblood culture and social background, find this pathway congenial, and their movement from the reservation usually solidifies a successful transformation. Whatever self-hatred they feel can be safely directed against the Indians with whom they do not wish to be identified, namely the lower class youth engaged in public violence and drunkenness.

Quite contrary to the views of most reformers, the very ethos and culture of the Indians sometimes allows successful adaptations to urban roles. In contemporary times, the Mohawk Indians who engage in high steel work constitute an outstanding example. The same warrior traits which brand the Camp Indian as undesirable are present among the Mohawk, but channeled in the context of a respected and well-paying occupational career. Mohawk men live and travel in male gangs. They drink, fight, and leave their families and children behind, but they work hard and under dangerous conditions, and contribute to maintain a stable and well integrated community. The Mohawk have achieved an occupational adjustment without undergoing a deracinating cultural assimilation. They have successfully created for themselves a niche in the complex interstices of modern industrial society.

Meanwhile, Indians are continuing to enter the urban environment. Some remain; some leave. Some make the attempt many times in their lifetimes. These peoples would doubtless find the adaptation easier if there were a functioning community (like "Cornerville" in Whyte, 1943) into which they could fit and where they could secure advice, food, shelter, and leads to employment. Without the existence of a community already functioning successfully—a North Gowanus rather than a Rapid City "camp"—the Indian migrant could surely use agencies of advice and assistance that are congenial to his style of interaction and could be concretely helpful. Cities like Chicago have several Indian centers which meet this need, at least to some extent. Clearly the need is more general.

SUGGESTED READINGS

Blumenfeld, Ruth. 1965. Mohawks: Round Trip to the High Steel. *TRANSaction* (November-December).

Boek, Walter E., and Jean K. Boek. 1959. The People of Indian Ancestry in Greater Winnipeg. Appendix I of *A Study of the Population of Indian Ancestry Living in Manitoba*, Jean H. Lagassé, director. Winnipeg: The Department of Agriculture and Immigration.

Freilich, Morris. 1958. Cultural Persistence among the Modern Iroquois. *Anthropos*, 53, 473–483.

————. 1970. Mohawk Heroes in Structural Steel, in *Marginal Natives: Anthropologists at Work*, ed. Morris Freilich. New York: Harper & Row, Publishers.

Gans, Herbert J. 1962. *The Urban Villagers: Group and Class in the Life of Italian-Americans*. New York: The Free Press.

Glazer, Nathan, and Daniel Patrick Moynihan. 1963. *Beyond the Melting Pot: The Negroes, Puerto Ricans, Jews, Italians, and Irish of New York City*. Cambridge, Mass.: The M.I.T. Press.

Hippler, Arthur E. 1969. *Barrow and Kotzebue: A Comparison of Acculturation in Two Big Villages in Northwest Alaska*. College, Alaska: Institute of Social, Economic and Government Research, University of Alaska. Mimeo'd.

Hodge, William H. 1969. *The Albuquerque Navajos.* Anthropological Papers of the University of Arizona, No. 11. Tucson: University of Arizona Press.

League of Women Voters. 1968. *Indians in Minneapolis.* Minneapolis: League of Women Voters.

Mitchell, Joseph. 1949. *The Mohawks in High Steel.* Orig. pub.: *The New Yorker,* Vol. 25. Reprinted in 1966 (with Wilson, *Apologies to the Iroquois*). New York: Random House, Inc., Vintage Books V-313.

Price, John A. 1968. The Migration and Adaptation of American Indians to Los Angeles. *Human Organization,* 27, 2 (Summer), 168–175.

Smith, Valene. 1966. Kotzebue: A Modern Alaska Eskimo Community. Unpublished Ph.D. dissertation, Department of Anthropology, University of Utah.

Suttles, Gerald D. 1968. *The Social Order of the Slum: Ethnicity and Territory in the Inner City.* Chicago: University of Chicago Press.

Wallace, Anthony F. C. 1951. *Some Psychological Determinants of Culture Change in an Iroquoian Community.* U.S. Bureau of American Ethnology, Bulletin 149, 59–76.

White, Robert A., S.J. n.d. *The Urban Adjustment of the Sioux Indians in Rapid City, South Dakota.* Mimeo'd progress report.

Whyte, William Foote. 1943. *Street Corner Society: The Social Structure of an Italian Slum* (2nd ed. 1955). Chicago: University of Chicago Press, Phoenix Books.

Wilson, Edmund. 1966. *Apologies to the Iroquois* (with Mitchell, *The Mohawks in High Steel*). New York: Random House, Inc., Vintage Books V-313.

Woods, Richard G., and Arthur M. Harkins. 1968a. *Attitudes of Minneapolis Agency Personnel Toward Urban Indians.* Minneapolis: University of Minnesota, Training Center for Community Programs. Mimeo'd.

———. 1968b. *Indian Employment in Minneapolis.* Minneapolis: University of Minnesota, Training Center for Community Programs. Mimeo'd.

IDEOLOGIES OF
INDIAN-WHITE RELATIONSHIPS

Throughout this book we have focused upon the ideologies or conceptual models (cf. Gordon, 1964) by which various Indian and White groups have related to each other. We began by noting that the diverse peoples of the Americas were lumped together and denominated as "Indians," while the equally diverse invaders and immigrants from Europe (or Africa) were lumped together as "Whites" (or "Negroes" or "Blacks"). With the passage of time, the Indian appellation has acquired a cultural as well as a social reality. In the U.S. today there is a widespread sense of

Ideology,

Identity, and

the "Indian

Problem"

Indian identity, bolstered by pan-Indian associations and pan-Indian cultural practices. Yet, throughout the Americas, most persons denominated as Indians share this identity only to a minor degree; most of the time they think of themselves as members of local bands of kith and kin, or of particular tribal groups, and not as something so vague and general as "Indian." (In like manner, their White counterparts do not think of themselves so much as "White" as they see their primary identity in terms of family, ethnicity, religious affiliation, or professional occupation.)

Given the bifurcation into Indian and White, the conceptual models for this interaction have ranged among genocide, innate inferiority, Euroconformity, melting pot, and cultural pluralism. Let us review each of these.

Genocide

Some of the invaders regarded the Indians as troublesome vermin that might beneficially be exterminated. Sometimes they conducted formal military campaigns emphasizing a scorched earth policy, slashing orchards, burning crops, wrecking buildings, and razing and ruining as they proceeded. Sometimes they relied upon biological warfare, sending the

174

Indians clothing known to be infected with smallpox, diphtheria, or other diseases to which Indians had little resistance. As a consequence, today there are large areas of the Americas where no Indians are to be found. From Newfoundland to Argentina, from the Caribbean to the Californias, are places where Indians were deliberately exterminated by peoples who thought the slaughter justifiable, or even moral. Almost no portion of the Western hemisphere and almost no period of time have been free from traces of this approach to Indian relationships. Even as recently as 1970, newspapers were reporting the use of dynamite, machine guns, and biological warfare within Brazil against bands of Indians who were few in number and primitive in technology.

Innate Inferiority

Some invaders thought of Indians as innately (racially) inferior beings who might be employed and exploited just as Europeans did cattle or other animals. This orientation is not inconsistent with slaughter, since a man holding this view might treat Indians as if they were game to be hunted (as did the men of DeSoto's expedition), but the goal here was sport, not systematic extermination of a pestiferous creature. The orientation is most consistent with slavery, and Spanish (and English) settlers did attempt to utilize Indians as enforced labor, but the Indians proved unsatisfactory for plantation type situations. In many cases the death toll among Indian laborers was excessively great, as they simply could not or would not adapt to conditions of confinement, brutal hardship, and forced labor. Despite the presence of an Indian population, plantation owners soon found that they had to turn elsewhere, beyond the Americas, for cheap and docile labor. The slave trade brought Africans by the hundreds of thousands into the Caribbean and the eastern coasts of the Americas. When the slave trade was abolished, indentured laborers were brought from Asia. In consequence, the overwhelming proportion of the population in areas like modern Guyana is either of African or Hindu descent, with only a small number of isolated and rural American Indians.

The ideology of Indian inferiority has remained dominant in many areas of the Americas. Persons in the upper classes in several Latin American countries speak of Indians as animals or brutes, while in many areas of the U.S. (e.g., Arizona, Oklahoma, the Dakotas) Indians are regarded by much of the populace as is the Negro in the Deep South, being derogated as dirty, drunken, and idle, and subjected to segregation in schooling, housing, and dining.

Euroconformity

At all times there have been men of conscience to protest against the foregoing ideological orientations. Missionaries (notably as early as the sixteenth century, the Dominican Bartolomé de Las Casas) argued that the Indian was a human being made in the image of God and endowed with an immortal soul. The duty of the invaders was to bring to him the message of the Gospels and to enlist him into the Christian world. Given the diversity of such missionaries and their national orientations, it would not be satisfactory to speak simply here (as does Gordon, 1964) of "Anglo-Conformity," and we might indeed have to speak of "Hispano-Catholic-Conformity" or "Anglo-Protestant-Conformity." (It is worth noting that Greek Orthodox missionaries from Russia labored in Alaska, and that German Mennonites have labored throughout the Americas, as have French and Portuguese Catholic and Dutch Calvinist.)

Within the Euroconformist ideology, the Indian was also regarded as inferior, but by virtue of his religious condition, not his racial constitution. According to this view, the Indian was an uncivilized heathen, and missionaries thought of themselves as fulfilling the blessed work of inducting him into the Christian church and thereby into the international community of civilized peoples. Instruction in the Spanish language and the Spanish culture of peasant life was coexistent with instruction in Spanish Catholicism (as in later centuries went corresponding instruction in the English language and English farming culture). Broadly speaking, these activities could be defined as educational, and the missionaries as engaged in a process of educating an entire community. Thus the Euroconformist ideology was manifested in a movement of missionizing and educating that has endured since the sixteenth century and has involved a great number of Catholic religious orders (e.g., Dominican, Jesuit, Augustinian) and a great diversity of religious denominations (e.g., Roman Catholic, Greek Orthodox, Methodist, Baptist, Pentecostal), as well as many persons and considerable funds. Some missionaries, of great nobility of character, came to appreciate the ethical and spiritual content of traditional Indian cultures and to relate to Indians as fellow human beings rather than moral inferiors. Others have exhibited the most extreme types of ethnocentric snobbery. Few of the missionaries made any effort to learn the native language of those they wished to recruit as their flock; few of those who made the effort did in fact learn to speak the language. Perhaps most significant is the fact that the mission system has continued to endure. In the U.S. today there are mission establishments for Indians which are over a century old; indeed, some tribes have been exposed for several centuries to missionaries of a particular denomination (considering, for example, that the Catholics came with the Spanish into the Southwest early in the sixteenth century, and the French into the Northeast in the seventeenth century). Thus, in numerous instances the relationship between White and Indian continues to be a variant of "Mission-Conformity."

In one sense, to speak of these as ideologies of conformity is misleading. What the missionaries and educators had in mind were not the actualities of the social life from whence their mission was supported. Indians were not to be transformed into replicas of conquistadores or English sailors, but into saintly Christian versions of those ethnic types. Recognizing the depravities of their European countrymen, the missionaries often tried to impose social isolation upon their Indian flock to shelter them from intimacy with such evil exemplars. During the seventeenth century, the Dominican missionaries tried to establish an ideal Catholic commonwealth in the isolation of Paraguay; Protestant missionaries in the U.S. during the nineteenth century tried to keep their Indian flocks isolated on reservations and away from the seductive examples of traders, soldiers, and explorers. If Whites who professed to be Christians engaged in numerous violations of codes governing sexual morality, Indians who were the target of the missionary effort were not to fall into that pit of vice.

The artificial isolation did not produce a race of Indian saints, but the insistence that Indians were to become ideal men has helped to disguise the magnitude of the transformations which the Indian peoples have made. Indians are today greatly different from what they once were (in earlier chapters we have outlined some of the representative transformations). They have adopted many of the cultural traits brought by the invaders, and have participated in further changes and evolutions of the national societies in which they are located. Yet there remains what is termed "an Indian problem" and an enduring image of an unchanging Indian (cf. Wax, 1968). To those who reason according to the Conformist conceptual model, the Indian appears to be a problem because he does not change—at least, not in the way and at the rate that they think he should.

Social scientists as well as missionaries and educators have oriented their thinking about a Conformist ideology. Many students of Indian affairs have postulated a simple continuum, at one pole of which is "the traditional Indian" and at the other pole "the middle class American." Then they have envisaged the progress of the Indian as an imaginary movement along that pathway leading to eventual assimilation. The Indian culture would gradually disappear as its various traits were replaced by corresponding traits of middle class American culture; the researcher could mark the "progress" of Indians as they moved along the continuum. We have already touched on many of the difficulties of this conceptualization, but we might note that it makes the U.S. (or other nations) appear as an artificial cultural unity, for it accepts the image of a middle class culture as normative for the nation. Some actual Indians in the actual United States have indeed assimilated into the middle class to such a degree that they are indistinguishable from their counterparts of Euroamerican ancestry. But many other Indians have been adapting themselves to a working class or lower class style of life.

The Caughnawaga men who work in high steel do so with the flair of the classical, itinerant, adventurous, autonomous band of craftsmen. They work in teams rather than as discrete individuals; they become bored with jobs and, regardless of pay, quit impulsively to labor on novel jobs in exotic localities; they travel as bachelor gangs, leaving wives and children at home; and so on. The pattern appears to be like the Indian war party, but it also shows marked similarities to lower class masculine subculture. Moreover, many characteristics regarded as peculiar vices or handicaps of Indians are actually widespread among lower class groups: subordination of the nuclear family to the peer societies of men and women and to larger kinship groupings; orientation of the peer society of young men toward "action" or "kicks" (including drink, casual sex, brawling, gambling, speed, and risky enterprise challenging to conventional authority); allegiance to particular persons rather than to abstract ideals or moral principles. As a tool of social scientific analysis, the conceptual model of Conformity suffers because it ignores (1) the diversity of cultures (or styles of living) within the nation as a whole, (2) the diversity of Indian societies, past and present, and (3) the multiform transformations of Indian societies.

Melting Pot

The alloying of Indians and Europeans has long been underway in countries like Mexico and Guatemala. A large mass of people have emerged—the Mestizos—who are mainly Indian in ancestry but who have adopted many Hispanic or European traits, such as speaking Spanish, wearing Western clothes, practicing a variant of Catholicism, and familial and kinship patterns. Some recognizably Indian traits remain, most conspicuously in the cuisine based on native American foods (maize, beans, chili peppers). The comparative magnitudes of European and Indian heritages have become a source of argument, not merely for historians of culture, but for ideologists of the national state. For a long time the dominant attitude of Mexican intellectuals was exemplified by José Vasconcelos, who argued that the Indian cultures had fallen before the stronger, more virile, culture of the Spaniards, so that the character of Mexico had been stamped by European civilization. Accordingly, the fate of such Indian groups as remained must be "Hispanic conformity." Opposed to these Europeanists have been the Indianistas (e.g., Manuel Gamio), who have argued that the Spanish, as persons or bearers of culture, have always been a small minority, and that the tenor of Mexican life, in the past and for the future, is Indian. This ideological argument as to the dominant ingredient in Mexico's melting pot translates into a practical argument concerning governmental policies toward the enclaved Indian peoples. If the heritage and destiny of Mexico are European, then programs for Indians must be Euroconformist (or assimilationist); but if the heritage and destiny are really Indian, then the program for peoples who have remained Indian (rather than becoming Mestizo) should capitalize on their cultural uniqueness.

Via Mexican-Americans, this ideological debate has become relevant to the situation of Indians in the U.S. Chicano militants have started to speak of the Southwest as *Aztlán* (an Aztec term), thus identifying themselves, in their rights and status, with the Indians who were overrun by Spaniards and other Euroamericans. They reject the legitimacy of the land claims of those presently considered owners of the land (whether local ranchers or the U.S. Forest Service), and they reject as well the Treaty of Guadalupe Hidalgo (1848) whereby the U.S. seized large areas of land which had long been settled and occupied by Mexican Americans (and Indian peoples).

There have been only a few instances when a melting pot conceptualization seemed to be actualizing itself within North America. The most notable "melt" is the case of the Métis, discussed in an earlier chapter, where French men and Indian women conjoined to create a society marginal to both the Euroamerican and the native Indian. However, with the passage of time, the Métis have been forced to assume the structural position of an Indian tribe, despite their French cultural heritage. Significantly, much recent Canadian administrative planning has concerned Indians, Eskimos, and Métis conjointly, despite the marked differences in culture which once distinguished them.

Parallel instances within the U.S. concern the Six Nations and the Cherokee. In each case there was a significant degree of intermarriage with Whites, especially at elite levels of the tribe, and concomitantly the marked rise of new political forms (formally organized "nations" or "republics" and "leagues of nations"). Each seemed to be evolving in a melting pot sense, creatively integrating traditional native traits with those of the European (invention of the Cherokee syllabary by Sequoyah exemplifies this creative integration). Yet in both instances it proved impossible to maintain a position of structural separateness and relative autonomy. The sovereignties of these "Indian Nations" were destroyed by political and military actions, and could no longer serve as the social crucibles wherein the cultural melting could occur. A bifurcation has come about among the contemporary Cherokee of northeastern Oklahoma. The elite group has evolved toward the conventional middle or upper class of the U.S., while the mass of people has retreated toward a separate cultural identity, and now constitute a depressed and oppressed ethnic lower class within that region.

Of course, a number of cultural inventions of the Indian peoples have been incorporated into the recent and contemporary culture of the U.S. (or the Western world generally). Most conspicuous are the domestications of certain plants (e.g., maize, beans, squash, pumpkins, potatoes) and the discoveries of uses of native wild plants (e.g., tobacco, rubber, quinine, coca). Yet, in the relationship that has developed between Indian and White, little or nothing of the ethos or social organization of Indian peoples has affected the emerging culture of American society Rather, a distorted image of the warrior-hunter aspect of native cultures has permeated American society via the movies and the Scouting movement. This has been accompanied by a thematic counterpointing of Indian-White relationships in which Indians are placed in a small handful of stock roles (e.g., villainous raider of peaceable settlers; noble redman defending his land; beautiful barbarian maiden trying to establish peace between the irascible males of two different cultures).

Eccentric versions of the ethos or social traits of Indian culture have occasionally crept into American or European culture by some intriguing and peculiar avenues. In Germany there are organizations built on such admiration of Plains Indian society that people come together during the summers to dwell in tipis and to enact, insofar as they can, the style of Indian living. A more dramatic version of this has developed among the "hippie" subculture of the U.S., wherein individuals model their dress, grooming, and even rituals after what they have read or seen among Indians; some hippies have even journeyed to live among Indian peoples (with what consequence it would be interesting to know). An older version of this relationship was built on the notion of the spiritual and therapeutic qualities of Indian medicine men. For a time there flourished among "spiritualists" the notion that the rites and lore of American Indians could assist them in such feats as establishing contact with the deceased; a century ago there was the kindred notion of the value of Indian medicines and healing practices. (Of course, there was some real grounding to this faith, inasmuch as Indian therapists had considerable skill, especially in dealing with physical injuries, wounds, and broken and dislocated bones, even though they had little lore for handling the microorganisms associated with the Europeans.)

Cultural Pluralism

In the period of European settlement of the Americas, the conception of cultural pluralism seemed at times highly appropriate. Indian societies would continue to function as such, providing they acknowledged the sovereignty of the European power. Not all Europeans or Indians were prepared to acquiesce in such an accommodation, but many a settler would have preferred that Indians live their lives in their own fashion and not challenge or interfere with him in his exploitation of local resources. Prior to the Civil War, the loose nature of federal integration within the U.S. made it plausible to consider offering statehood to the Delaware in 1778, while the Cherokee and other tribes were later to attempt to secure the privileges of representation in the Congress. It should be borne in mind that the Indians were regarded in federal law as "domestic dependent nations," and it was their character as "nations" which made it customary and meaningful to deal with them according to the conventions of international diplomacy, including sending ambassadors and negotiating treaties.

The pluralist scheme gradually declined in favor, and the notion arose in the U.S. that the Indians would disappear, either through natural extinction or assimilation into the general population. It was only with the rise of the orientation of "cultural relativism" in anthropology, and of cultural pluralism as a framework for dealing with immigrants to the U.S., together with the work of ethnographers among Indians, that the cultural uniqueness of the remaining tribes came to be recognized and respected. As we have described earlier, this movement achieved a position of federal power when John Collier became Commissioner of Indian Affairs in 1933. Collier spearheaded a program to assist the tribes in increasing their financial base and political strength, and in working out for themselves their cultural and social destinies. While his program encountered many vicissitudes (and much opposition from within the Indian Service), it has nonetheless left a residue of accomplishment and ideology that remains influential.

Especially in the Indian area, the orientation of cultural pluralism usually arouses fervent criticism, some of it ethnocentric and simple-minded, but some quite sophisticated. The simple-minded criticism derives from the conformist ideological orientation, which perceives Indian societies as unchanging, or changing only insignificantly, and believes that

Indians can improve their lot—or "progress"—only by becoming like middle class Americans imbued with the ethos of individualistic competition (the secularized Protestant ethos). In this view, anthropologists are guilty of a nostalgic approach to Indian affairs and wish to maintain Indian culture in an encapsulated and traditionalistic form, the better to perform their ethnographic researches. This criticism distorts the cultural pluralist orientation, the followers of which perceive that Indian societies have been changing and adapting. They also are aware that many peoples of the world have continued to possess distinctive institutions and subcultures while participating actively and successfully in the affairs of a larger society or nation state. The Jews within many European countries, the Chinese and Hindus in African and Asian countries, and many other ethnic and religious groups have existed as quasiautonomous minorities and been useful members of the body politic. The U.S. today includes distinct linguistic and religious groupings, such as the Hutterites, or communities of Orthodox (Chasidic) Jews, who constitute vivid illustrations that peoples may retain a distinctive culture and ethos (quite unlike the secular Protestant ethos) and remain valuable members of society. It may also be noted that Yugoslavia has not only several officially recognized languages but even a corresponding set of separate school systems, and nonetheless functions with marked effectiveness as a nation in the modern world.

A more sophisticated critique of cultural pluralism applied to Indian affairs comes from those (including some anthropologists) who assert that whatever was distinctive and valuable in Indian cultures has now vanished, and that what is observed on Indian reservations is fundamentally a "culture of poverty." This criticism seems most empirically sound as applied to Indians of the eastern and midwest regions of the U.S., especially those who have been living in small bands with little social isolation from their neighbors. These critics note the disappearance of the native language, traditional ceremonials, aboriginal systems of kinship and affinity, and traditional arts and crafts, and contend that other anthropologists have been deluding themselves by mistaking for distinctive Indian traits practices which are recent responses to conditions of deprivation, political impotence, and lower socioeconomic status. This argument leads to the assumption that Indians, as any lower class people, need drastic assistance and encouragement in order to be transformed into prosperous and successful Americans.

The countercritiques take two forms, the structural and the cultural. The structural counter chooses to ignore the relevance of the degree of uniqueness of Indian culture. Many pan-Indian political groups, especially the more radical ones, argue that Indians must organize as a unique and distinct people. Even if the Indian cultures have deteriorated, they contend that Indians can only improve their lot if they organize on the basis of their uniqueness and attempt to regain the rights which they were once assured were theirs. These groups argue further that those who assert that Indians have lost their cultures are serving the cause of various interest groups who would seek to deprive Indians of whatever modest rights and privileges yet remain to them, justifying their expropriations with the declaration that these are "special privileges" which were defensible only when Indians were a distinct people.

The cultural counterpoints to the numerous instances in which Indians remain culturally distinct, most notably their languages and their ethos. Advocates of this countercritique note that dissolution of these remnants of distinct Indian culture and identity will provoke more problems than it will resolve. Were Indian cultures totally to disappear, Indians would not emerge as prosperous middle class Americans but as disorganized and deracinated proletarians. Moreover, the problems which agencies such as the schools have in dealing with Indians testifies to Indian cultural uniqueness and social solidarity. Rather than attempt to dissolve these linkages further, the goal should be to strengthen them, so that Indians can feel free to make their own choices, whether this means they remain culturally and socially distinct, socially distinct but culturally assimilated, or culturally and socially assimilated.

Indian Communities and Heirship Law

Suppose that a major foreign power, such as the Soviet Union, were to say to the citizens of the State of California: We estimate that your state is worth so many billions of dollars; dividing this per capita would mean a hundred thousand dollars for each individual; if you will take this sum, we will reserve for you an adequate area of the presently unoccupied area of the Mohave Desert, and help you to build adequate homes there. Of course, Californians and all Americans would reject the offer with disdain, but a number of lower class impoverished folk would be tempted by the thought of receiving a hundred thousand dollars apiece.

Preposterous as this example may seem, it does illustrate how the U.S. has consistently dealt with Indian societies, in the past and even today. Instead of considering rights, duties, privileges, and responsibilities interwoven in a complex net of social relationships, the outsider's approach in the example is simply to view the membership of each person in the society as if it were a case of heirship to a piece of property (cf. Clifton, 1965). By this procedure, the member of the society is encouraged to view his position one-sidedly—solely in terms of rights, privileges, and rewards—and not in terms of the reciprocities, duties, responsibilities, and obligations which are an invariable counterpart of social existence. Moreover, the federal procedure is continually being repeated in a large variety of contexts. A person who can show that he is "of Indian blood" (of a quarter degree or more) may be eligible for various kinds of benefits (health, education, employment with the federal government, and so on), regardless of whether he participates in an Indian community or contributes to its existence. From the point of view of lawmakers and the courts, this individual is heir to the property rights of Indians, and the benefits accrue to him. In similar fashion, when it is proposed by some agency to sell off reservation property, the issue is usually presented as an heirship matter to all those listed on the tribal rolls, regardless of where they live and the nature of their participation in tribal life. Confronted by an opportunity to gain cash from their status as tribal members, many individuals are tempted to vote in favor of sale; this is more likely to be true if they reside away from the reservation and seldom participate in tribal affairs. Clearly, continued application of this Anglo-Saxon heirship logic is an effective way to disrupt the economy and functioning of a tribal society.

Summary

Many of the Indian groups which were present at the time of the Spanish invasion have disappeared. Some were exterminated, and others died as their ecological basis was undermined. Some groups were assimilated in a process characterized by intermarriage either with other Indian groups, with Whites, or with Negroes. The melting pot as an actuality has been most evident in a few Latin American countries, notably Mexico and Guatemala, where aboriginal and Spanish cultures have blended into an intermediate—Mestizo—configuration. Within the U.S., the Anglo-conformist orientation has generally been dominant in the agencies and persons dealing with Indians. The small number of Indians and their atomization into discrete linguistic and cultural bands, not to mention their relative poverty and lack of sophistication, have made it hard for them to resist these pressures.

However, even in the U.S. a surprising number of recognizable Indian peoples with recognizably Indian traits have remained. Some pan-Indian leaders have been arguing for a cultural pluralist orientation, and they have received the support of many anthropologists active in Indian affairs. On the other hand, many governmental employees and other persons continue to argue that there is no cultural choice for the Indians except assimilation, even though they may remain structurally organized as distinct associations.

PROBLEMS OF INDIVIDUAL
AND COMMUNAL IDENTITY

The social organization of traditional Indian societies can be divided into two classes: those which were small in size and egalitarian in status, and those which were large and complex—civilized societies—and led by elites. Invasions and conquests disrupted the second kind of societies and left a great many that had been, or reverted toward, the first type. In consequence, the tradition of an Indian elite capable of exercising political and intellectual leadership has disappeared or sharply declined. The small societies which have endured lack the notion of hierarchy and of political or military leadership. Many of the customs of these societies seem as if they were designed to redistribute the wealth within the community, and ethnologists have referred to them as "leveling rituals." For example, in some Plains bands, the death of a significant individual is marked by a funeral ceremony in which the family of the deceased gives away large quantities of goods, even to the point of utter destitution; in many Central American villages, men with age move toward ceremonial offices marked with great honor, but requiring elaborate expenditures that may consume the capital of a lifetime; in many Plains societies, anyone acquiring a large amount of goods is expected to distribute a substantial portion in the ceremonial "giveaways." Many other native customs which impressed White visitors—e.g., the sexual hospitality of the traditional Eskimo—were but an aspect of the egalitarian ethos which preserves interpersonal harmony and social solidarity by sharing valuables among the members of the small band or community.

Within the small egalitarian community, individual achievement as extolled by the Protestant ethos and individualistic competition as lauded by capitalist ideology can only be regarded as immoral. Individuals do achieve, and sometimes even compete, but the achieving and competing occur within a moral context which assures that the loser will not be ashamed and that harmonious relationships will be maintained. The proper and moral competition is between groups, not within them; the consequence of such competition is to strengthen bonds, not disrupt them. Hence, the preachments of missionaries, educators, or other reformers, in which the youngster is urged to act as a self-sufficient economic individual (by withholding his money from friends and relatives, saving it in the bank, being thrifty in his expenditures, advancing his own in-

dividual career in disregard of others), can only be received as incomprehensible messages challenging the moral fabric of the social group. The
visions called forth by these preachments would, if taken seriously, arouse
horror or contempt; but what does occur is that they are placed in the
alien category of being White or "acting White."

Many observers have become sensible of the Harmony Ethos (cf.
Gulick, 1960, pp. 131 f.), and some astute reformers, such as Commissioner John Collier, have tried to structure their programs on the co-
operativeness and egalitarianism characteristic of Indian societies. But a
caution is necessary, for while it is tempting to place these bands in the
same context as the Hutterite colony or the Israeli kibbutz, there is an
enormous difference in *social organization* and *religious ideology*. Sustained by a religious (or nationalistic) ideology, the colonies (and the
kibbutzim) have evolved systems of formal organization which have enabled them to work as efficient units with complex divisions of social
labor. Indian bands, especially in their involution under reservation conditions, have tended toward anarchic egalitarianism based on primary
(and informal) linkages. To function as modern communal societies, they
would have to develop social forms to handle the elaborate division of
social labor structured about modern intellectual and technical skills.

Although it is a common inference, it would be incorrect to assume
that these anarchically egalitarian Indian societies had no leadership. As
Paul Radin polemicized so long ago (1927), even the small egalitarian
bands did generate their intellectuals and "philosophers." But this status
was advisory rather than executive, and it was reserved for men of age,
experience, and personal self-discipline. The moral authority of this role
has been preserved in some reservation communities, despite all manner
of onslaughts, but all too often the authority has been drastically undercut by such devolutions as the loss or degradation of the native language.
Among the Chippewa of Minnesota the native language has all but disappeared; it still flourishes among the Sioux of the Dakotas as a domestic
tongue, but it has lost much of the spiritual and intellectual resources
that it once possessed. In consequence, the elderly Indian of traditional
philosophical wisdom cannot discourse on any level of moral profundity
with his son, while with his grandsons and great-grandsons he sometimes
can scarcely communicate at all. In a sense, the conditions of reservation
life have decapitated the upper levels of native intellectuality and spiritual leadership from the levels of popular existence. (A parallel process
has been occurring among the Spanish speaking peoples of the U.S. Southwest, where their suppression by the Anglos—exemplified by prohibitions
attached to usage of Spanish in the public schools—has degraded the
language into a lower class dialect whose speakers do not relate to the

higher intellectual culture of Spanish tradition. In consequence, Chicano children appear in school as "culturally deprived," and their Spanish fluency is a handicap rather than an asset. The schools bemoan the existence of these "educational problems," while across the border in Mexico the cousins of these children are flourishing in schools that appear technically far inferior.)

Erosion of the basis of traditional authority of the aged has not afforded much opportunity for the young and innovative. Like most small communities, Indian societies tend to be conservative, and this has been accentuated by conditions of reservation poverty and oppression. Many institutions—mission churches, the Indian Service, and most recently the Office of Economic Opportunity—have approached reservations with a notion of transforming them by instructing and converting their youth, who in turn would become the leaders of modernized Indian societies. However, most Indian adults have continued to respect the wisdom of age and experience and have defined youth as a time for frivolity and irresponsibility. They have not been inclined to defer to the opinions of youngsters whose years of off-reservation schooling have served to detach them from the painful struggles of daily reservation living. In consequence, those Indian youth who thought of themselves as returning home to lead their peoples have had to reconsider and affiliate with a pan-Indian agency (such as the Indian Service or B.I.A.). Only in those urban areas where there are no organized Indian communities and "leadership" often consists of confrontations staged for the mass media have Indian youth been able to assume the position of spokesmen for Indians (even though some critics contend that they still do not "lead" anyone—cf. Harkins and Woods, 1969).

With the foregoing as prologue, we now turn to a sketch of some of the prevailing modes of individual adaptation and evolution by U.S. Indians. As a heuristic device, we will employ the notion of "types" of Indians, even while recognizing that individual Indians do not themselves fit such neat categorizations. Nonetheless, the typology allows a certain convenience and economy in presentation.

Indian Youth as Seen by a Militant

The identity pressures described rather abstractly in the preceding paragraphs become more meaningful when presented in the passionate prose of a talented (now deceased) young Indian spokesman. For the reader unfamiliar with the sophisticated radical critiques which have recently been formulated by young Indians, the following analysis by the late Clyde Warrior of "Five Types of Young Indians" may be of interest and

provide a contrast to the typology presented in this chapter. At the time
he wrote this essay, Warrior was an officer of N.I.Y.C., and the essay appeared in the journal of the Council, *ABC: Americans Before Columbus*,
II, 4 (December 1964). A few parts of the essay are omitted, and what is
reprinted here is with the kind permission of Della Warrior (Clyde's
widow) and of Robert V. Dumont, Jr. (who in 1964 was an officer of
N.I.Y.C. and an editor of *ABC*).

> Among American Indian youth today there exists a rather pathetic scene,
> in fact, a very sick, sad, sorry scene. This scene consists of the various
> types of Indian students found in various institutions of learning through-
> out American society. It is very sad that these institutions, and whatever
> conditioning takes place, creates these types. For these types are just
> what they are, types, and not full, real human beings, or people.
>
>   *TYPE A—SLOB OR HOOD.* This is the individual who receives his
> definition of self from the dominant society, and unfortunately, sees this
> kind in his daily relationships and associations with his own kind. Thus,
> he becomes this type by dropping out of school, becomes a wino, steals,
> eventually becomes a court case, and is usually sent off. If lucky, he
> marries, mistreats his family, and becomes a real pain to his tribal com-
> munity as he attempts to cram that definition (of himself) down the
> society's throat. In doing this, he becomes a Super-Slob. Another Indian
> hits the dust through no fault of his own.
>
>   *TYPE B—JOKER.* This type has defined himself that to be an Indian
> is a joke. An Indian does stupid, funny things. After defining himself,
> from cues society gave him, he proceeds to act as such. Sometimes he
> accidentally goofs-up, sometimes unconsciously on purpose, after which
> he laughs, and usually says, "Well, that's Indian." And he goes through
> life a bungling clown.
>
>   *TYPE C—REDSKIN "WHITE-NOSER" OR THE SELL-OUT.* This
> type has accepted and sold out to the dominant society. He has accepted
> that definition that anything Indian is dumb, usually filthy, and immoral,
> and to avoid this is to become a "LITTLE BROWN AMERICAN" by
> associating with everything that is white. He may mingle with Indians,
> but only when it is to his advantage, and not a second longer than is
> necessary. Thus, society has created the fink of finks.
>
>   *TYPE D—ULTRA-PSEUDO-INDIAN.* This type is proud that he is
> Indian, but for some reason does not know how one acts. Therefore he
> takes his cues from non-Indian sources, books, shows, etc., and proceeds
> to act "Indian." With each action, which is phony, we have a person
> becoming unconsciously phonier and phonier. Hence, we have a proud,
> phony Indian.
>
>   *TYPE E—ANGRY NATIONALIST.* Although abstract and ideological,
> this type is generally closer to true Indianness than the other types, and
> he resents the others for being ashamed of their own kind. Also, this
> type tends to dislike the older generation for being "Uncle Tomahawks"
> and "yes men" to the Bureau of Indian Affairs and whites in general. The
> "Angry Nationalist" wants to stop the current trend toward personality
> disappearance, and institute changes that will bring Indians into con-

temporary society as real human beings; but he views this, and other problems, with bitter abstract and ideological thinking. For thinking this [he] is termed radical, and [he] tends to alienate himself from the general masses of Indians, for speaking what appears, to him, to be truths.

None of these types is the ideal Indian. . . .

It appears that what is needed is genuine contemporary creative thinking, democratic leadership to set guidelines, cues and goals for the average Indian. The guidelines and cues have to be based on true Indian philosophy geared to modern times. This will not come about without nationalistic pride in one's self and one's own kind.

This group can evolve only from today's college youth. Not from those who are ashamed, or those who have sold out, or those who do not understand true Indianism. Only from those with pride and love and understanding of the People and the People's ways from which they come can this evolve. And this appears to be the major task of the National Indian Youth Council—for without a people, how can one have a cause?

This writer says this because he is fed up with religious workers and educationalists incapable of understanding, and pseudo-social scientists who are consciously creating social and cultural genocide among American Indian youth.

I am fed up with bureaucrats who try to pass off "rules and regulations" for organizational programs that will bring progress.

I am sick and tired of seeing my elders stripped of dignity and low rated in the eyes of their young.

I am disturbed to the point of screaming when I see American Indian youth accepting the horror of "American conformity," as being the only way for Indian progress. While those who do not join the great American mainstream of personalityless neurotics are regarded as "incompetents and problems."

The National Indian Youth Council must introduce to this sick room of stench and anonymity some fresh air of new Indianness. A fresh air of new honesty, and integrity, a fresh air of new Indian idealism, a fresh air of a new Greater Indian America.

How about it? Let's raise some hell!

The Socially Conservative Indian

If he has been reared in a functioning if impoverished Indian community, the most simple and natural path of life for an Indian is to continue within it, linking his personal fate to its system of primary relationships and its communal sharing of goods and services (an excellent description of such a community can be found in Rohner and Rohner, 1970). Since numerous educators, welfare workers, and missionaries devote themselves to combating this type of adaptation, the individual must elude their moralizing; he will be regarded by such types as a "typical Indian" who lacks initiative, incentive, will power, and drive. True to their analysis, he will never be rich or successful by middle class standards, barring some happy accident that enriches all members of his band. Sometimes (perhaps frequently) he will be hungry or miserable, but so long as his band can preserve its unity, he will have the security of belonging, a corresponding sense of personal identity, and at least a minimal standard of living. Regular employment may be troublesome, unless he encounters an employer who takes sufficient interest in him to build a personal (or familial) relationship; under these circumstances he is likely to develop into a conscientious employee.

For some generations, reformers have been forecasting that rural Indian communities will die out and these types of Indians will disappear. Although each generation does witness the emergence of new threats to reservation communities, so far they have maintained themselves. The misapprehension of the reformers is caused in part by their focus on specific cultural traits, and their assumption that the continuity of the conservative community is dependent upon these traits. But, as this book has emphasized, "Indianness" is not a function of specific traits. The Indian is labeled here as "conservative" by virtue of his *social* relationships; he may otherwise watch television and drive Detroit automobiles, as do Americans of every other ethnicity. These relationships constitute a tough and flexible community, and it would be rash to forecast its disappearance.

The White Indian

The Indian who is socially conservative draws cues to his conduct from members of his Indian band (in sociological jargon they are his "reference group"). In contrast, the White Indian is cued into middle class Americana. He typically thinks of his Indianness as a matter of particular cultural traits which were rejected by his parents and grandparents, and he is oriented toward building his personal career and the social success of his own nuclear family. His personal identity is not established as a participant in a band of kith and kin, but (in the fashion of middle class Americans) is composed via his individual accomplishments within the institutions of the larger society—the schools, bureaus, and corporations. In the modern climate of occupational opinion, the White Indian is likely to continue to list himself as "Indian" on schedules where there is an entry for "race," because by doing so he may gain various perquisites and benefits, such as scholarships, medical care, even preference for employment. He may even find a desirable career as part of that Mixedblood elite (discussed above) which mediates between external agencies and rural tribal communities. If he should adopt this role, he may build his career out of attempting to "shapeup" Indians. In the past, a natural affiliation for such an individual was the Indian Service, from whose vantage point of power and influence he could contrast the virtues of his own achieving self with the irresponsibility and drunkenness of "backward" or "residual" Indians.

An alternate resolution for these White Indians is assimilation. While accurate data have not been compiled, even the most superficial acquaintance with Indian affairs leads to two observations. First, some significant proportion of Indian young men and women are marrying Whites; second, some significant proportion of Mixedblood Indians are assimilating into general middle class society, retaining virtually nothing in the way of social affiliation or cultural identification with Indian peoples. Intermarriage need not lead to assimilation, but the heirship definition of Indianness in terms of blood quanta—as written into law and utilized in court decisions—makes it almost inevitable that the children of intermarriage will not be defined either by themselves or by others as "Indian." Conceivably, assimilation could be avoided if the married couple were to reside within an Indian community and raise their children among Indian children. But the actual tendencies of intermarriage seem to be consciously toward assimilation. Among some Indian peoples the elders, especially the women, urge their children to marry White because of their bitter personal experience that Indian identity is a social handicap, or because they believe that Whites have proven to be socially and economically more stable marriage partners.

Given the high rate of natural increase among most Indian peoples, a sizable rate of out-marriages and assimilation can occur without leading to a diminution in numbers. Nevertheless, the tendency is worthy of note, and it has been having a noticeable effect on some tribal groups.

Generalized Indians

Several centuries of federal and mission pressures have detached many Indians from their ties to local bands of kith and kin, and moved them toward a generalized Indian identity. Especially among children who have spent years with Indians of a variety of tribes in federal and mission boarding schools where they were subjected to authoritarian rule, the tendency has been to emerge with a strong sense of identity as an "Indian" who has social linkages to school peers rather than to rural tribal bands. An Indian boarding school tends to affect its students just as any total institution does its inmates, and just as distinct syndromes develop among prisoners ("prisonization") or among those confined to therapeutic institutions ("hospitalization"), so do correspondingly distinct attitudes develop among those confined to boarding schools. There is particularly a strong sense of acclimatization to institutional living, and it is no accident that many of those graduated from the system have turned around and entered it as employees.

A generalized sense of Indian identity also tends to emerge among children who are the product of intertribal marriages, or who are raised in an urban environment where the Indians with whom they and their parents associate derive from a multiplicity of tribes. It may emerge among persons whose natal community has been so damaged by poverty, or removal because of dam construction, or tribal termination, or the pressure of federal and mission programs, or some combination of these, that there remains no stable community within which they can participate. The individual who lacks community membership but suffers all the other miseries of the Indian condition—poverty, undereducation, lack of skills, institutional abuse—is likely to drift into a lower-lower class existence characterized by personal disorganization.

The problem for the generalized Indian is that his role and his relationships with other Indians are in the very process of creation. It is instructive to compare the cultural and political developments in new nations, such as Tanzania, Ghana, or Nigeria, with those among the Indians of North America. Tribes in the new African nations have continued to exist, and large proportions of the population continue to derive their personal identities and social being from participating in the lives of tribal communities. On the other hand, the processes of formal education and interaction with the greater world have helped to create a stratum of people who no longer participate in tribal communities and do not define themselves primarily as tribesmen. In the African case, this kind of individual—a generalized member of his nation—has been finding social roles within the government. The problem in the American situation is more difficult. Exteriorly, the generalized Indian confronts an audience largely accustomed to defining as Indian only those who are poor, uneducated, and politically impotent; interiorly, from within the Indian world, he lacks a stable base of support from an organized Indian population. Thus, the exterior society imposes continual pressure to betray his identity—to deny his Indianness, to confess that he feels morally superior to the mass of Indians, to characterize his involvement in Indian affairs as if it were a unidirectional expression of charity, and so on.

There has emerged a class of "militants" who aggressively challenge these notions and insist upon their Indianness, despite their lack of participation in rural Indian life. Their situation is akin to that of the "marginal men" described by Park (1928), Hughes (1949), and others. It is indicative of the pressures and temptations that they feel that their vocabulary so frequently employs such terms as "fink," "cop out," and "sell out." Identity for a member of a traditional Indian band was given and irrevocable; for the generalized Indians who are the product of mass society, the status of "Indian" can only be maintained by a forceful act of will in the face of pressure and hostility, both from within and without the Indian world.

SOLUTIONS TO
THE "INDIAN PROBLEM"

Long before this final section of the final chapter, the alert reader will have realized that, rather than the "Indian Problem," there is a set of diverse problems involving the *interrelationships* of Indians and non-Indians in a broad ecological and institutional context. While it makes some sense to say that "Indians will have to solve their own problems" or that "Indians should be allowed to solve their own problems" (the form of utterance depending on whether the speaker is a White reformer or an Indian nationalist), inasmuch as the problems involve a range of interrelationships, they cannot be "solved" either by Whites or Indians alone. Like most human beings, Indians have always tried to deal with their own problems as they encountered them, but many features of their present problems are beyond their control. Even when this is not so, they are handicapped by poverty, social discrimination, and the restrictive nature of many governmental policies.

Most rural Indian communities (reservation or otherwise) have been trying to sustain themselves in an ecologically and economically difficult environment, while at the same time they have been harassed by a political and legal framework uncongenial to tribal existence. Relative to reservation communities, the federal Congress (and at its authorization the state legislatures) exercises powers for which there is nothing comparable involving private corporations, local governments, or individual enterprises. No business enterprise is quite so subject to the whim of governmental bodies as is an Indian tribe. Nor has any business enterprise or any normal local governmental unit been so subjected to the destructive onslaught of the Army Corps of Engineers and its allies in building dams, altering river courses, and flooding landsites. On top of this, application of the principles of heirship law serves to encourage formation of Indian parties which have a vested interest in the termination of organized community life, while having no correlative responsibilities for their fellow Indians. (Think how destructive it would be to organized business activity if the stockholders of a corporation had the power and opportunity to dissolve it and distribute its assets per capita simply by a majority vote

at any time.) Given the difficult ecological situation, the political impotence vis-à-vis governmental agencies, and the continual threat of physical
and organizational dissolution, it is little wonder that Indians have a
difficult time in sustaining formally organized tribal life. It is in some
sense amazing that their communities have continued to function as well
as they have during the past century.

Much discussion about the "Indian Problem" really centers about
poverty. Some critics and reformers (both Indian and White) attribute
widespread Indian poverty to Indian customs, cultures, or personality,
and specify "the solution" to "the problem" as instillation of new customs, culture, or personality in place of the traditional. This reformist
orientation is itself highly "traditional," for it has characterized the mission churches, the Indian Service, the B.I.A., and now the Office of Economic Opportunity (O.E.O.). Although the ideological proclamations of
the O.E.O. declared that it was designed to assist lower class communities
in bettering their lot, a large proportion of O.E.O. funds and effort went
into programs, such as Head Start, premised on the theory that the way
to eliminate poverty was to alter the nature of those who were poor (cf.
Wax and Wax, 1968). Equally traditional of these reformist programs has
been their being aimed at the young (e.g., Head Start, Neighborhood
Youth Corps). Many adult Indians want employment and seek it desperately, but their communities receive only governmental programs directed at their children.

Long ago, pioneer sociologist Georg Simmel (1908) argued that poverty was not an absolute state but a relationship. Certain peoples, such
as the hunting and gathering tribes of North America or the frontiersmen
who displaced them, have lived under conditions of great hardship and
yet not been classified as "poor." Hardship becomes defined as "poverty"
only when it is linked in a socioeconomic system with those who are
better off—the *rich*—thus establishing an asymmetric relationship. In Simmel's day, this relationship was epitomized by charitable giving, which
was distinguished from gift exchanges among peers (as at weddings and
births) by the norm that these gifts were not to be reciprocated. The poor
were the objects of benevolent activity by the rich. In contemporary
America, the poor have become the objects (or targets?) of rehabilitative
programs whose design and control rest outside of their communities. (If
the poor were to reciprocate by designing programs to "rehabilitate" the
communities of the rich, this would constitute "revolution.") The latent
consequence of most such programs is disruption of the system of economic and social interdependence within the Indian community. Most
stable working class communities (all over the world) are built on the
solidarity and interdependence of the single-sexed peer society of kith

and kin, yet most rehabilitative programs seek to fractionate that society by emphasizing the isolated nuclear family. The majority of these programs are designed to raise the Indian standard of living by propelling Indians into styles of living beyond their means. For example, a federally sponsored housing project within a reservation community will typically divide Indians into isolated living units based on the nuclear family, and require of each such family a monthly payment far beyond previous levels of family income. The housing looks nice and is in many ways far more pleasant than the cabin or shack it replaces. Some Indian families may desire such housing, and for them it should be made as available as it is for other groups in this country. But for other elements of the Indian population, the design and location of the residence serves to disrupt the kin-based system of exchange and interdependence, thus making the family far more dependent on the money economy without providing any guarantees of employment or income.

Since beggers (i.e., the poor) cannot be choosers, this kind of project is brought to the reservation as if it were a benevolent gift, and its glitter dazzles the eyes of the poor, who do not immediately perceive the intent of those who designed and "donated" the project. (It is rare when a housing project takes some note of the desires of the poor, and I have yet to hear of an Indian project which began with an analysis of the living and sharing practices of the reservation people and then developed a program of improvement with them, taking into full consideration their estimated cash incomes.) Some projects have required volunteer Indian labor as a form of commitment by the local folk, and yet in most cases the commitment has not been met, even by the family whose residence is under construction (cf. Bee, 1969).

Since poverty is an integral part of the U.S. socioeconomic system, it makes little sense to speak of "abolishing poverty." Nevertheless, it is eminently feasible to assist an ethnic group, or an Indian tribe, in improving its position *relative to other groups* (although it should be recognized that these other groups will oppose that movement because it erodes their situation of vantage and power). The relative position of an ethnic group cannot be improved if the implicit condition of the betterment of any individual is his deracination. If every Indian who betters himself must become an "ex-Indian"—detached from his natal group—then there is no way to reduce that group's poverty short of its total elimination.

It is not easy for an Indian group to improve its socioeconomic position relative to other groups in the U.S. (cf. Wax and Wax, 1968). Most reservations lack resources, and most Indian communities lack capital. Wage labor would offer a pathway whereby some Indians might at least

move from the lowest class to a stable working class existence, except that
the world as a whole is in a state of chronic underemployment and under-
utilization of human labor. Characteristically, most varieties of stable
skilled labor in the U.S. have been subjected to monopolistic restriction,
whether by the unions or by educational and training requirements that
are frequently irrelevant to actual performance on the job (cf. the requirements for teacher certification in most school systems). The current
conflict between Black and White ethnic organizations over employment
in the construction trades serves to demonstrate that the skilled working
class cannot be entered by an isolated Negro male who has simply acquired the particular skills needed for the job. Rather, the ethnic group
as an organized force has to seize control of some aspect of the economic
enterprise or win some degree of political strength, because otherwise
that isolated man will never be hired or allowed to work. In this respect,
most O.E.O. programs are impractically and idealistically designed. Training procedures which disrupt the strength of local peer associations of
young men serve to subvert the very possibility of winning employment.

It will be difficult for Indians to better their socioeconomic situation unless they organize to increase their share of political power. But
as we have indicated, a multitude of difficulties hinder such organization.
Traditional Indian allegiances and affiliations were to local tribal groups,
and not to something as general and abstract as "Indian." Moreover, it
has been difficult for an appropriate organizational form to emerge which
allowed both for the tribal and the individual nature of Indianness. The
N.C.A.I. is the most general vehicle, and yet, like the federal Congress
of the early twentieth century, its representatives include persons whose
claims to membership are highly dubious, since they have secured their
status on the basis of a disenfranchised (Indian) population. Precisely
because they are unchecked by any democratic electoral process, some of
these representatives—particularly those from the so-called "Civilized
Tribes"—have achieved positions of relatively great power, and have utilized it to commit the N.C.A.I. to some reactionary political position
(e.g., declarations against civil rights agitation and for "total victory" in
Vietnam).

As Indians have become urbanized, a multitude of other political
associations have emerged, most based in a particular urban area. While
some of these associations issue a newsletter or newspaper, few have any
deep penetration among the mass of Indian people, and most draw a disproportionate element from among disaffected youth. To the extent that
such associations assist Indians in making an adjustment to urban life, or
win concessions for the Indian populace generally, or provide the basis

for a sense of Indian self-respect, they can be extremely valuable. However, it should be cautioned that some are merely vehicles for the personal aggrandizement of "Indian leaders" who have made a career of performing before the mass media and on the conference and lecture circuit (cf. Harkins and Woods, 1969).

In addition to the other handicaps which have been reviewed in the course of this chapter and this book, there is the present legal-juridical framework concerning the role of ethnic minorities in the U.S. The tenor of legislation and court decisions of the past generation has been hostile to the efforts of ethnic nationalists of any persuasion or location, whether Black Panthers in Oakland, Black Muslins in Manhattan, Chasidic Jews in Williamsberg, Hutterites in the Dakotas, Amish in Iowa, Polish Catholics in Chicago, or White segregationists in Alabama. Insofar as any of these groups would like to establish a complement of institutions reserved for their own people, they consistently run athwart of the law and find themselves ineligible for the federal or state support so necessary in the present American fiscal system. Perhaps because of governmental traditions (once rooted in treaty clauses), most American Indian communities have withstood these pressures better than any other ethnic groups, but even they have increasingly encountered a disposition in the Congress to justify special programs for Indians only on the grounds of poverty, and otherwise to assert the evils of "special legislation" or "special privilege" and the necessity for treating all citizens alike. Indians attempting to maintain life as organized tribal bodies while securing various forms of state recognition and assistance are being impeded by federal pressures for "desegregation."

Sociologists have typically referred (as have we in this book) to the ideology of "cultural pluralism," but the issue here is "social pluralism": whether, or to what extent, the American governmental system can recognize, deal with, and accord privileges to ethnic groups (or communities) as intermediaries between itself and its citizens (cf. Park, 1939). In a certain sense, the issue concerns the extent to which the U.S. is going to become a *mass society*—composed of isolated social atoms for whom ethnicity is an accidental cultural quality—or whether it will continue to allow a variety of forms of ethnic organizations and community. Because of the historically peculiar position of the American Indians, it may well be that their struggles for group cohesion will have ramifications for the destiny of the nation as a whole. Those of us who fear the complete massification of American society thus have reason to be glad that Indians maintain themselves as such, and that there continues to be the "Indian Problem."

SUGGESTED READINGS

Bee, Robert L. 1969. Tribal Leadership in the War on Poverty: A Case Study. *Social Science Quarterly* (December), 676–686.

Clifton, James A. 1965. The Southern Ute Tribe as a Fixed Membership Group. *Human Organization*, 24, 4 (Winter), 319–327.

Gordon, Milton M. 1964. *Assimilation in American Life: The Role of Race, Religion, and National Origins.* New York: Oxford University Press, Inc.

Gulick, John. 1960. *Cherokees at the Crossroads.* Chapel Hill: Institute for Research in Social Science, University of North Carolina.

Harkins, Arthur M., and Richard G. Woods. 1969. *The Social Programs and Political Styles of Minneapolis Indians: An Interim Report.* Minneapolis: University of Minnesota, Training Center for Community Programs. Mimeo'd.

Hughes, Everett Cherrington. 1949. Social Change and Status Protest: An Essay on the Marginal Man. *Phylon,* 10 (First Quarter), 58–65. Reprinted in *Where Peoples Meet: Racial and Ethnic Frontiers,* by Everett C. Hughes and Helen M. Hughes. New York: The Free Press, 1952.

Park, Robert Ezra. 1928. Human Migration and the Marginal Man. *Phylon,* 10 (First Quarter), 58–65. Reprinted in *Race and Culture, Collected Papers of Robert Ezra Park,* Vol. I, ed. Everett C. Hughes *et al.* New York: The Free Press, 1950.

———. 1939. Symbiosis and Socialization: A Frame of Reference for the Study of Society. *American Journal of Sociology,* 45, 1–25. Reprinted in *Human Communities: The City and Human Ecology, Collected Papers of Robert Ezra Park,* Vol. II, ed. Everett C. Hughes *et al.* New York: The Free Press, 1952.

Radin, Paul. 1927. *Primitive Man as Philosopher.* New York: Appleton.

Rohner, Ronald, and Evelyn C. Rohner. 1970. *The Kwakiutl, Indians of British Columbia.* New York: Holt, Rinehart and Winston, Inc.

Simmel, Georg. 1908. The Poor (trans. Claire Jacobson). *Social Problems,* 13, 2 (1965), 140–148.

Wax, Murray L. 1968. The White Man's Burdensome Business. *Social Problems,* 16, 1 (Summer), 106–113.

———, and Rosalie H. Wax. 1968. The Enemies of the People, in *Institutions and the Person: Essays Presented to Everett Cherrington Hughes,* ed. Howard S. Becker *et al.* Chicago: Aldine Publishing Company.

Bibliographic and Related Source Materials

While numerous specific references have been mentioned at the end of each chapter, there are additional materials which would be of use to readers. For those contemplating ethnohistorical researches, there are several excellent guides to the literatures and materials; for those wishing to understand contemporary Indian activities, there is periodical literature which is not always subscribed to or listed by university libraries. I have also indicated sources for films, maps, and sound recordings, as well as general and academic information.

BIBLIOGRAPHIES AND REFERENCE WORKS

Berry, Brewton. 1969. *The Education of American Indians: A Survey of the Literature.* Prepared for the Special Subcommittee on Indian Education of the Committee of Labor and Public Welfare, U.S. Senate. 91st Congress, 1st Session. Washington, D.C.: U.S. Government Printing Office.

Costo, Rupert, ed. 1970. *Textbooks and the American Indian* (American Indian Historical Society). San Francisco: Indian Historian Press, Inc.

Dockstader, Frederick J. 1957. *The American Indian in Graduate Studies: A Bibliography of Theses and Dissertations.* New York: Museum of the American Indian, Heye Foundation.

Hippler, Arthur E. 1970. *Eskimo Acculturation: A Selected Annotated Bibliography of Alaskan and Other Eskimo Acculturation Studies.* Fairbanks: Institute of Social, Economic and Government Research, University of Alaska.

Klein, Bernard, and Daniel Icolari, eds. 1967. *Reference Encyclopedia of the American Indian.* New York: B. Klein. An uneven collection of materials, not always carefully sifted, but valuable for its listings of areal offices of the B.I.A., of museums, libraries, local associations, tribal councils, and so on.

Murdock, George Peter, ed. 1960. *Ethnographic Bibliography of North America* (3rd. ed.). New Haven: Human Relations Area Files. An indispensable resource for anyone proposing to review the history of a particular Indian group; the listings are by region of North America, and within each region by tribe; an ethnohistorical map accompanies the volume.

Newberry Library, Chicago. 1961. *Dictionary Catalog of the Edward E. Ayer Collection of Americana and American Indians*. 16 vols. Boston: G. K. Hall and Co.

Peabody Museum of Archaeology and Ethnology, Harvard University. 1963. *Author and Subject Catalogues of the Library*. 54 vols. Boston: G. K. Hall and Co.

Snodgrass, Marjorie P, compiler. 1968. *Economic Development of American Indians and Eskimos: 1930 through 1967*. Departmental Library, Bibliography Series No. 10. Washington, D.C.: U.S. Department of the Interior. Multilithed. Lists 1,595 studies, plans, surveys, etc., classified by subject area, e.g., "Fish and Wildlife Development," and indexed by Reservation area.

Stanley, Samuel, and William C. Sturtevant, compilers. 1969. *Selected References on Present-day Conditions Among U.S. Indians*. Center for the Study of Man, Smithsonian Institution, Washington, D.C., 20560.

U.S. Bureau of Indian Affairs. 1968. *Answers to Your Questions about American Indians*. Washington, D.C.: U.S. Government Printing Office. This 42-page pamphlet contains a variety of useful information, including a modest bibliography which lists some key governmental publications, a listing of the 32 best known museums with Indian collections, plus "answers" to the more usual elementary "questions."

COMPILATIONS OF PAPERS
AND MATERIALS

Cunningham, Jinkie, ed. 1969. "Cree Studies." *Western Canadian Journal of Anthropology*, 1, 1.

Kellogg, Frazier, compiler. 1969. *Toward Economic Development for Native American Communities, A Compendium of Papers*. Submitted to the Subcommittee in Economy in Government of the Joint Economic Committee, Congress of the U.S. 91st Congress, 1st Session, Joint Committee Print. Washington: U.S. Government Printing Office. 2 vols.

Lurie, Nancy O., and Stuart Levine, eds. 1965. "The Indian Today." *Midcontinent American Studies Journal*, 6, 2 (Fall). Reprinted with additions, Penguin Books, 1970.

Owen, Roger C., James J. F. Deetz, and Anthony D. Fisher, eds. 1967. *The North American Indians: A Sourcebook*. New York: The Macmillan Company. Mainly ethnohistorical, organized regionally; has final section of seven papers on "The Indian in the Modern World." Also lists 251 educational films on the Indian.

Simpson, George, and J. Milton Yinger, eds. 1957. "American Indians and American Life." *The Annals of the American Academy of Political and Social Science*, 311 (May).

Spicer, Edward H., ed. 1961. *Perspectives in American Indian Culture Change: Studies in the Acculturation of the Yaqui, Rio Grande Pueblos, Mandan,*

Navaho, Wasco-Wishram, and Kwakiutl. Chicago: University of Chicago Press.

U.S. Senate. 1968–69. Hearings Before the Subcommittee on Indian Education of the Committee on Labor and Public Welfare, Parts 1–5, 90th Congress, 1st and 2nd sessions; Parts 1, 2, and Report (90-501) 91st Congress, 1st session. Washington: U.S. Government Printing Office, 1969.

Voget, Fred, ed. 1962. "American Indians and their Economic Development." *Human Organization,* 20, 4.

Wax, Murray L., *et al.* 1964. "Formal Education in an American Indian Community," Supplement, *Social Problems,* 11, 4 (Spring).

FILMS

Whether commercial or academic, films about American Indians range from the absurd to the superb, but most are in the former category. While commercial films usually suffer from a failure to comprehend Indian cultures and values, the academic films often attempt to portray static societies, unchanging in their ways. Since 1963 the *American Anthropologist* has been conducting a section of "Film Reviews," and persons interested in reading professional evaluations should turn to their columns. Within the American Anthropological Association (1703 New Hampshire, NW, Washington, D.C., 20009) there has developed a Program in Ethnographic Film oriented toward improving the nature and use of anthropological films. While this program is general and not specifically focused upon American Indians, its leadership should be able to assist in the location of materials that might be sought by readers of this volume.

MAPS

Kroeber, Alfred L. *Distribution of Indian Tribes of North America.* Southwest Museum, Highland Park, Los Angeles, Calif., 90042.

Tax, Sol, *et al.* 1960. *The North American Indians: Distribution of Descendants of the Aboriginal Population of Alaska, Canada, and the United States* (4th ed.). Department of Anthropology, University of Chicago, 60637 (25″ × 29″, black and white).

U.S. Bureau of Indian Affairs. *Indian Tribes, Reservations, and Settlements in the United States.* Reissued by Indian Rights Association, 1505 Race Street, Philadelphia, Pa., 19102.

U.S. Department of the Interior. 1965. *Indian Land Areas.* Washington, D.C.: U.S. Government Printing Office, 20402.

Voegelin, C. F., and F. M. Voegelin. 1966. *North American Indian Languages.*

Prepared and Printed by Rand McNally & Co. for the American Ethnological Society. A large wall map, 4′ × 6′, multicolor, indicating aboriginal distributions of language phyla and families from the Arctic to Central America.

PERIODICALS

Since some of these periodicals are erratic in publication and subscription price, only the name of the periodical and the name and address of the publisher (as of 1970) are given.

ABC: Americans Before Columbus, National Indian Youth Council, 3102 Central, S.E., Albuquerque, N.M., 87106.

Akwesasne Notes, Rooseveltown, N.Y., 13683. Essentially a clipping and reproducing service, assembling materials on American Indians from most of the major newspapers and popular journals in the U.S.; of great value to anyone attempting to keep informed on current happenings.

The Indian, American Indian Leadership Council, Route 3, Box 9, Rapid City, South Dakota, 57701.

Indian Affairs, Newsletter of the Association on American Indian Affairs, Inc., 432 Park Avenue South, New York, N.Y., 10016. In the 1930's and 1940's this was one of the most active associations in the field; since then it has been overshadowed by the emergence of associations organized by Indians themselves.

The Indian Historian, American Indian Historical Society, 1451 Masonic Avenue, San Francisco, Calif., 94117. A.I.H.S. has developed a press and is issuing a variety of books on Indian affairs, both past and present.

Indian Truth, Indian Rights Association, 1505 Race Street, Philadelphia, Pa., 19102. Founded in 1882, this is one of the senior associations concerned with Indian affairs. It has close ties with the American Friends Service Committee, and it suffers from the liabilities of having grown out of the tradition of benevolent concern by White religious and reformist groups.

ONAS Newsletter, Organization of Native American Students, Box 40, Wesleyan Station, Middletown, Conn., 06457.

Rainbow People, P.O. Box 469, Gresham, Oregon, 97630. (Alternate address: Caughnawaga, Quebec, P.O. Box 362, Iroquois Land)

The Sentinel, National Congress of American Indians, 1346 Connecticut Avenue N.W., Washington, D.C., 20036.

United Scholarship Service News, P.O. Box 18285, Capitol Hill Station, Denver, Colo., 80218.

The Warpath, United Native Americans Inc., P.O. Box 26149, San Francisco, Calif., 94126.

In addition to the periodicals listed above, there are many others issued either by organized tribes (e.g., *The Oglala War Cry*) or by local associations (e.g., *The Cherokee Report* of the Original Cherokee Community Organization, Tahlequah; *The Choctaw Times,* Nashville) as well as by urban Indian centers, museums devoted to American Indians, and university centers (e.g., Institute of Indian Studies, University of South Dakota). I have not investigated whatever publications may issue from the Indian-Eskimo Association of Canada (Toronto) and the Canadian Indian Youth Council; reports on the weekly program *Indian Magazine* may be received from Radio Features, Canadian Broadcasting Corporation, Box 600, Toronto, Ontario.

SOURCES OF INFORMATION

Anthropological Research. Center for the Study of Man, Smithsonian Institution, Washington, D.C., 20560; The Ethnology Division of the National Museums of Man, National Museum of Canada, 360 Lisgar Street, Ottawa; The Northern Science Research Group, Department of Indian Affairs and Northern Development, Ottawa; Museo Nacional de Antropología de México, Calzada de la Milla, Bosque de Chapultepec, Mexico 5, D.F.

Scholarships, Educational Assistance. Most activities are coordinated by the United Scholarship Service, P.O. Box 18285, Denver, Colo., 80218. Graduate education is the special province of the National Indian Training and Research Center, 510 Lindon Lane, Tempe, Arizona, 85281.

The Federal Government. While the Bureau of Indian Affairs (1951 Constitution Avenue, Washington, D.C., 20242) is the natural center to approach for information about many current programs, many different agencies have been and are involved with one or another aspect of Indian affairs. Of major importance is the Indian Health Service of the U.S. Department of Health, Education, and Welfare. There is also an Indian Desk in the U.S. Office of Economic Opportunity. Within the Department of Commerce, the Bureau of the Census has responsibility for securing basic demographic information about Indians. In addition, the Community Relations Service of the U.S. Department of Justice and the U.S. Civil Rights Commission each have special interests in the legal situation of Indians and in discrimination against Indians. Within the Office of Education there is an office of Special Programs for the Disadvantaged, which coordinates programs concerned with Indians and other minorities.

U.S. Congress. First are the hearings before congressional committees. Particularly in hearings before the Appropriations Committee, the individual governmental agencies usually take pains to present evidence about their activities, effects, and the costs of their services. Besides this, there are special investigatory subcommittees, such as the Special Subcommittees on Indian Education of the Committee on Labor and Public Welfare of the U.S. Senate, 90th and 91st Congress. (This subcommittee was chaired first by Robert F. Kennedy and then, after his death, by his brother Edward.) Earlier, there was an extensive review of the legal situation of American Indians undertaken by the Subcommittee on Constitutional Rights of the Committee on the Judiciary, U.S. Senate, 88th Congress (this subcommittee was chaired by Senator Sam Erwin). Much more material is apt to appear in these published hearings than the average student is likely to elicit via a letter or even a visit to a governmental agency. Besides the hearings before committees or subcommittees, there are the speeches of congressmen, which sometimes reveal or highlight data that might otherwise be buried in agency files.

SOUND RECORDINGS

American Indian Soundchief, 1415 Carlson Drive, Klamath Falls, Ore. 97601.
Canyon Records, 6050 N. 3rd Street, Phoenix, Ariz. 85012.
Folkway Records, 165 West 46th Street, New York, N.Y., 10036.
Indian House, P.O. Box 472, Taos, New Mexico, 87571.

ANTHROPOLOGICAL AND ETHNOHISTORICAL TEXTBOOKS

This is an abbreviated listing of some of the better books among the numerous writings about Indians, their traditional cultures, and their histories.

Driver, Harold E. 1961. *Indians of North America*. Chicago: University of Chicago Press. Organized topically, with headings such as "Horticulture," "Crafts," "Clothing," and "Marriage and the Family."
Eggan, Fred. 1966. *American Indians: Perspectives for the Study of Social Change*. Chicago: Aldine Publishing Company. Sophisticated and not for the novice in the study of kinship, but highly illuminating in its portrait of the growth of anthropological comprehension of traditional Indian practices and their changes through time.
Hagan, William T. 1961. *American Indians*. Chicago: University of Chicago Press. Brief, focusing on interrelationship of Indian and White.
Oswalt, Wendell H. 1966. *This Land Was Theirs*. New York: John Wiley & Sons, Inc. Ethnohistorical accounts of ten representative tribal groupings, including the Pawnee, Tlingit, Hopi, and Iroquois.
Spicer, Edward H. 1969. *A Short History of the Indians of the United States*. New York: Van Nostrand Reinhold Company. In addition to a brief history, there are documents which reveal how Indians and their White contemporaries each regarded affairs and forecast their outcomes.
Underhill, Ruth Murray. 1953. *Red Man's America: A History of Indians in the United States*. Chicago: University of Chicago Press. Organized regionally and historically, each chapter covering a different region and its peoples, with special emphasis upon contact history.

Federal Expenditures in the Name of American Indians

The tables which follow show the magnitude of federal expenditures during the late 1960's for programs designed for or rationalized on the basis of their impact upon American Indian populations. Since fiscal analysis is not my area of specialty, these tabulations are presented without comment. However, they should indicate to the reader the sums of monies involved and the various federal, state, and tribal agencies through which they are being funneled. The original source of these tables is the U.S. Bureau of Indian Affairs, and some of their interpretive comments have been included to enable the reader to understand the nature of the expenditures and the form in which a request is made of the federal Congress.

TABLE B–1

TOTAL FEDERAL FUNDING OF
INDIAN RESERVATION PROGRAMS FOR
FISCAL YEARS 1968–1969
(IN THOUSANDS OF DOLLARS)

	Fiscal Year 1968	Fiscal Year 1969
I. Agriculture, Dept. of		
1. Farmers Home Adm.	3,570	3,500
2. Agr. Stabilization and Conservation Services	3,870	3,870
3. Consumer and Marketing Services	2,242	2,424
4. Rural Electrification Adm.	1,845	1,845
5. Soil Conservation Service	566	566
6. Federal Extension Service	31	31
Total	12,124	12,236
II. Commerce, Dept. of		
Economic Development Adm.		
1. Public Works	15,611	21,600
2. Business Loans (includes Working Capital Guarantees)	2,495	7,500
3. Planning Grants	555	500
4. Technical Assistance	205	400
Total	18,866	30,000

205

| | Fiscal Year | |
	1968	1969
III. Economic Opportunity, Office of		
1. Legal Services	1,331	1,100
2. Upward Bound	1,225	1,875
3. Work Experience (adm. HEW)	2,310	500
4. VISTA	1,800	2,100
5. Head Start	6,697	6,200
6. Neighborhood Youth Corps (adm. Labor)	4,354	5,800
7. Community Action	13,000	15,000
8. FHA-OEO Loans	900	350
9. Job Corps	2,336	1,255
10. Operation Mainstream (adm. Labor)	1,410	1,300
11. New Careers (adm. Labor)	230	3,000
Total	35,593	38,480
IV. HEW (except PHS), Dept. of		
Office of Education		
1. PL 89–10 Elementary and Secondary Education	9,376	9,459
2. PL 89–874 Aid to School Districts		
(operation and maintenance)	18,000	18,720
3. PL 81–815 Aid to School Districts (construction)	2,000	0
4. Other	481	1,143
Total	29,857	29,322
V. Housing and Urban Development, Dept. of		
1. Public Housing (annual contributions)	1,123	621
2. Neighborhood Facilities	1,895	485
3. Sec. 701—Planning Grants	192	4
Total	3,210	1,110
VI. Interior, Dept. of (except B.I.A.)		
1. Bureau of Reclamation	206	209
2. Bureau of Sport Fisheries and Wildlife	950	1,147
3. Bureau of Commercial Fisheries	834	844
4. U.S. Geological Survey	716	750
Total	2,706	2,950
VII. Labor, Dept. of		
Manpower Development and Training Act	1,845	2,300
VIII. Small Business Admn.	107	509
Total other agencies	104,308	116,907
IX. B.I.A.	245,333	241,073
X. P.H.S.	104,068	121,751
1. Indian Health Activities	85,280	95,880
2. Construction of Indian Health Facilities	18,788	25,871
Total federal funding	453,709	479,731

SOURCE: U.S. Bureau of Indian Affairs, May 1969.

ESTIMATED OBLIGATIONS IN BUDGETS OF
OFFICE OF EDUCATION FOR ASSISTING INDIAN CHILDREN
AND IN PUBLIC HEALTH SERVICE FOR
ASSISTING INDIANS, FISCAL YEARS 1968–1970
(IN THOUSANDS OF DOLLARS)

	1968	1969	1970 (est.)
Office of Education			
Assistance for Indian Children:			
School assistance in federally affected areas (off reservations)			
Maintenance and operation PL 874	18,000	18,720	17,506
Construction PL 874	2,000	—	—
Elementary and secondary educational activities (primarily on reservation)			
Educationally deprived children (Title I)	8,907	9,825	9,825
Supplementary educational centers and services (Title III)	297	326	230
Library resources (Title II)	142	73	—
Handicapped (Title II)	30	60	60
Other			
Manpower development and training	1,749	1,760	1,760
Miscellaneous	481	1,143	1,018
Total—Office of Education	31,606	31,907	30,399
Public Health Service:			
Indian health services	85,280	95,202	101,179
Construction of Indian health facilities			
Sanitation facilities	8,173	15,975	19,113
Other	10,615	2,539	7,885
Total—Public Health Service	104,068	113,716	128,177

SOURCE: U.S. Office of Education, May 1969, OASC (13).

TABLE B–3

DEPARTMENT OF THE INTERIOR, BUREAU OF INDIAN AFFAIRS: EDUCATION AND WELFARE SERVICES

Appropriation, 1968	$126,478,000	
Second supplemental appropriation, 1968	5,732,000	
Total appropriation, 1968		$132,210,000
Total available, 1968		132,210,000
Appropriation, 1969	140,693,000	
Supplemental appropriation, 1969	1,452,000	
Pay cost supplemental, 1969	2,843,000	
Total appropriation, 1969		144,988,000

Summary of Increases and Decreases, 1970	Base for 1970	Increase in 1970	
Educational assistance, facilities and services:			
Assistance to pupils in non-federal schools	$14,552,000	$ 6,548,000	
Operation of federal school facilities	81,933,000	7,584,000	
Community development and adult education	1,333,000	950,000	+ 15,082,000
Welfare and guidance services:			
Direct welfare assistance	10,435,000	3,150,000	
Social services	4,547,000	—	
Welfare housing	3,671,000	1,975,000	+ 5,125,000
Relocation and adult vocational training:			
Provide for additional trainees in relocation and adult vocational training	24,376,000	19,650,000	+ 19,650,000
Maintaining law and order:	4,141,000	600,000	+ 600,000
Increase, 1970			+ 40,457,000
Budget estimate, 1970			185,445,000

EDUCATION AND WELFARE SERVICES:
ANALYSIS BY ACTIVITIES

Activity	Fiscal Year 1968	Fiscal Year 1969		
		Total Appropriation	Pay Cost Supplemental	Amount Available
1. Educational assistance, facilities and services	$ 89,245,983	$ 95,459,000	$2,359,000	$ 97,818,000
2. Welfare and guidance services	19,573,387	18,456,000	197,000	18,653,000
3. Relocation and adult vocational training	20,788,400	24,177,000	199,000	24,376,000
4. Maintaining law and order	2,982,657	4,053,000	88,000	4,141,000
Contract authorization	−1,300,000	—	—	—
Applied to contract authorization	910,163	—	—	—
Unobligated balance lapsing	9,410	—	—	—
Total	$132,210,000	$142,145,000	$2,843,000	$144,988,000

TABLE B-5

DEPARTMENT OF THE INTERIOR, BUREAU OF INDIAN AFFAIRS:
COMPARATIVE STATEMENT OF 1969 APPROPRIATION AND 1970 BUDGET ESTIMATE

Appropriations and Activities	Fiscal Year 1969			Fiscal Year 1970 (est.)	Increase (+) or Decrease (−) 1970 Compared with 1969
	Appropriation	Pay Cost Supplemental	Amount Available		
Education and welfare services:					
1. Educational assistance, facilities, and services	$ 95,459,000	$2,359,000	$ 97,818,000	$112,900,000	+$15,082,000
2. Welfare and guidance services	18,456,000	197,000	18,653,000	23,778,000	+ 5,125,000
3. Relocation and adult vocational training	24,177,000	199,000	24,376,000	44,026,000	+ 19,650,000
4. Maintaining law and order	4,053,000	88,000	4,141,000	4,741,000	+ 600,000
Total	$142,145,000	$2,843,000	$144,988,000	$185,445,000	+$40,457,000
Resources management:					
1. Forest and range lands	$ 5,570,000	$ 190,000	$ 5,760,000	$ 6,360,000	+$ 600,000
2. Fire suppression and emergency rehabilitation	140,000	–	140,000	140,000	–
3. Agricultural and industrial assistance	8,878,000	272,000	9,150,000	10,700,000	+ 1,550,000
4. Soil and moisture conservation	5,759,000	216,000	5,975,000	5,975,000	–

5. Maintenance of roads	4,101,000	185,000	4,286,000	4,286,000	—
6. Development of Indian arts and crafts	569,000	10,000	579,000	579,000	—
7. Management of Indian trust property	7,449,000	261,000	7,710,000	7,774,000	+ 64,000
8. Repair and maintenance of buildings and utilities	16,395,000	474,000	16,869,000	17,988,000	+ 1,119,000
9. Operation, repair, and maintenance of Indian irrigation systems	1,379,000	11,000	1,390,000	1,390,000	—
Total	$ 50,240,000	$1,619,000	$ 51,859,000	$ 55,192,000	+$ 3,333,000
Construction:					
1. Buildings and utilities	$ 19,414,000ª	—	$ 19,414,000	$ 17,500,000	—$ 1,914,000
2. Irrigation systems	5,921,000	—	5,921,000	5,873,000	— 48,000
Total	$ 25,335,000	—	$ 25,335,000	$ 23,373,000	—$ 1,962,000
Road construction (liquidation of contract authorization):					
Federal-aid highway roads	$ 18,000,000	—	$ 18,000,000	$ 20,000,000	+$ 2,000,000
General administration expenses	4,767,000	$ 246,000ᵇ	5,013,000	5,113,000	+ 100,000
Revolving fund for loans	450,000		450,000	—	— 450,000
Grand total	$240,937,000	$4,708,000	$245,645,000	$289,123,000	+$43,478,000

ªTransferred to other accounts.

ᵇRepresents transfer from Pollution Control Operation—Research Federal Water Pollution Control Administration.

EDUCATIONAL ASSISTANCE, FACILITIES, AND SERVICES

Subactivity	F.Y. 1968 Amount Available	F.Y. 1969 Amount Available	F.Y. 1970 Amount Available	Increase (+) or Decrease (−) 1970 compared with 1969
A. Assistance to pupils in nonfederal schools: Public schools:				
a. Navajo peripheral	$ 1,604,300	$ 1,620,000	$ 1,800,000	+$ 180,000
b. Other	8,336,296	9,932,000	15,452,000	+ 5,520,000
Higher education	2,245,880	3,000,000	3,848,000	+ 848,000
Total	$12,186,476	$14,552,000	$ 21,100,000	$ 6,548,000
B. Federal facilities				
Boarding schools	$58,182,098	$61,483,000	$65,617,000	+$ 4,134,000
(no. of pupils)	(39,550)	(39,900)	(40,900)	(+1,000)
Day schools	13,992,880	16,289,000	18,639,000	+ 2,350,000
(no. of pupils)	(16,249)	(17,750)	(19,390)	(+1,640)
(no. of units)	(609)	(644)	(679)	(+35)
Special services:				
a. Program direction	2,024,302	2,311,000	2,611,000	+ 300,000
b. Transportation of boarding school students	914,022	900,000	900,000	−
c. Indian school boards			300,000	+ 300,000
Summer programs	959,205	$ 950,000	1,450,000	+ 500,000
Total	$76,022,507	$81,933,000	$ 89,517,000	$ 7,584,000
C. Adult education and community development	$ 1,037,000	$ 1,333,000	$ 2,283,000	+$ 950,000
Total	$89,245,983	$97,818,000	$112,900,000	+$15,082,000

A. Assistance to pupils in nonfederal schools: F.Y. 1969, $14,552,000; F.Y. 1970, $21,100,000; increase, $6,548,000. The increase consists of:

Increase (+) or Decrease (—)		Total Program	Total Positions	Explanation
Amount	Positions			
(1) $+ 180,000	—	$ 1,800,000	—	To meet increased costs of peripheral dormitory program
(2) +5,520,000	—	15,452,000	—	To meet normal program increases and provide kindergarten opportunities for reservation children
(3) + 848,000	4	3,848,000	4	To meet increased need for college scholarship grants to Indian youth
+6,548,000	+4			

Need for Increase: Public Schools. Increased enrollment and educational costs continue to require substantially higher amounts of Johnson-O'Malley funds. It is also apparent that the differing backgrounds of the many tribal groups necessitate a variety of approaches and the development of divergent materials if linguistic and cultural interferences are to be removed. Additional funds are being provided to support programs which train public school teachers of Indian children, encourage participation of Indian parents in school affairs, and provide home-school counselors to serve as a link between the school and Indian home.

1. The increase of $180,000 requested for the peripheral program is based upon the prior year's expenditures for educational services.

2. The increase of $5,520,000 for State contracts is the result of negotiations with States.

Under the terms of existing State Plans, in view of estimated enrollment increases of about 8 per cent and sharp increases in operating costs, the amount needed to fund the program will be greater in 1970. Enrollment is expected to rise from 66,000 to 71,000. To support this increase and provide the necessary education services, an additional $3,220,000 is required.

An increase of $2,300,000 is requested for the establishment and operation of kindergartens in schools which serve Indian children from reservation homes. Many Indian children who attend public schools come from an environment that has limited association with the dominant culture and in many instances adults in the home have not attained a literacy level. Children from these homes enter school greatly handicapped because of their language/cultural problems. In order to provide these children with the benefits of earlier school experience in developing skills and learning processes it is planned in fiscal year 1970 to provide financial assistance for public school kindergarten operations in accordance with the Act of April 16, 1934 (48 Stat. 596), as amended.

Eight States in the Johnson-O'Malley program include kindergarten in their regular education program. School districts which do so are eligible to apply for State aids and funds through Public Law 874 and would require only approximately 50 per cent support from the Bureau. In fiscal year 1970 there will be 33 such units. Full Bureau financing will be required for the remaining 74 units.

TABLE B-7

1970 ALLOCATIONS—EDUCATION

	Non-Federal Facilities			Federal Facilities	Grand Total
	JOM[a]	Higher Education	Total		
Aberdeen Area	$ 1,870,000	$ 425,000	$ 2,295,000	$ 9,081,000	$ 11,376,000
Albuquerque Area	260,000	330,000	590,000	4,173,000	4,763,000
Anadarko Area	48,000	400,000	448,000	5,628,000	6,076,000
Billings Area	540,000	210,000	750,000	887,000	1,637,000
Juneau Area	2,584,000	393,000	2,977,000	9,832,000	12,809,000
Minneapolis Area	1,121,000	203,000	1,324,000	81,706	1,405,706
Muskogee Area	1,030,000	860,000	1,890,000	3,150,000	5,040,000
Navajo Area	3,825,000	273,000	4,098,000	37,711,000	41,809,000
Phoenix Area	3,792,000	492,000	4,284,000	7,610,000	11,894,000
Portland Area	955,000	215,000	1,170,000	1,915,000	3,085,000
Sacramento Area	35,000	—	35,000	—	35,000
Cherokee	—	15,300	15,300	1,015,200	1,030,500
Miccosukee	—	—	—	64,000	64,000
Seminole	28,000	19,880	47,880	86,120	134,000
Institute of American Indian Arts	—	—	—	994,000	994,000
Teacher recruitment	—	—	—	214,000	214,000
Central Office (includes Instructional Service Center, Brigham City; Public School Relations and School Facilities, Albuquerque)	—	—	—	2,403,000	2,403,000
Undistributed	364,000	11,820	375,820	172,974	548,794
Clearing account	—	—	—	4,307,000	4,307,000
Grand total	$16,452,000	$3,848,000	$20,300,000	$89,325,000	$109,625,000

SOURCE: U.S. Bureau of Indian Affairs, 1970.

[a] "JOM" refers to Johnson O'Malley Act of 1934 (48 Statute 596), which authorizes payments to states and other agencies operating instructional institutions serving Indian pupils (MLW).

Reference Materials on
Indian Population, Education,
and Health

Herewith are printed tables and discussion deriving from federal sources and indicating such matters as growth of Indian population from 1890 to 1960, the size of the population of Indians served by the B.I.A. (as of 1968), the schools attended by Indian children, and the death rates of Indians by age.

ESTIMATES OF THE INDIAN POPULATION
SERVED BY THE BUREAU OF
INDIAN AFFAIRS: SEPTEMBER 1968[1]

The [following] tables provide population estimates of Indians resident on, or adjacent to, Federal reservations. Table [C–1] reports the population for each of the 25 reservation States, and also for each of the 12 regional administrative units of the Bureau. Table [C–2] shows total Indian population for individual reservations, grouped by State. The reservation name is listed first, followed by the name of the Agency office with Bureau jurisdiction. Reservations crossing State lines are listed under the State where the majority reside. However, the population is prorated among the states to arrive at the State total in Table [C–1.]

Who is an Indian? The statistics here pertain to what might be called "administrative" or "official" Indians who are eligible for services from the Bureau of Indian Affairs. Generally speaking, they are members of tribes with Federal trust land, who have one-quarter or more Indian blood and who live on a Federal reservation or nearby. Other definitions of "Indian" are possible—for example, the Census Bureau employs a cultural definition, counting persons who report themselves as Indian (or who are so regarded by the community) regardless of tribe or residence. Different definitions lead to different statistics, so there is no one answer to the question, "How many Indians are there?"

These tables do not include all Indians in the United States. They

[1]Reprinted from U.S. Bureau of Indian Affairs, 1969.

TABLE C–1

ESTIMATES OF INDIAN POPULATION
ON OR ADJACENT TO FEDERAL RESERVATIONS,
BY STATE AND AREA: SEPTEMBER 1968
(INCLUDES ALASKA NATIVES)

Bureau of Indian Affairs Total   452,000

State

Alaska[a]	55,400	Nebraska	2,500
Arizona	105,900	Nevada	4,400
California	6,600	New Mexico	74,500
Colorado	1,600	North Carolina	4,600
Florida	1,200	North Dakota	13,600
Idaho	5,100	Oklahoma[b]	72,400
Iowa	500	Oregon	2,800
Kansas	1,000	South Dakota	30,000
Louisiana	300	Utah	5,700
Michigan	1,000	Washington	16,000
Minnesota	10,400	Wisconsin	6,500
Mississippi	3,200	Wyoming	4,100
Montana	23,100		

Administrative area

Aberdeen Area	45,900	Muskogee Area	59,300
Albuquerque Area	28,800	Navajo Area	120,300
Anadarko Area	17,600	Phoenix Area	44,600
Billings Area	27,200	Portland Area	23,700
Juneau Area	55,400	Sacramento Area	5,100
Minneapolis Area	18,400	Central Office	5,800

SOURCE: U.S. Bureau of Indian Affairs, 1969.

Note: Details may not add to totals because of rounding. Adjustments made for the States where reservations overlap into another State.

[a]Includes all Indians and Natives in Alaska.

[b]Includes former reservation areas in Oklahoma.

exclude Indians who are not members of tribes with trust land under Federal jurisdiction and members of such tribes no longer living on or adjacent to Federal reservations. In the 1960 census, about 200,000 Indians, roughly one-third of all those in the United States, were not included in the service population; the number is probably higher now.

Special legislation governs eligibility in Alaska and Oklahoma. In Alaska, the figures include all Alaskan Natives—that is to say, Aleuts and Eskimos as well as American Indians. Very few are living on reservations, and the term "adjacent" refers to all the rest of Alaska. In Oklahoma, the area covered is composed of former reservations. In both States, the Bureau's responsibility extends to the population shown in the table.

TABLE C–2

ESTIMATES OF INDIAN POPULATION
ON OR ADJACENT TO FEDERAL RESERVATIONS,
BY RESERVATION: SEPTEMBER 1968

State and Reservation	B.I.A. Agency	Indian Population	State and Reservation	B.I.A. Agency	Indian Population
Alaska (includes all Indians and Natives)			Florida		
Anchorage District	Anchorage	13,650	Big Cypress	Seminole	300
Bethel District	Bethel	12,700	Brighton	Seminole	260
Fairbanks District	Fairbanks	8,350	Hollywood		
Nome District	Nome	9,950	(Dania)	Seminole	400
Southeast District	Southeast	10,800	Miccosukee	Miccosukee	230
Arizona			Idaho		
Ak-Chin			Coeur d'Alêne	Northern Idaho	320
(Maricopa)	Pima	230	Fort Hall	Fort Hall	3,040
Camp Verde	Truxton Canyon	690	Kootenai	Northern Idaho	60
Cocopah	Colo. River	100	Nez Perce		
Colorado River	Colo. River	1,680	(Lapwai)	Northern Idaho	1,510
Fort Apache	Fort Apache	6,000	(see also Duck Valley, listed in Nevada)		
Fort McDowell	Salt River	330	Iowa		
Gila Bend	Papago	260	Sac and Fox	Sac & Fox Office	500
Gila River	Pima	7,420	Kansas		
Havasupai	Truxton Canyon	370	Iowa	Horton	270[d]
Hopi	Hopi	5,940	Kickapoo	Horton	320
Hualapai	Truxton Canyon	1,030	Potawatomi	Horton	470
Kaibab	Hopi	140	Sac and Fox	Horton	20[e]
Navajo: total	Navajo Area	(119,500)	Louisiana		
Arizona part	Navajo Area	68,700	Chitimacha (est.)	Choctaw	270
Papago	Papago	5,290	Michigan		
Salt River	Salt River	2,260	Bay Mills	Great Lakes	250
San Carlos	San Carlos	4,650	Hannahville	Great Lakes	140
San Xavier	Papago	660	Isabella (Saginaw)	Great Lakes	220
Yavapai	Truxton Canyon	90	Keweenaw Bay		
(see also Ft. Yuma, listed in Calif.)			(L'Anse and		
California			Ontonagon)	Great Lakes	400
Agua Caliente	Palm Springs	70[a]	Minnesota		
Fort Mohave	Colo. River	300	Fond du Lac	Minnesota	740
Fort Yuma	Colo. River	1,220[b]	Grand Portage	Minnesota	210
Hoopa Valley	Hoopa	800	Leech Lake	Minnesota	2,800
Morongo	Riverside	220	Lower Sioux	Minnesota	110
Round Valley			Mille Lac	Minnesota	830
(Covelo)	California	270	Nett Lake	Minnesota	680
62 Other reserva-			Prairie Island	Minnesota	90
tions and	Calif., Hoopa,		Prior Lake	Minnesota	20
rancherias (est.)	and Riverside	3,720	Red Lake	Red Lake	2,740
Colorado			Upper Sioux	Minnesota	80
Southern Ute	Southern Ute	660	White Earth	Minnesota	2,050
Ute Mountain	Ute Mountain	1,140[c]	(see also Winnebago, listed in Wisconsin)		

State and Reservation	B.I.A. Agency	Indian Population
Mississippi		
Choctaw	Choctaw	3,180
Montana		
Blackfeet	Blackfeet	6,540
Crow	Crow	3,820
Flathead	Flathead	2,800
Fort Belknap	Fort Belknap	1,800
Fort Peck	Fort Peck	4,250
Northern Cheyenne (Tongue River)	Northern Cheyenne	2,440
Rocky Boys	Rocky Boys	1,460
Nebraska		
Omaha	Winnebago	1,370
Santee	Winnebago	240
Winnebago	Winnebago	740
(see also Iowa and Sac and Fox, listed in Kansas)		
Nevada		
Duck Valley	Nevada	880ᶠ
Duckwater	Nevada	80
Dresserville	Nevada	160
Fallon Col. and Res.	Nevada	200
Fort McDermitt	Nevada	370
Goshute	Nevada	160ᵍ
Moapa River	Nevada	70
Pyramid Lake	Nevada	400
South Fork	Nevada	90
Walker River	Nevada	390
Yerington Col. and Res.	Nevada	170
Yomba	Nevada	60
12 Other reservations and colonies (est.)	Nevada	1,600
New Mexico		
Acoma	Southern Pueblos	1,920
Alamo (Puertocito)	Navajo Area	1,030
Canoncito	Navajo Area	740
Cochiti	Southern Pueblos	490
Isleta	Southern Pueblos	2,030
Jemez	Southern Pueblos	1,380
Jicarilla	Jicarilla	1,500
Laguna	Southern Pueblos	2,880

State and Reservation	B.I.A. Agency	Indian Population
New Mexico (Cont.)		
Mescalero	Mescalero	1,690
Nambe	Northern Pueblos	200
Navajo: total	Navajo Area	(119,500)
New Mexico part	Navajo Area	46,700
Picuris	Northern Pueblos	80
Pojoaque	Northern Pueblos	40
Ramah	Zuni	1,060
Sandia	Southern Pueblos	180
San Felipe	Southern Pueblos	1,340
San Ildefonso	Northern Pueblos	420
San Juan	Northern Pueblos	790
Santa Ana	Southern Pueblos	400
Santa Clara	Northern Pueblos	710
Santo Domingo	Southern Pueblos	1,940
Taos	Northern Pueblos	1,190
Tesuque	Northern Pueblos	300
Zia	Southern Pueblos	380
Zuni	Zuni	5,040
North Carolina		
Cherokee (Qualla Boundary)	Cherokee	4,640
North Dakota		
Fort Berthold	Fort Berthold	2,660
Fort Totten (Devils Lake)	Fort Totten	1,750
Turtle Mountain	Turtle Mt.	6,990
(see also Standing Rock, listed in South Dakota)		
Oklahoma (includes former reservation areas)		
Absentee Shawnee	Shawnee	950
Cheyenne-Arapaho	Concho	3,400
Cherokee	Tahlequah	9,600
Chickasaw	Ardmore	5,250
Choctaw	Talihina	9,900
Creek	Okmulgee	12,600
Eastern Shawnee	Miami	(see Agcy T.)
Fort Sill Apache (see Kiowa-Commanche-Apache)		
Iowa	Shawnee	60
Kaw	Pawnee	(see Agcy T.)
Kickapoo	Shawnee	550
Kiowa-Comanche-Apache and Ft. Sill Apache	Anadarko	5,100

State and Reservation	B.I.A. Agency	Indian Population	State and Reservation	B.I.A. Agency	Indian Population
Oklahoma (Cont.)			Washington		
Miami	Miami	(see Agcy T.)	Chehalis	Western Wash.	190
Miami Agency	Miami	8,350	Colville	Colville	2,950
Osage	Osage	3,250	Hoh	Western Wash.	40
Otoe-Missouri	Pawnee	(see Agcy T.)	Kalispel	Northern Idaho	120
Pawnee	Pawnee	(see Agcy T.)	Lower Elwah	Western Wash.	130
Pawnee Agency	Pawnee	3,700	Lummi	Western Wash.	670
Ponca	Pawnee	(see Agcy T.)	Makah	Western Wash.	520
Potawatomi	Shawnee	500	Muckleshoot	Western Wash.	340
Quapaw	Miami	(see Agcy T.)	Nisqually	Western Wash.	190
Sac & Fox	Shawnee	600	Nooksak	Western Wash.	260
Seminole	Wewoka	7,000	Port Gamble	Western Wash.	120
Seneca-Cayuga	Miami	(see Agcy T.)	Port Madison	Western Wash.	190
Tonkawa	Pawnee	(see Agcy T.)	Puyallup	Western Wash.	170
Wichita	Anadarko	1,800	Quileute	Western Wash.	300
Oregon			Quinault	Western Wash.	940
Burns-Paiute	Warm Springs	150	Shoalwater	Western Wash.	20
Celilo Village	Warm Springs	30[a]	Skokomish	Western Wash.	220
Umatilla	Warm Springs	980	Spokane	Colville	680
Warm Springs	Warm Springs	1,620	Squaxon Island	Western Wash.	130
South Dakota			Swinomish	Western Wash.	360
Cheyenne River	Cheyenne River	4,160	Tulalip	Western Wash.	450
Crow Creek	Pierre	1,150	Yakima	Yakima	7,010
Flandreau	Flandreau	150	Wisconsin		
Lower Brule	Pierre	580	Bad River	Great Lakes	420
Pine Ridge	Pine Ridge	11,060	Lac Courte		
Rosebud	Rosebud	7,160	Oreilles	Great Lakes	730
Sisseton	Sisseton	1,940	Lac du Flambeau	Great Lakes	900
Standing Rock	Standing Rock	4,710[h]	Mole Lake	Great Lakes	110
Yankton	Yankton	1,260	Oneida	Great Lakes	1,670
Utah			Potawatomi	Great Lakes	230
Navajo: Total	Navajo Area	(119,500)	Red Cliff	Great Lakes	430
Utah part	Navajo	4,100	St. Croix	Great Lakes	290
Skull Valley	Uintah & Ouray	30	Stockbridge-		
Uintah & Ouray	Uintah & Ouray	1,270	Munsee	Great Lakes	450
Washakie	Fort Hall	L	Winnebago	Great Lakes	1,330[i]
(see also Goshute listed in Nevada and			Wyoming		
Ute Mountain in Colorado)			Wind River	Wind River	4,110

SOURCE: U.S. Bureau of Indian Affairs, 1969.

L means less than 10.

[a] 1967 data.   [b] 3% in Arizona.   [c] 21% in Utah.

[d] 37% in Nebraska.   [e] 47% in Nebraska.   [f] 25% in Idaho.

[g] 39% in Utah.   [h] 47% in North Dakota.   [i] 4% in Minnesota.

The population resident within the reservation boundaries may include many non-Indian people. However, only Indians are counted in the tables.

The statistics are labeled "Estimates" because they are not based to any major extent on actual population surveys as of the given date. The figures for each reservation are supplied by the local staff, using the data sources available. Some sources are very accurate, such as the membership lists maintained by some tribes, but other sources are less so. Generally speaking, data for the Navajo Area, the State of Oklahoma (Anadarko Area and Muskogee Area), and the State of Alaska (Juneau Area) are considered the least accurate and the most difficult to improve because of the large population scattered over enormous areas.

Since 1900 the Indian population has more than doubled itself. However, the rate at which it is currently growing cannot be precisely determined. Because of a lack of comparability between the U.S. Censuses of 1950 and 1960, the recorded increase in this period does not reflect actual growth. It is believed that the Indian population is increasing at a rate between 1.7 and 2 per cent a year, a rate slightly higher than that for the total population of the United States (see Tables C–3, C–4, and C–5).

In order to understand the growth of the Indian population, we should examine its fertility characteristics (Table C–6) as compared to those of the U.S. population considered as a whole (U.S. All Races). The birth date for "U.S. All Races" is seen to have declined from a figure of 25 (per 1,000) in 1957 to less than 18 in 1967, which constitutes a decrease of one-fourth. In contrast, the rate for "Indian and Alaska Natives" rose steadily from a figure of 37 in 1955 to over 43 in 1964. In that year, the birth rate of native peoples was more than double that of the U.S. population as a whole. Since that year, there has been a steady decrease in both Indian and Alaskan native races, especially in the latter.

The infant death rate among Indians and Alaska Natives combined declined about 48 per cent between 1955 and 1967, from 62.5 to 32.2 per thousand live births. Over the same period, the U.S. All Races rate dropped 15 per cent. In 1955 the Indian and Alaska Native rate was 2.4 times as large as the U.S. All Races rate. In 1967, in spite of the significant improvement mentioned above, it was still 1.44 times as high as the U.S. All Races rate. The Alaska Native rate fluctuated between 18 and 80 per cent above the Indian rate over the 13-year period (see Table C–7).

Because of the wide difference in age distribution between the Indian and Alaska Native population and the country as a whole (median ages about 17 and 28, respectively), crude death rates are not entirely

TABLE C–3

UNITED STATES INDIAN AND ALASKA
NATIVE POPULATIONS, 1890–1961[a]

Year	U.S. Excluding Alaska	Federal Indian Reservation States	Alaska Natives
1960	509,100	455,000	42,500[b]
1950	421,600[c]	375,300[c]	33,900
1940	334,000	316,300	32,500
1930	332,400	315,900	30,000
1920	244,400	231,300	26,600
1910	265,700	250,900	25,300
1900	237,200	226,300	29,500
1890	248,300	235,500	25,400

SOURCE: U.S. Department of Commerce, Bureau of the Census, U.S. Census of Population, 1960, PC (1) 1B and PC (2) 1C.

[a]The self-enumeration procedures used in the 1960 U.S. Census resulted in more persons of mixed Indian and non-Indian ancestry being returned as Indian than in earlier Censuses when race was determined by observation of the enumerator.

[b]Final count from 1960 Census, as shown in U.S. Bureau of Census report, Nonwhite Population by Race. Includes 5,800 Aleuts, 22,300 Eskimos, and 14,400 Indians.

[c]In 1950, the published figure of 343,000 was adjusted for underenumeration of persons with mixed blood and those classified in the "All other" races category who had been previously returned as Indian.

TABLE C–4

ENROLLMENT OF INDIAN CHILDREN
AGES 6–18 IN TYPE OF SCHOOL, 1967–1968

Type of School	Indian Children, Ages 6–18[a]	
	No.	%
	152,088 =	100
Federal	46,725	30.7
Public	87,361	57.4
Mission and other private	8,544	5.6
Total all schools	142,630	93.7
Not enrolled[b]	6,616	4.4
Information not available[c]	2,842	1.9

SOURCE: U.S. Bureau of Indian Affairs, Statistics Concerning Indian Education, Fiscal Year 1968.

[a]Data are for children for whom the B.I.A. has educational responsibility as enumerated by B.I.A. agencies in its Annual School Census of Indian children.

[b]Mostly Navajo children living in remote areas.

[c]Children recorded at their own agencies but who reside off the reservation.

221

TABLE C-5

AMERICAN INDIANS BY STATES (NUMBER AND PERCENTAGE ATTENDING SCHOOL AT INCREASING LEVELS OF ISOLATION, FALL, 1968, ELEMENTARY AND SECONDARY SCHOOL SURVEY)

State	Total No. of Students	Total No. of American Indian Students	% of Total Students	American Indians Attending Minority Schools									
				0-49.9%		50-100%		80-100%		95-100%		100%	
				No.	%	No.	%	No.	%	No.	%	No.	%
Continental U.S.	43,353,567	177,464	0.4	109,540	61.7	67,924	38.3	53,528	30.2	29,654	16.7	11,177	6.3
Alabama	770,523	39	0	6	15.4	33	84.6	33	84.6	0	0	0	0
Alaska	71,797	6,808	9.5	4,866	71.5	1,942	28.5	1,768	26	1,192	17.5	607	8.9
Arizona	366,459	14,431	3.9	5,827	40.4	8,604	59.6	6,781	47	388	2.7	7	0
Arkansas	415,613	414	.1	414	100	0	0	0	0	0	0	0	0
California	4,477,381	13,986	.3	12,284	87.8	1,702	12.2	599	4.3	182	1.3	7	.1
Colorado	519,092	1,366	.3	1,211	88.6	155	11.4	66	4.8	11	.8	0	0
Connecticut	682,361	204	0	194	95.1	10	4.9	4	2	0	0	0	0
Delaware	123,863	10	0	10	100	0	0	0	0	0	0	0	0
District of Columbia	148,725	31	0	6	19.4	25	80.6	23	74.2	10	32.3	0	0
Florida	1,340,665	1,455	.1	1,389	95.5	66	4.5	20	1.4	8	.5	2	.1
Georgia	1,001,245	323	0	189	58.6	134	41.4	134	41.4	134	41.4	134	41.4
Idaho	174,472	1,699	1	1,564	92.1	135	7.9	0	0	0	0	0	0
Illinois	2,252,321	1,804	.1	1,602	88.8	203	11.2	60	3.3	28	1.6	5	.3
Indiana	1,210,539	544	0	464	85.3	80	14.7	14	2.6	8	1.5	5	.9
Iowa	651,705	418	.1	415	99.3	3	.7	0	0	0	0	0	0
Kansas	518,733	1,392	.3	1,374	98.7	18	1.3	2	.1	1	.1	0	0
Kentucky	695,611	47	0	46	97.9	1	2.1	0	0	0	0	0	0

Louisiana	817,000	213	0	202	94.8	11	5.2	0	0	0	0	0	0
Maine	220,336	1,132	.5	332	29.3	800	70.7	467	41.2	67	5.9	67	5.9
Maryland	859,440	169	0	169	100	0	0	0	0	0	0	0	0
Massachusetts	1,097,221	430	0	407	94.7	23	5.3	11	2.6	5	1.2	0	0
Michigan	2,073,369	4,404	.2	4,267	96.9	137	3.1	75	1.7	44	1	4	.1
Minnesota	856,566	5,748	.7	5,702	99.2	46	.8	0	0	0	0	0	0
Mississippi	456,532	112	0	104	92.9	8	7.1	3	2.7	3	2.7	3	2.7
Missouri	954,596	278	0	264	95	14	5	8	2.9	6	2.2	4	1.4
Montana	172,059	5,015	3.9	2,472	49.3	2,543	50.7	2,275	45.4	325	6.5	81	1.6
Nebraska	266,342	824	.3	743	90.2	81	9.8	32	3.9	13	1.6	0	0
Nevada	119,180	2,454	2.1	1,870	76.2	584	23.8	235	9.6	64	2.6	64	2.6
New Hampshire	132,212	29	0	29	100	0	0	0	0	0	0	0	0
New Jersey	1,401,925	311	0	258	82.9	53	17.1	10	3.2	4	1.3	1	.3
New Mexico	271,040	19,742	7.3	3,048	15.4	16,694	84.6	12,241	62	3,420	17.3	1,638	8.3
New York	3,364,090	5,710	.2	3,795	66.5	1,915	33.5	1,791	31.4	1,738	30.4	557	9.8
North Carolina	1,199,481	14,021	1.2	2,916	20.8	11,105	79.2	10,587	75.5	10,585	75.5	4,272	30.5
North Dakota	115,995	1,523	1.3	1,165	76.5	358	23.5	0	0	0	0	0	0
Ohio	2,400,296	736	0	684	92.9	52	7.1	31	4.2	9	1.2	4	.5
Oklahoma	543,501	24,003	4.4	23,630	98.4	373	1.6	70	.3	18	.1	6	0
Oregon	455,141	3,601	.8	3,108	86.3	492	13.7	487	13.5	0	0	0	0
Pennsylvania	2,296,011	411	0	409	99.5	2	.5	1	.2	0	0	0	0
Rhode Island	172,264	143	.1	143	100	0	0	0	0	0	0	0	0
South Carolina	603,542	404	.1	341	84.4	63	15.6	62	15.3	62	15.3	62	15

SOURCE: *Congressional Record*, Senate, February 28, 1970, p. S2665. This table originated in the Department of Health, Education, and Welfare (whose Secretary was then Robert Finch). In explaining the significance of this table, the Department stated:

American Indians surveyed attended school at a rate of 61.7 per cent in schools of predominantly white, nonminority enrollment, while 16.7 per cent were in 95 through 100 per cent minority schools. These 177,464 American Indian students did not include some 52,400 American Indian students who attended schools administered by the Interior Department's Bureau of Indian Affairs.

223

TABLE C–6

NUMBER AND RATE OF LIVE BIRTHS: INDIANS AND ALASKA NATIVES
IN 24 RESERVATION STATES, AND U.S., ALL RACES
(CALENDAR YEARS 1955–1967, RATES PER 1,000 POPULATION)

Year	Indian and Alaska Natives		Indian (23 Res. States)		Alaska Native		U.S. All Races	
	Number	Rate	Number	Rate	Number	Rate	Number	Rate
1955	17,028	37.1	15,304	36.1	1,724	49.3	4,047,295	24.6
1956	17,947	38.0	16,040	36.9	1,907	51.5	4,163,090	24.9
1957	18,814	39.3	16,982	38.6	1,832	47.7	4,254,784	25.0
1958	19,371	39.9	17,428	39.2	1,943	48.7	4,203,812	24.3
1959	20,520	41.7	18,616	41.4	1,904	45.9	4,244,796	24.0
1960	21,154	42.5	19,188	42.2	1,966	45.6	4,257,850	23.7
1961	21,664	42.8	19,570	42.3	2,094	48.6	4,268,326	23.3
1962	21,866	42.7	19,770	42.1	2,096	48.6	4,167,362	22.4
1963	22,274	43.0	20,142	42.4	2,132	49.5	4,098,020	21.7
1964	22,782	43.3	20,794	43.1	1,988	45.7	4,027,490	21.0
1965	22,370	41.7	20,352	41.5	2,018	43.4	3,760,358	19.4
1966	21,100	38.7	19,154	38.5	1,946	41.1	3,606,274	18.4
1967	20,658	37.4	18,948	37.5	1,710	35.5	3,520,959	17.8

SOURCE: *Indian Health Trends and Services*, 1969. Washington, D.C.: Program Analysis and Statistics Branch of the Indian Health Service, U.S. Department of Health, Education, and Welfare.

TABLE C–7

INFANT DEATHS AND DEATH RATES: INDIANS AND ALASKA NATIVES
IN 24 RESERVATION STATES, AND U.S., ALL RACES
(CALENDAR YEARS 1955–1967, RATES PER 1,000 LIVE BIRTHS)

Year	Indian and Alaska Native		Indian		Alaska Native		U.S. All Races	
	Number	Rate	Number	Rate	Number	Rate	Number	Rate
1955	1,065	62.5	936	61.2	129	74.8	106,903	26.4
1956	1,066	59.4	900	56.1	166	87.0	108,183	26.0
1957	1,136	60.4	989	58.2	147	80.2	112,094	26.3
1958	1,123	58.0	989	56.7	134	69.0	113,789	27.1
1959	1,016	49.5	870	46.7	146	76.7	112,088	26.4
1960	1,064	50.3	914	47.6	150	76.3	110,873	26.0
1961	961	44.4	827	42.3	134	64.0	107,956	25.3
1962	967	44.2	827	41.8	140	66.8	105,479	25.3
1963	972	43.6	864	42.9	108	50.7	103,390	25.2
1964	856	37.6	747	35.9	109	54.8	99,783	24.8
1965	872	39.0	740	36.4	132	65.4	92,866	24.7
1966	822	39.0	722	37.7	100	51.4	85,516	23.7
1967	666	32.2	571	30.1	95	55.6	79,028	22.4

SOURCE: *Indian Health Trends and Services, op cit.*

satisfactory for mortality comparisons. It is preferable to compare age-adjusted races, which are designed to eliminate the effect of differences in age composition. Indian and Alaska Native 1967 age-adjusted rates were higher than U.S. All Races age-adjusted rates for eight out of the twelve leading causes of Indian and Alaska Native death. Rates for these eight causes ranged from 2.1 times as high as the U.S. rate (diabetes mellitus and suicide) to 8.0 times as high (tuberculosis, all forms). Two causes showed definitely lower rates for Indians and Alaska Natives—diseases of the heart and malignant neoplasms. It must be noted, however, that these two conditions are generally associated with the older age groups. Proportionately fewer Indians and Alaska Natives reach the high age groups where these causes become so important. For all causes combined, the

TABLE C–8

CRUDE AND AGE-ADJUSTED DEATH RATES FOR THE TWELVE LEADING
CAUSES OF DEATH AMONG INDIANS AND ALASKA NATIVES
IN 24 RESERVATION STATES COMPARED WITH U.S., ALL RACES
(CALENDAR YEAR 1967, RATES PER 100,000 POPULATION)

	Crude Rates		Age-Adjusted Rates[a] and Ratio		
Cause of Death	Indian and Alaska Native	U.S., All Races	Indian and Alaska Native	U.S., All Races	Ratio: Indian to U.S.
All causes	863.8	935.7	1,049.9	734.5	1.4
Accidents	180.9	57.2	216.8	55.0	3.9
Diseases of the heart	140.0	364.5	199.4	270.6	0.7
Malignant neoplasms	70.9	157.2	101.1	129.3	0.8
Influenza and pneumonia (excl. newborn)	53.5	28.8	51.3	21.2	2.4
Certain diseases of early infancy	49.4	24.4	18.5	20.9	0.9
Vascular lesions affecting CNS	48.8	102.2	67.2	71.2	0.9
Cirrhosis of the liver	38.9	14.1	59.6	13.4	4.4
Homicide	19.9	6.8	26.6	7.7	3.5
Diabetes mellitus	19.4	17.7	29.0	13.8	2.1
Suicide	17.0	10.8	23.1	11.1	2.1
Tuberculosis, all forms	16.3	3.5	23.9	3.0	8.0
Gastritis, etc.	14.5	3.8	9.9	3.0	3.3
All other	194.4	144.8	223.4	114.3	2.0

SOURCE: *Indian Health Trends and Services, op. cit.*

[a]Adjusted to 1940 U.S. total resident population. Figures for U.S. All Races differ from those published by the National Center for Health Statistics because of differences in the age groupings used in making the adjustments.

Indian and Alaska Native age-adjusted rate was 40 per cent above the U.S. All Races rate (see Table C–8).

Indians and Alaska Natives in general die at earlier ages than the overall U.S. population. This is pointed out by Table C–9, which gives the percentage distribution, by age, of deaths for calendar year 1967. The table shows that as great a percentage of deaths occurred under age 1 among Indians and Alaska Natives (14 per cent) as occurred under age 45 among the U.S. All Races. Another striking feature is that more than 60 per cent of the deaths for the whole country were at age 65 or over, whereas only half that percentage (33 per cent) were at age 65 or over among Indians and Alaska Natives.

Age-specific death rates for accidents show that Indian and Alaska Native rates are highest relative to those of the U.S. All Races from ages 25 to 54. Overall, the 1965–1967 average Indian and Alaska Native rate was 3.1 times as high as the U.S. rate. But for the age groups 25–34, 35–44, and 45–54, Indian and Alaska Native rates were four and one-half to five and one-half times those for all races. As Table C–10 shows, the same pattern held true six years earlier. Comparison between the two periods shows that Indian and Alaska Native rates decreased only in the age group 45–54, and not much at that. U.S. All Races rates increased for each age group except under 15 (see Table C–10).

TABLE C–9

NUMBER OF DEATHS AND PER CENT DISTRIBUTION
BY AGE: INDIANS AND ALASKA NATIVES
IN 24 RESERVATION STATES, AND U.S.,
ALL RACES (CALENDAR YEAR 1967)

Age	Indian and Alaska Native		U.S. All Races	
	No.	%	No.	%
All ages	4,776	100.0	1,851,323	100.0
Under 1	666	13.9	79,028	4.3
1– 4	204	4.3	13,506	0.7
5–14	120	2.5	16,893	0.9
15–24	356	7.5	37,706	2.0
25–34	390	8.2	34,786	1.9
35–44	431	9.0	74,039	4.0
45–54	465	9.7	165,041	8.9
55–64	552	11.6	294,162	15.9
65–74	716	15.0	437,919	23.7
75 and up	867	18.2	697,656	37.7
Unknown	9	0.2	587	0.0

SOURCE: *Indian Health Trends and Services, op. cit.*

TABLE C–10

ACCIDENT AGE-SPECIFIC DEATH RATES:
INDIANS AND ALASKA NATIVES
IN 24 RESERVATION STATES, AND U.S.,
ALL RACES (RATES PER 100,000 POPULATION)

Age	Indian and Alaska Native 1965–1967 Avg.	U.S. All Races 1966	Ratio: Indian to U.S.	Indian and Alaska Native 1959–1961 Avg.	U.S. All Races 1960	Ratio: Indian to U.S.
All ages	180.8	58.0	3.1	159.8	52.3	3.1
Under 15	80.7	27.4	2.9	80.2	28.3	2.8
15–24	247.0	67.1	3.7	192.9	56.0	3.4
25–34	285.8	51.9	5.5	248.7	43.0	5.8
35–44	253.4	47.9	5.3	217.4	40.9	5.3
45–54	249.5	55.6	4.5	258.5	49.8	5.2
55–64	260.7	67.3	3.9	235.3	59.0	4.0
65 and up	326.7	156.2	2.1	281.6	153.6	1.8

SOURCE: *Indian Health Trends and Services, op. cit.*

Index

236

INDEX